D0651539

# The Changing Face of Japanese Retail

The 1990s saw dramatic change in the Japanese corporate sector, as the bubble economy ended and Japan moved into recession. The employment practices of many companies are changing as they struggle to restructure and avoid bankruptcy. This book examines shifts in employment structure, working practice, and recruitment strategies in Japanese retail, through a case study of one major chain store, Nagasakiya. It reviews the company's attempts to cope with the challenges of deregulation, intensifying competition and falling consumption, which have combined to create a climate in which some major Japanese retail companies may fail to survive.

Issues discussed in the book include gender in the workplace; changing notions of corporate community; and the impact of Japan's recent recession. Through the unique insight gained during fieldwork as an employee of Nagasakiya, Matsunaga explores the impact of these changes on recruitment and training processes, as well as on company–employee and inter-employee relations. In particular, the research presented here focuses on the increasing numbers of part-time female staff in Japanese retail. It challenges the conventional view of such staff, who have often outlasted their senior male colleagues, as peripheral to the workforce, and asks whether a rethink of 'the Japanese employment system' is now overdue.

*The Changing Face of Japanese Retail* provides a fascinating insight into changing employment practices in Japanese retail. It is a valuable and accessible resource for students and academics in Japanese studies, anthropology, business studies, and women's studies.

**Louella Matsunaga** lectures in the social anthropology of Japan at Oxford Brookes University.

**Industrial Harmony in Modern Japan: The Intervention of a Tradition**
*W. Dean Kinzley*

**Japanese Science Fiction: A View of a Changing Society**
*Robert Matthew*

**The Japanese Numbers Game: The Use and Understanding of Numbers in Modern Japan**
*Thomas Crump*

**Ideology and Practice in Modern Japan**
*Edited by Roger Goodman and Kirsten Refsing*

**Technology and Industrial Development in Pre-war Japan: Mitsubishi Nagasaki Shipyard, 1884–1934**
*Yukiko Fukasaku*

**Japan's Early Parliaments, 1890–1905: Structure, Issues and Trends**
*Andrew Fraser, R.H.P. Mason and Philip Mitchell*

**Japan's Foreign Aid Challenge: Policy Reform and Aid Leadership**
*Alan Rix*

**Emperor Hirohito and Shôwa Japan: A Political Biography**
*Stephen S. Large*

**Japan: Beyond the End of History**
*David Williams*

**Ceremony and Ritual in Japan: Religious Practices in an Industrialized Society**
*Edited by Jan van Bremen and D.P. Martinez*

**Understanding Japanese Society: Second Edition**
*Joy Hendry*

**The Fantastic in Modern Japanese Literature: The Subversion of Modernity**
*Susan J. Napier*

**Militarization and Demilitarization in Contemporary Japan**
*Glenn D. Hook*

**Growing a Japanese Science City: Communication in Scientific Research**
*James W. Dearing*

**Architecture and Authority in Japan**
*William H. Coaldrake*

**Women's *Gidayû* and the Japanese Theatre Tradition**
*A. Kimi Coaldrake*

**Democracy in Post-war Japan: Maruyama Masao and the Search for Autonomy**
*Rikki Kersten*

**Treacherous Women of Imperial Japan: Patriarchal Fictions, Patricidal Fantasies**
*Hélène Bowen Raddeker*

# The Changing Face of Japanese Retail

## Working in a chain store

**Louella Matsunaga**

London and New York

First published 2000 by Routledge
11 New Fetter Lane, London EC4P 4EE

Simultaneously published in the USA and Canada
by Routledge
29 West 35th Street, New York, NY 10001

*Routledge is an imprint of the Taylor & Francis Group*

© 2000  Louella Matsunaga

Typeset in Baskerville by
Prepress Projects Ltd, Perth, Scotland
Printed and bound in Great Britain by
TJ International Ltd, Padstow, Cornwall

*British Library Cataloguing in Publication Data*
A catalogue record for this book is available
from the British Library

*Library of Congress Cataloging in Publication Data*
Matsunaga, Louella, 1959–
    The changing face of Japanese retail : working in a chain store/
    Louella Matsunaga.
        p. cm.
    Includes bibliographical references and index.
    ISBN 0-415-22975-8
    1. Retail trade – Japan. 2. Stores, Retail – Japan. 3. Nagasakiya
    (1948) – History. I. Title.

HF5429.6.J3 M38 2000
381′.12′0952–dc21    00-042482

R0176371682

# Contents

# Illustrations

## Figures

## Tables

# Preface

At the beginning of the new century, Japan, widely seen as a 'miracle country' in the late 1950s and the early 1960s, was struggling out of its 1990s recession, which was particularly acute between 1997 and 1999. The 1990s were a time of turbulence in Japanese politics and in the economy, and pressure for restructuring has been strong. Grave weaknesses in the banking system were revealed in the form of a massive overhang of bad debt inherited from the boom period of the late 1980s and subsequent collapse. An ambitious programme of reform of the political system was announced by the Hosokawa coalition government, which replaced single-party rule by the Liberal Democratic Party (LDP) in 1993, but the path towards implementing reform proved to be far from smooth. Indeed, after a brief period out of office, the LDP was soon back in power as part of a succession of coalition arrangements, during which period it gradually clawed back its dominant political position. Even at the start of the new century, however, the LDP was still unable to run the country without help from other parties and, curiously enough, this help was beginning to bring about results in the form of the implementation of a reformist agenda. In particular, the dominant role of the government bureaucracy over policy-making was now being challenged through parliamentary legislation. Even the 1946 Constitution, which had inhibited Japan from acting as a 'normal nation' in defence matters, was now to be the subject of scrutiny by parliamentary commissions. Nevertheless, uncertainties remained and were being compounded. Obuchi's prime ministership ended prematurely in April 2000: he suffered a severe stroke and died six weeks later. His successor, Mori, was soon in political trouble after declaring that Japan was a 'country of the gods, centred on the Emperor', and with an election imminent the political future appeared unstable.

The Nissan Institute/Routledge Japanese Studies Series seeks to foster an informed and balanced, but not uncritical, understanding of Japan. One aim of the series is to show the depth and variety of Japanese institutions, practices, and ideas. Another is, by using comparisons, to see what lessons, positive or negative, can be drawn for other countries. The tendency in commentary on Japan to resort to outdated, ill-informed, or sensational stereotypes still remains and needs to be combated.

Ever since James Abegglen published *The Japanese Factory* in 1958, commentators outside Japan have come to regard Japanese factory organisation with a mixture of awe and incomprehension. The factory as 'family' and the factory as 'community' have been frequent images, with the notion of harmonious and dedicated striving for common goals holding attraction in societies wracked by strikes and demarcation disputes (e.g. Britain in the 1970s). Ironically, however, what seemed a big part of the recipe for economic dynamism and growth between the 1960s and the 1980s has more recently been subjected to criticism as a brake on creativity and innovation, e.g. the comparative slowness of Japan to shift its economy from rigidities, for instance the reluctance of 'traditional' Japanese firms to shed labour in the interests of profitability.

In this book Dr Matsunaga examines in close detail a chain store which in the 1990s was declining in economic viability, and in 2000 actually faced bankruptcy. Unlike many better-known industrial names, this company counted many 'temporary' women employees among its workforce and, although they did not have the degree of job security enjoyed by their male colleagues, in Dr Matsunaga's view, they were hardly peripheral to the workforce, or even, in a real sense, temporary. Thus, while the 'permanent–temporary' dichotomy was difficult to sustain, the idea of 'ingroup versus outgroup' seemed equally problematic. Indeed, Dr Matsunaga makes good use of the notion of 'permeability' to describe the boundaries between the firm, other firms, and the broader community.

This is an innovative work, which will take its place as a significant contribution to our understanding of the changing Japanese commercial scene at the outset of the twenty-first century.

J. A. A. Stockwin

# Acknowledgements

This book has been a long time in the making, and I have incurred a great many debts along the way. For taking me on in the first place, my thanks to Brian Moeran, my first supervisor for my doctoral research, on which this book is largely based. For encouraging me through to the finish, my thanks to Professor Abitoh Itoh of Tokyo University, who helped to guide me during my fieldwork, and to the many excellent teachers who were then at SOAS, University of London, especially Kaoru Sugihara, Lionel Caplan, David Parkin, and most of all Lola Martinez, who took on my supervision for the writing up part of the project. I am also grateful to my colleagues in recent years at King's College, London, the Nissan Institute and the Institute of Social and Cultural Anthropology at Oxford University, and the Anthropology Department of Oxford Brookes University for support and intellectual stimulation, and for spurring me on to get something into print. Particular thanks are due to Roger Goodman and Joy Hendry for their faith in this project.

For financial support during my doctoral research I am indebted to SOAS and the Sanwa Bank Foundation for help with my fieldwork costs, to the University of London for financing my tuition, and to the Royal Anthropological Institute for a Radcliffe-Browne award towards the costs of writing up. I have also benefited from the generous support of the Anthropology Department at Oxford Brookes University, which enabled me to make a return visit to Japan in 1999 in order to do some much needed updating of the original research in the changed conditions of the post-bubble economy. For help in transcribing interviews I am grateful to Hillary Stevens and Yoko Myers, and my thanks also to Kumiko Helliwell for her help in seeking the relevant copyright authorisations.

While doing the research for this book, I have also been bringing up two young children. My thanks to them for putting up with a frequently distracted mother, to my husband for all his support, and to the many friends and family in England and Japan whose help has made it possible. I would particularly like to thank Emi Sumitomo, Patricia Oe, Kumie Kojima, and Hideko Koyanagi in Japan, and Marilyn Crawley in England for friendship, moral support, and help with childcare – sometimes in very trying circumstances.

My father in England, and my mother-in-law in Japan have also helped more than I can say.

Arranging access to conduct a study of this kind in a company is never easy. I owe an enormous debt to Imagawa-sensei and Mr Sekiguchi in Koganei, Tokyo, for introducing me to Nagasakiya, and for continuing to help with access and useful contacts over the years. But most of all, I would like to thank the branch manager who first agreed to let me work in the company, and all the people I worked with at Nagasakiya for their willingness to let me participate in so many areas of company life, and to talk to me at length about their experiences in the company. I hope this book succeeds in conveying some of the complexity of their working lives.

Louella Matsunaga
September 2000

# Notes

Every effort has been made to contact copyright holders for their permission to reprint material in this book. The publishers would be grateful to hear from any copyright holder who is not here acknowledged and will undertake to rectify any errors or omissions in future editions of this book.

Where Japanese names appear in the text they are written according to Japanese convention, with the family name first, followed by the first name. For names of people, places, and companies no macrons have been used, otherwise macrons are used to indicate long sounds in Japanese.

In order to protect the anonymity of the many employees who were willing to talk to me about their experiences, good and bad, of working in Nagasakiya, pseudonyms have been used throughout for Nagasakiya employees. The company itself, and the branch in which I worked, appear under their real name, and I am most grateful to Nagasakiya for permission to use the company name in this book.

# 1 The changing face of the Japanese company

In February 2000, the Japanese press reported a major bankruptcy in the retail sector. The company involved, Nagasakiya, was not well known outside Japan, but within Japan it had at one time been one of the leading companies in the chain store sector, and it was also one of the most long-established chain store groups in Japan. This was the largest bankruptcy to date in Japan's retail sector, with projected debts for the Nagasakiya group of 380 billion yen (*Japan Times* weekly news roundup 12–18 February 2000). Nagasakiya filed for protection from its creditors under the Corporate Rehabilitation Law and announced that it was making efforts to rescue and rebuild the company. However, the press speculated that this event heralded the acceleration of a process of 'natural selection' in the chain store sector, in which weaker groups, such as Nagasakiya, would go under, with the profitable parts of their business bought up by rivals (*Asahi Shinbun* 15 February 2000).

This bankruptcy had a particular poignancy to me, as I had worked at Nagasakiya during the early 1990s, an experience that formed the basis of my doctoral research and of this book. It had long been clear that Nagasakiya was in decline, and on my return visit in 1999 an atmosphere of gloom prevailed in the company. Although the emphasis at that time was officially on efforts to rebuild the company, the pessimism of some of the middle management was reflected in the parting remark made to me by one manager, 'It would be nice if Nagasakiya still exists when you next visit ...'

Although Nagasakiya should not be seen as a 'typical' Japanese company – indeed part of the argument of this book is that no such thing exists – it is an interesting case to examine in more depth in that its own rise to prosperity and subsequent decline can be seen as an extreme example of the effect of fluctuations in the wider economy on individual Japanese companies. Also, in the changing ways in which Nagasakiya has represented itself over the course of the 1990s, we can see how these economic fluctuations refract wider, more general discourses in Japan of 'the company' and of company–employee relations. A marked shift is evident in particular in the ways in which large Japanese companies sought to project themselves at the beginning of the 1990s, at the time of labour shortage and the bubble economy, and, subsequently, as recession began to bite. To give the background to these changes, this chapter begins with an overview of the ways in which 'the Japanese company' has been imagined in the post-war period, and the importance of the company as a particularly potent symbol of modern Japan, before returning to the particular case of Nagasakiya, its recent decline, and the implications of the Nagasakiya case for the wider study of Japanese companies.

## Imagining 'the Japanese company'

In a televised debate on Japanese society, broadcast by the BBC during the Japan Festival in Britain in 1991, Asada, a Japanese philosopher, argued that, of the various great 'isms', the one that characterised Japan was not capitalism but corporatism.[1] This statement is perhaps indicative of the importance of Japan's large companies not only in the Japanese economy, but also in prevailing images of Japan in the post-war period, both at home and abroad. As Yoshino (1992) has persuasively argued, 'the Japanese company is regarded by businessmen and others as the microcosm of uniquely Japanese society, and ... 'company men' as the typical bearers of the 'uniqueness' of Japanese culture' (Yoshino 1992: 183).

The broad features of what is sometimes called 'the Japanese employment system' have become well-known worldwide, and the core characteristics of this system – lifetime employment (that is employment from graduation until retirement), pay by seniority, and enterprise unionism – have been extensively discussed (see, for example, Clark 1979; Crawcour 1978). Sometimes called the three pillars of the Japanese employment system, these features have been linked to a fourth, somewhat more nebulous, characteristic, the view of companies as communities (Clark 1979; Dore 1987; Sako 1997) or bounded units (Nakane 1970), which in some way bind together and 'envelop' their members (Nakane 1970: 15).

This idea of the company as a bounded unit has been expressed in different ways over the course of the past century or so, but with some recurring motifs. From the late nineteenth century onwards, the metaphor of the company as family has been widely evoked, both by industrialists and by academic commentators. For example, the Tokyo Chamber of Commerce observed in 1898 that, 'in our country, relations between employers and employees are just like those within a family' (Marshall 1967: 57), while in a later generation the pre-privatisation Japan National Railways referred to itself as 'one family' (Noguchi 1990). In the early period of industrialisation, at least, this notion of company as family was not merely one promoted by management, but was also taken up by employees campaigning for better treatment, who used it as a tool to criticise management who fell short of these ideals (T. C. Smith 1988).

In the post-war period influential academic writers such as Hazama (1963) and Nakane (1970) have again drawn on the metaphor of company as family or household (*ie*). In populist writing, too, the firm as family has continued to be a much-used image – one example among many can be found in the writing of Morita, co-founder of Sony, who states in his best-selling book *Made in Japan*, 'the most important mission for a Japanese manager is to … create a familylike feeling within the corporation, a feeling that employees and managers share the same fate.' (Morita 1987: 130).

Other commentators have, however, been more sceptical of this analogy. Writing in the 1970s, Cole (1971) comments that the idea of company as family is a view 'promoted by Japanese management' and warns that 'this analogy diverts the observer from the actual relationships within the Japanese firm' (Cole 1971: 12). Clark (1979), in his classic study, *The Japanese Company*, is also critical of the family analogy – tracing the historical development of the ideology of familism he concludes by remarking that the 'firm as family' analogy is no longer often made; perhaps, he suggests, because of the changes in the Japanese family itself during the post-war period (Clark 1979: 41). Noguchi (1990), writing on the then Japan National Railways, again questions the idea of the firm as family, concurring with Cole (1971) that this is a management-promoted ideology.

Most recently, this debate has been returned to by Kondo (1990) in her study of a small family-run business in downtown Tokyo. Taking an interpretive approach, Kondo moves beyond the argument of whether or not Japanese firms are 'really' like families, instead seeking to examine the varying ways in which the metaphor of the family is evoked and contested. This approach has important implications for the study of Japanese companies, however it is limited in so far as Kondo is examining a small family-run firm in which face-to-face relationships are the rule. The context thus differs in important ways from that of large companies, where most employees may never meet, and in some ways the family analogy is thus harder to sustain. In Nagasakiya, for example, male managers dismissed the family analogy on the grounds that the company was too big to be like a family.

Another prominent theme in the writing on Japanese companies, especially in the 1970s and 1980s, was that of harmony and consensus. Notable examples here are Rohlen (1973, 1974) and, in a more populist vein, Vogel (1979), Ouchi (1981), Pascale and Athos (1981), as well as the earlier, and very influential, work of Abegglen (1958). In these writings there is a shift in emphasis from the company as family to the company as community, a view also stressed by Abegglen and Stalk (1985) and Dore (1987). This notion of the company as community again draws on Nakane (1970) in depicting companies as bounded units where the difference between insider and outsider is stressed.

Rohlen (1974), for example, describes the various ways in which a large Japanese bank creates and affirms its own distinctive identity and asserts the difference between members and non-members. Examples he gives of this process include the spiritual training undergone by new recruits, the ceremony in which they are welcomed into the company, and a wealth of symbolism associated with the company, including a company song and motto. Thus, although the new recruits may not have met, and indeed may never meet, all of their fellow employees, there is still a sense of a common belonging to a single organisation, which, according to Rohlen, has considerable emotional force for many of these new recruits. Anderson's (1991) concept of the 'imagined community' (evoked in the context of a discussion of nationalism) seems relevant here, where although most of the members of the community may never meet nevertheless there is an image of the community to which they belong in the mind of all (Anderson 1991: 6).

However, in the 1980s and 1990s, there was a reaction against this depiction of Japanese companies as harmonious, consensual entities, in which members are linked by a common identity and common interests. A new strand of writing emerged examining conflict in the workplace (for example Mouer and Sugimoto 1981; 1986; Kamata 1982; Pharr 1984; Tanaka 1988; Turner 1995) and questioning whose perspective is represented by the earlier, more normative accounts. Noting that the chief defining characteristics of the so-called Japanese employment system – lifetime employment, seniority pay, and enterprise unionism – have only ever applied consistently to a minority of the Japanese workforce (the permanent male employees of large companies), an increasing number of writers from the 1980s onwards began to examine the working lives of those outside this elite group.

Numerous studies have appeared of working women in Japan (e.g. Cook and Hayashi 1980; McLendon 1983; Pharr 1984; Lo 1990; Kondo 1990; Saso 1990; Brinton 1992, 1993; Lam 1992; Hunter 1993; Roberts 1994; Kawashima 1995; Ogasawara 1998), and other researchers have described small and medium-sized enterprises (e.g. Chalmers 1989; Kondo 1990; Roberson 1998), and part-time or short-term employees (Kamata 1982; Tanaka 1988; Kondo 1990; Shirahase 1995) as well as the relatively recent phenomenon of foreign illegal employees (Oka 1994). At the same time, more research is being done on companies in previously neglected sectors of the Japanese economy, for example (at the time) state-owned industry (Noguchi 1990), retail (Creighton 1988, 1991, 1992, 1996, 1998; Moeran 1998; Ueno 1998), and advertising (Moeran 1996).

A move can thus be seen in the anthropology of Japanese companies that reflects trends in the anthropology of Japan in general, from an emphasis on the normative and the consensual in early works such as Nakane (1970) to a concern with conflict and alternative perspectives (some examples in the general anthropology of Japan include Mouer and Sugimoto 1981, 1986; Ben Ari and Eisenstadt 1990; Krauss *et al.* 1984). This in turn echoes trends in the wider literature on the anthropology of organisations (albeit with a marked time lag), where a similar shift can be seen from work concerned with consensus (the Human Relations school – dominant from the mid-1920s to the 1950s) to studies focusing on conflict (the Manchester shop floor studies of the 1950s and 1960s) (Wright 1994: 5–14).

The notion of the Japanese employment system itself has also been subjected to intense scrutiny from very varied disciplinary perspectives. In the field of organisation studies, an interest in large, very successful, companies, apparently underpinned by a radically different system of employment, has contributed to a burgeoning interest in 'corporate culture' (Alvesson 1993: 3). However, at the same time as many management theorists have reproduced a fairly stereotyped view stressing the difference between Japanese companies and their counterparts elsewhere (see, for example, Hickson and Pugh 1995), analysts from other disciplines, such as economics, have argued that these differences are exaggerated and have queried the portrayal of Japanese companies and the Japanese employment system as being distinctive (Koike 1983, 1988). And from another perspective, anthropologists and sociologists, including many of those who have contributed to the recent research on non-elite sectors of the economy referred to above, have questioned the extent to which an idealised system, covering at the most 20–30 per cent of the population of Japan, can fairly be referred to as 'the Japanese employment system' (see, for example, Brinton 1993: 13–15; Kondo 1990: 49–50; Roberson 1998: 4–6).

Much of this debate, however, has been overshadowed by recent events with the demise of Japan's bubble economy and a number of high-profile company failures. Deregulation is under way in the financial sector, and there have also been changes in the ways in which Japanese companies in general are run and are perceived. Whether or not the so-called Japanese employment system can survive these changes, even among the elite to whom it is supposedly most applicable, is very much a subject of debate (see, for example, Inoue 1997; Kaneko 1997; Yahata 1997) and is one of the issues addressed in this book. Once seen as emblematic of Japan's economic success, Japan's large companies now provide powerful images of Japan's economic woes. Nagasakiya's recent bankruptcy is one of a number of high-profile bankruptcies in Japan since the mid-1990s, some of which have also been widely reported outside Japan. One of the most striking images shown on British television of Japan's emergent economic crisis was that of the managing director of Yamaichi Securities, until then one of Japan's big four securities firms, offering tearful apologies for his company's bankruptcy in 1997. If the idea of 'the Japanese company' is still a powerful symbol of Japan, the resonances of that symbol have shifted.

In this rapidly shifting context, how can the study of Japanese companies best be approached? Are the linked ideas of 'the Japanese employment system' and of companies as communities still tenable? One possibly fruitful line has been suggested by Kondo (1990). Kondo aligns herself with the interpretative approach of Geertz (1973), moving away from a view of culture as a static given, something 'out there' for an anthropologist to discover, towards a consideration of culture as process, a system of negotiated meanings.[2] The emphasis accordingly shifts away from a normative description of company structure towards an attempt to convey the varying viewpoints of those involved.

Kondo (1990: 35–6) explicitly rejects the search for an 'irreducible essence' and insists that 'meaning can never be fixed', but is constantly recreated, ever shifting and dependent on context. In this, her work links up with that of other anthropologists currently writing on Japan (for example Hendry 1987, 1993; Bachnik and Quinn 1994) who seek to examine the varying ways in which Japanese people represent the world and the society in which they live and reject the positivist search for an essential core beneath the layers of representation, or 'wrapping' (Hendry 1993). A similar shift is also evident in the anthropology of organisations, where earlier positivist debates on whether organisations should be studied in terms of consensus or of conflict have given way to a current interest in organisation as process (Alvesson 1993; Wright 1994).

If the focus is thus to shift to an examination of how the idea of a company is constructed, contested, and negotiated by its employees, a new set of issues emerges. Some writers have questioned whether it is valid to continue to consider the company (or a company) as the object of analysis. Does taking the company as the focus of study not tend to assume what needs to be demonstrated, that is, that the company is a significant bounded entity, with some sort of internal unity and cohesion? Alvesson (1993), writing on organisations generally, warns, 'organizations are complex entities, and it is not certain that the most apparent and widely espoused beliefs, values, and symbols will cover the overall cultural patterns or even those that are of greatest significance for individuals in understanding their work situations' (Alvesson 1993: 63). He goes on to suggest, borrowing again from Geertz (1973), that perhaps we should study '*in* organizations', rather than attempting to study organisations themselves as if they were closed and coherent units (Alvesson 1993: 120).

Turning back to research on companies in Japan, Roberson (1998) has suggested that there may also be a class dimension to be considered, with blue collar workers in small and medium-sized firms far less likely to find the focus of their lives in the workplace than are their white collar counterparts. He questions the notion of the firm as community, and suggests that instead of assuming that membership of a company creates a significant boundary we should take a wider view of employees' lives, both inside and outside the workplace, and also incorporate a study of movement between companies. In this approach, the focus becomes that of the life-course and the role that employment may play in this, a topic that has also been explored by Plath (1983), Kondo (1990), and, for women employees, by Brinton (1992, 1993).

Another aspect that clearly needs to be explored in more depth is the way in which representations of the company may shift over time, and with the influence of wider economic changes. Here, the notion of the company as community has come under particular scrutiny. Tabata (1998) points out that the idea of the company as community has not been universally seen in a positive light in Japan. A series of critical publications in the late 1980s and early 1990s in Japan pointed out the downside of a system in which the male salaried employee is expected to dedicate himself to his company, becoming a *kaisha ningen*, or company person, and simultaneously to a large extent forfeiting control over his own personal and family life (Kumazawa 1989; Uchihashi and Sataka 1991; Saito 1993 cited in Tabata 1998: 201). Tabata goes on to argue that as the so-called 'lifetime employment' system in Japan has come under threat in the post-bubble economy of the 1990s the idea of the firm as community also becomes problematic, in so far as this idea is based on 'job security and workers' commitment' (Tabata 1998: 200)

The question of what becomes of the idea of the company as community in the post-bubble economy has also been taken up by Sako (1997). Sako defines the Japanese company community as comprising members with common interests and a shared 'social identity', which, she argues, 'derives from the relative homogeneity of the quality of labour within the firm, both by attribute (i.e. gender) and by ability and educational achievements' (Sako 1997: 5). She argues that this is then reinforced by the welfare benefits and the employment security provided by the firm. She particularly stresses the issue of employment security, arguing that, 'if employees wish to stay on in the firm but the firm is unwilling to offer employment security, no community would emerge' (Sako 1997: 4). Sako also states that the characteristics of the company as community she identifies mean that the members of this community are 'usually male regular workers' (Sako 1997: 5). However, she goes on to state that the boundaries of the corporate community are changing in two important ways.

First, she suggests that they are expanding to include the subsidiaries of large companies as well as the core company itself as, in the post-bubble economy, lifetime employment is redefined as meaning employment within the enterprise group, rather than within a single company. Second, she suggests that the boundary between what she terms 'core' and 'periphery' in the workforce can no longer be so clearly drawn. Drawing on Wakisaka's (1997) research, which shows that the average length of service of part-time women workers in Japan is increasing, Sako suggests that 'some part-time workers in Japan are clearly treated as quasi-members of the firm as community' (Sako 1997: 10).

To treat the company as a clearly bounded community thus presents some evident difficulties. Where the boundaries are drawn and who is included within the boundary are areas of ambiguity and contestation, and they are subject to change over time. Attempts such as that made by Sako (1997) to define the notion of company as community inevitably lead to a host of exceptions and qualifications that tend to undermine the initial definition. How can a description of Japanese companies as community encompass both the homogeneous images generated of the corporate community and the internal diversity and complexity of the workforce? And, looking back at Roberson's (1998) objections to the notion of company as community, how is one to reconcile the view of the company as enveloping its employees with a life-course-based perspective showing a range of individual employment trajectories constrained by factors such as gender, class, size of company, and economic conditions?

## Anthropological perspectives on community, boundaries, and identity

The idea of the Japanese company as community thus appears problematic for two principal reasons. First, the boundaries of the corporate community are not fixed, and second the company means different things to different people. However, before the view of company as community is dismissed out of hand, it is worth taking a closer look at exactly what we mean by community. From an anthropological perspective, Cohen (1985), drawing on Barth (1969), has argued that rather than trying to define a community in an 'objective' way, for example by using a list of traits, or characteristics, it is more fruitful to look at it as a fluid category, subject to continual redefinition and re-negotiation. He further argues that the boundary of the community itself is also a contextually variable and shifting phenomenon. Cohen writes:

> The boundary represents the mask presented by the community to the outside world; it is the community's public face. But the conceptualization and symbolization of the boundary from within is much more complex … in the public face, internal variety disappears or coalesces into a simple statement. In its private mode, differentiation, variety, and complexity proliferate … the boundary thus symbolises the community to its members in two quite different ways: it is the sense they have of its perception by people on the other side – the public face and 'typical' mode – and it is their sense of the community as refracted through all the complexities of their lives and experience – the private face and idiosyncratic mode.
>
> Cohen (1985: 75)

Although Cohen's formulation is intended as a general analysis of communities and their boundaries, it seems apt as a description of large Japanese companies. The company's public face, at least in certain contexts, will tend to show the company in simple terms – the ideal, or normative, model of Japanese company life. From this viewpoint, the idea of the company as a bounded community may seem unproblematic. However, the private face shows a more complex and varied picture. This also accords well with the important emic categories in Japan of inside and outside (*uchi* and *soto*), and the linked pairs of *honne* (how things 'really' are – the unofficial and private realm)[3] and *tatemae* (how things are supposed to be – the official or public realm), and *ura* (backstage – that which lies beneath the surface) and *omote* (surface) as described extensively by Doi (1973, 1985), Kondo (1990) Bachnik (1992), and Bachnik and Quinn (1994).

As Bachnik (1992, 1994) and Kondo (1990: 31) discuss in some detail, these pairs are all very much relational concepts rather than absolutes, and they may also vary depending on context. For example, as far as the outside–inside pairing is concerned, the boundary between the two is always shifting, and an insider in some contexts may not be an insider in others. This, again, seems to fit rather well with Cohen's (1985) argument that the boundaries of community are subjective, variable, and subject to interpretation and negotiation.

In untangling the idea of company as community, then, context is crucial. We need to know much more about who says what about the company, when, and in what situation. And this needs to be done in tandem with an examination of the external economic constraints within which the company operates. What sorts of representations of the company arise in what sorts of contexts? Which employees are seen as more appropriate to speak for the company to outsiders and why? If, as it would appear from the literature on Japanese companies, there is a hegemonic discourse of 'the Japanese company', how does this discourse gain authority and become 'officialised'?[4] How do other sorts of discourses become muted? What is the role of gender in all this? How are the boundaries between inside and outside marked in the company context, and how do these boundaries shift? What views of the individual employee are implied in the discourses generated of and by the company? How does the individual employee relate to the wider company? And how do representations of company life and identity shift over time?

## The case study: Nagasakiya

In what follows, these questions are addressed through a case study of Nagasakiya, the chain store whose bankruptcy was referred to at the beginning of this chapter. Before recent events, Nagasakiya presented a picture in many ways familiar from descriptions of other large Japanese companies. For example in terms of size and structure, it clearly fell within the large company category[5] and was far too large for face-to-face relationships between all employees to be possible. In 1999 its full-time employees numbered over 2,500 with a further 6,000 or so part-timers, and it was part of an extended corporate group with a number of subsidiary companies and its own company union. Regular full-time staff in the company were recruited straight from school (in the case of female employees) or university (in the case of male, and, for a short period, a small number of female employees), or, more rarely, junior college (both male and female recruits). The ideal within Nagasakiya was that male employees should then remain with the company until retirement, although this ideal has come under particular strain in recent years (see pp. 25–6, 159–67).

However, as a retail company Nagasakiya also differs in a number of respects from companies in the better-documented manufacturing and financial sectors. A large proportion of its employees are women and are classified as part-timers; a classification reflecting less the (only slightly) fewer hours that they work compared with regular employees than the fact that they are not considered as full members of the company; they therefore receive lower wages, calculated at an hourly rate, fewer benefits, and in most cases are not members of the company union. Even for male regular employees, career paths in Nagasakiya, particularly for older employees, in practice show considerable divergence from norms described for large companies in other sectors of the Japanese economy. This is especially noticeable in the uneven application of the ideal of lifetime employment, owing in large measure to the changing employment needs created by Nagasakiya's initial rapid growth and subsequent decline.

In a number of ways the special features of Nagasakiya also make it particularly interesting. As a company with a majority of female employees, it offers a chance to reassess views of the Japanese corporate mainstream that depict women workers as marginal. As a company that has seen rapid growth and subsequent decline, it provides a case study of the influence of economic factors on company employment policy and on the career paths of individual company employees. It also provides an opportunity to examine the ways in which one company has, over the past forty years, continually sought to reinvent itself, and of the importance of corporate image and prestige (or lack of it) in the process of recruitment and within the company.

Returning to the linked issues of community, identity, and boundaries, as a company with a large number of employees classified as 'part-time' or 'temporary', the boundaries of Nagasakiya are not as clear cut as may be the case in large Japanese companies in other sectors. Some sections of the workforce are quite fluid, although this fluidity does not neatly correspond either to gender or to employment status, as will be discussed further below (pp. 26–30). Nagasakiya thus offers a context in which a range of viewpoints and experiences of the workplace may be examined and contrasted, and the varying perceptions of the company by a range of different sorts of employees may be assessed.

Many of these apparently unusual features of Nagasakiya have implications in the context of the changing Japanese economy that go beyond the specific case study outlined here. For one thing, in Japan, as in most highly developed post-industrial economies, over the last thirty years the percentage of those engaged in manufacturing has declined. By 1997, the percentage of employed persons in Japan working in wholesale, retail, restaurants, and hotels had risen to 22.5 per cent, just ahead of those engaged in manufacturing, which employed 22 per cent of the working population (Japan Institute of Labour 1998a: 23). A closer look at employment in retail and service industries would seem to be overdue.

Another aspect of Nagasakiya that is of increasing relevance to working life in Japan as a whole is its high proportion of female employees, especially those classified as part-timers. Female labour force participation in Japan as a whole has risen markedly during the post-war period, with employment of older women re-entering the workforce as part-time employees after having children showing a sharp increase from the 1960s onwards. Brinton (1993: 10) notes that the entry of these women to the workforce filled a need for cheap labour, and the low cost of these employees, who are paid a relatively low hourly rate and enjoy few of the benefits on offer to regular full-time staff, continues to be an important consideration for employers such as Nagasakiya. There is also evidence that employment of part-time staff in the retail sector in particular, but also to a lesser extent in finance, transport and communication, and the service industries has increased further in the post-bubble economy.[6] This is probably in part because of their lower cost in wages and other benefits, and also because the employer is not generally seen as having a responsibility to ensure the continued employment of part-time staff in adverse economic conditions, thus making it notionally easier to lay off this type of employee. The experience of the women rejoining the workforce as part-timers is therefore an increasingly important area to consider in any description of work and company life in Japan.

The research presented here begins with a description in Chapter 2 of Nagasakiya itself, its history, and its place within the retail sector in Japan. Chapters 3–6 follow through the experience of a new recruit to the store in the early 1990s, from recruitment, through the initial training, to daily work within the company. Chapters 7 and 8 consider the importance of gender and age in Nagasakiya, and contain narratives about the employment experiences of a range of employees, including some accounts of employees' and ex-employees' experiences of the restructuring Nagasakiya has undertaken in the post-bubble economy. The last chapter returns to the issue of the company as community and considers the implications of this study for some of the broader theoretical areas of debate on Japanese companies and the ways in which they are represented.

The organisation of the book moves from outside-oriented representations of Nagasakiya to the more complex area of internal debates and the viewpoints of employees, in order to both give a sense of how an individual's perception of the company may shift as his/her relationship with the company develops and highlight some of the differences between idealised official representations and more informal and personal accounts. However, I am not concerned here with producing an account of the 'real' Nagasakiya beneath the surface, but rather with looking at how varying ideas of the company and membership of the company are generated by different people in different contexts. Anderson (1991) writes, 'communities are to be distinguished not by their falsity/genuineness, but by the style in which they are imagined' (Anderson 1991: 6). This book, then, is an examination of the varying, and changing, ways in which one large Japanese company has been imagined, and of the shifting positions of individual employees within the larger corporate context.

# 2 Nagasakiya and the retail sector in Japan

## The retail sector in Japan

As is now well known, Japan's retail sector has a relatively high proportion of small family-run outlets – in 1997 nearly 50 per cent of retail outlets had only one or two employees. However, it would be misleading to depict Japan as primarily a nation of small shops. Large-scale stores also have a long history in Japan, going back over 100 years, and large retail groups dominate in economic terms, with a far higher proportion of total sales.

The earliest large stores in Japan were called *hyakkaten*, literally one hundred goods store, or *depāto*, from the English 'department store'. The Meiji era (1868–1912) department stores were often stores that had expanded during this period from pre-Meiji origins as small family-run dry goods stores. For example, Takashimaya, now one of the most prestigious of the department stores, began in 1831 as a small shop dealing in materials for kimonos, run by a Mr Iida and his wife; the oldest department stores can trace their history back to the seventeenth century.

The development of these stores into department stores in the late nineteenth and early twentieth centuries has been well documented, as has the subsequent history of department stores in Japan (Moeran 1998; Ueno 1998), and need not detain us here. The important point to stress in this context is that from early in their history the department stores sought to present themselves as far more than simple marketplaces where goods could be obtained. Rather, they constructed images that, although varying in some important respects among the different stores, have in common an emphasis on the store as cultural mediator (Creighton 1998). Japanese department stores introduce new goods from abroad; showcase arts and crafts from both Japan and abroad, including both art exhibitions and the marketing of (generally high-priced, luxury) products such as pottery or kimono; and in more general terms create built environments which in themselves become meeting places, centres for leisure, and even tourist attractions. By the early twentieth century Mitsukoshi had become an attraction on the standard tourist itinerary of Tokyo after a successful advertising campaign in which it linked up with the Imperial Theatre using the slogan 'Today the Imperial, tomorrow Mitsukoshi' (Seidensticker 1983: 113); several generations later, in the 1980s, young and fashion-conscious Japanese were flocking to admire the new and architecturally innovative Seibu department store in downtown Tokyo on their days off.

One consequence of the development of department stores into 'a dream world' (Moeran 1998: 142) marketing the luxurious and the exotic has been that the department stores have largely vacated the lower end of the market. Also, they have tended to cluster either in the centre of large cities or, for the later generation of stores which developed alongside the railway lines, on railway hubs. For those living in suburban or provincial areas, therefore, department stores have remained venues for a special outing, sometimes requiring a lengthy journey, or, frequently, places to buy a special gift in one of Japan's gift-giving seasons.[1] They are not places to buy daily necessities, nor do they market themselves as such. The personnel manager of Takashimaya explained to me:

> We aim to show people how they can create a beautiful living environment. If you want a coffee cup you can admire for its beauty, you can find one here. If you just want something to drink coffee out of, you can go to a chain store.

Chain stores, in contrast, are a relatively recent innovation in Japan, dating only from the post-war era. In the pre-war period, the retail sector comprised the department stores on the one hand and small family-owned retail outlets on the other. As the number of department stores began to grow, there was pressure from the small retailers for protective legislation that would restrict the establishment of further large outlets. This eventually resulted in the Department Store Law of 1937, which recognised the advantages that a large scale conferred on the department stores and sought to protect smaller retailers by requiring a permit for the opening or expansion of any department store, defined as 'any single retail store dealing in a variety of goods that contained more than 1,500 m² of floorspace' (Upham 1989: 6).

This legislation lasted a mere ten years – in the immediate aftermath of the war such regulation was seen as undesirable and the 1937 law was repealed in 1947. In the 1950s economic recovery began, and competition in the retail sector again began to intensify. In 1956 the lobbying of small and medium-sized retailers' groups for protection against the renewed menace of the department stores resulted in a new Department Store Law. This followed the same lines as the 1937 law and re-introduced the permit system while retaining the same definition of a department store. As Upham (1989) points out, this law in fact served the interests of both the existing department stores and the smaller retailers. It protected the former from new competitors entering their section of the market while effectively producing a zoning system whereby small retailers could operate free from competition from large-scale outlets as long as they were outside the main urban shopping centres.

By the 1960s a new kind of large-scale store was emerging, taking advantage of a loophole in the existing regulatory system. These stores called themselves *sūpā* (from the English, supermarket) or *chēn stōa* (chain stores), and in their overall organisation and marketing strategy they were based on US chain stores such as J. C. Penny's. Mostly founded in the 1950s as small family businesses specialising in one type of product, often food or clothing, they expanded in the 1960s to become general merchandise stores, offering a range of goods similar to those on sale at department stores. They were able to expand in size by housing several legally independent entities within a single building, thus bypassing the 1956 law's provision that no single retail unit of more than 1,500 m² could be established without a permit. In doing so, they were able to exploit a gap in the retail sector between the prestigious department stores operating mainly in downtown areas, and the small and medium-sized retailers.

The new chain stores aimed to sell a wide range of goods cheaply and to serve a wider geographical area than that served by the department stores. American chain stores provided the model for both type of merchandise and marketing, and management structure, with a highly centralised management dictating policy to a number of standardised outlets. The areas particularly targeted were provincial centres that lacked department stores and the new suburbs of Tokyo and other large Japanese cities. The suburbs had until then been poorly served by large retailers, and new chain stores were built alongside the stations of the commuter railway lines, in a similar way to the earlier generation of 'railway' department stores but on a smaller scale, and serving the suburbs rather than the main commuter hubs. In cases where a single company owned both a department store and a group of chain stores (for example the Seibu Saison group, which owns both the Seibu department stores and the Seiyu supermarkets, as well as other speciality stores, and was formerly part of the same organisation as the Seibu railway company),[2] chain store branches were opened at intervals along the suburban lines, with department stores at the main commuter hubs in the centre of the city and at a few important suburban shopping centres, as well as the downtown shopping areas.

The chain stores were able to undercut smaller retailers by making use of the advantages of large scale, and they undercut the department stores by adopting a number of distinctive strategies relating to capital investment, merchandise sold, and staffing. First, equipment investment was minimised; for example, display units, flooring, and lighting were then and remain now much less elaborate and luxurious in the chain stores than in the department stores. Second, chain stores purchased merchandise at low cost, on the whole avoiding the brand-named luxury goods on sale in the department stores. Goods were then sold at a minimal profit margin, the aim being to achieve high overall profits through high sales of competitively priced goods.

The chain stores also adopted a 'self-service' system, using relatively large numbers of part-time staff with little sales training. Under this system, the goods are laid out for the customers' ease of access, who simply help themselves and then take the goods chosen to the nearest cash desk. Although staff are available to provide help and advise if necessary, the staffing levels are lower than in the department stores, and less sales training is given. Such training as is provided for chain store staff is more concerned with the basics of greeting customers, wrapping merchandise, ordering goods, operating the cash desk, and doing necessary paperwork.[3] Another innovation was that of employing large numbers of part-time staff, paid substantially lower wages than full company members, so that the overall wage bill was reduced.[4]

The strategy adopted by the chain stores was spectacularly successful. Between 1965 and 1969 this type of store doubled in number, and their sales increased nearly fivefold (Duncan 1974: 89). In the same period, department stores increased in number by only just over 25 per cent while doubling their level of annual sales. By the early 1970s, chain stores had made severe inroads into the areas of distribution previously covered by small retailers. They were also in a position to challenge the department stores for primacy in terms of turnover, if not in terms of prestige.

Against the background of the rapid expansion of the chain stores, both department stores and smaller retailers began lobbying again for the revision of the existing law on large-scale stores, resulting in the enactment of the Large Stores Law of 1973. This law replaced the permit system with a system of notification and adjustment, and it redefined the type of store targeted from a single unit occupying more than 1,500 m$^2$ of floor space to any building with more that 1,500 m$^2$ of retail space, regardless of whether the occupants of the building are strictly speaking a single legal entity.

Under this system, MITI (The Ministry of International Trade and Industry) had to be notified of the intention to construct any new building falling under the umbrella of the 1973 law, after which MITI had to put up a public notice of this intention and notify the local Chamber of Commerce. The decision on whether or not to recommend that the store be allowed to open as planned was then to be taken by MITI in consultation with local small retailers, but they also had to take into account the interests of local consumers. It was originally anticipated that this entire process would take seven to eight months.

Initially, the new law did not have much effect on the continued expansion of large stores, and the number of large stores in Japan almost doubled between 1973 and 1978 (Upham 1989: 14). In addition, many of the chain stores once more found a way to circumvent the law by opening new branches of just under 1,500 m$^2$. This situation led to further demands from small retailers for the law to be strengthened, and in the subsequent decade measures were passed extending the scope of the law from stores over 1,500 m$^2$ to stores over 500 m$^2$ (1978) and modifying the adjustment process to allow for more extended consultation with local retailers. MITI's role was effectively reduced to that of providing a formal rubber stamp once local retailers had consented.[5] These changes led to extensive delays in the opening of new large stores, often of seven or eight years or longer, and in some cases the large retailers gave up their plans to open new branches altogether in the face of concerted local opposition.[6]

However, as with the Department Store Laws of 1937 and 1956, the impact of the 1973 law was not entirely unfavourable to the large-scale stores, as it had the effect of protecting existing market leaders and preventing the entry of new competitors into the market. This led to a mixed attitude among chain store executives at the prospect of the repeal of the law, with the President of Daiei, the largest of the chain stores, opposing repeal, and the president of Uny, frozen in a middle-ranking position among the chain stores by a tightening of the adjustment system in the 1980s, supporting deregulation. One chain store official commented:

> To put it bluntly, the Large Stores Law is like a depression cartel for superstores. If we didn't have it and were forced to compete freely, there would be a major restructuring among the major companies via mergers and acquisitions.
>
> *'Gekishin' ima, ryūtsu kawaru* ('Severe Earthquake' now, distribution changes), quoted in Upham (1989: 32)

In fact, some restructuring had already occurred. The 1970s saw an intensifying of competition in the retail sector, despite the protective action of the 1973 legislation, as speciality store chains, catalogue shopping, discount stores, and convenience stores all began operations. A trend for all these different types of retail operation to operate under a single umbrella emerged, usually linked with one of the big chain stores. Also, many chain stores responded to the 1973 oil shock and the consequent slowing down of the economy by opting for diversification, partly through expanding into various retail niches and partly through assuring themselves of supplies of low-cost merchandise by setting up subsidiary manufacturing companies.

Another trend in the 1970s and 1980s was for the chain stores to follow the department stores' lead in making themselves over as cultural/family entertainment centres. Small amusement parks sprang up on chain store roofs, in an analogous fashion to those built on department stores in the 1930s, and one chain store, Seiyu, established a reputation for itself in both the theatre and film-making. Some chain stores also began to challenge the department stores for custom at the upper end of the market, selling luxury goods and acquiring franchises for the distribution of foreign brand-name goods; for example, Aeon, the group that owns the Jusco chain stores, acquired the rights to distribute Laura Ashley goods in Japan in the late 1980s and Body Shop goods in 1990 (Larke 1994: 214).

By the early 1990s the major chain stores had each formed their own conglomerate retail group, typically including convenience stores, discount stores, leisure-related services, and speciality shops, and sometimes a department store, as well as the original general merchandise store at its centre. Several of these groups were highly profitable, far more so than many of the prestigious older stores in the department store sector, and they were even able to launch take-over bids for their higher-status competitors, e.g. when the Hoyokado retail group made an unsuccessful attempt to acquire Isetan in 1993 (Larke 1994: 224). The opinion of a number of commentators at this point was that the prospects of the chain store sector were far brighter than those of the department store sector, particularly given the liberalisation of the Large Store Law in the 1990s, which looked set to open the way for the continued and accelerated expansion of these (relative) newcomers to Japanese retail.[7]

In 1990, under pressure from the US government to make changes to the distribution system in Japan, the Japanese government announced that the Large Stores Law would be reformed. First, the implementation of the law was relaxed by reducing the adjustment period for seeking official approval before opening a store to eighteen months. At the same time, small adjustments were made to the sales area permitted without seeking approval, the opening hours, and the number of days stores had to be closed each year. In a further change, taking effect in January 1992, the adjustment period before opening a new store was streamlined and further reduced to a maximum of twelve months. In an effort to placate smaller retailers, the government also brought in legislation to support small local shops, including extra funding to enable the construction of shopping centres composed of small and medium-sized retailers.

The immediate result of these successive changes to the Large Store Law was a marked increase in applications to open new large stores between 1990 and 1992. For some chain stores this was accompanied by a series of closures of older, smaller branches. The trend among chain stores was initially to close smaller outlets alongside suburban railway stations, and instead to open large out-of-town shopping and leisure centres with parking facilities,[8] to attract families looking to combine shopping with entertainment for children.

At the same time as this relaxation in the law looked set to create fresh opportunities for the expansion of the chain store sector, Japan's post-bubble recession began to bite, and consumption began to slow down. Initially, the chain stores benefited in some ways from the slowdown, at the expense of the department stores. As consumers sought to cut their expenditure, many turned away from department stores to their cheaper competitors, even for items such as gifts, for which, as explained above, department stores had previously tended to be the preferred choice. In 1992 the sales of end-of-year gifts (*oseibo*) in chain stores rose while those in department stores fell (Larke 1994: 206). However, as the recession continued, the chain store sector also began to be adversely affected. In 1993, the combined sales of Japan's top 500 retailers showed close to zero growth (Nihon Keizai Shinbun 1999: 132), and the remainder of the 1990s was marked by poor sales figures and the efforts by all of the major large retail companies to restructure. Although many of the chain stores continued to expand their sales space, they did not shown a commensurate growth in sales and have increasingly sought to restructure their personnel and wage systems in response. This has tended to lead to more widespread adoption of merit-based rather than seniority-based pay, and also to an increase in the number of part-time staff, in an effort to cut the wage bill. The problems faced by retailers were exacerbated by the increase in consumption tax from 3 per cent to 5 per cent in 1997, further depressing sales. In 1998, of the ten top-ranking chain store companies, only four – Itoyokado, MyCal, Uny, and Maruetsu – made a profit, with the loss makers including such big names as Daiei and Seiyu (Nihon Keizai Shinbun 1998: 14).

On another front, pressure to further loosen, or abolish, the restrictions placed on the opening of large-scale stores has continued. In 1996, the US government asked for a further review of the Large Store Law and asked the World Trade Organization to arrange bilateral talks with Japan; by 1997 both the US government and the EU (European Union) were putting pressure on Japan to abolish the Large Store Law entirely. This put the Japanese government in a difficult position, particularly as the Japanese Chamber of Commerce opposed the abolition of the law. In the end, the solution found was to replace the Large Store Law with the Large Store Location Law (*Daitenritchihō*) coupled with legislation aimed at reviving town centres.

The Large Store Location Law, which came into effect in June 2000, ostensibly differs from the Large Store Law in that the aim of the new law is to protect the local environment and to benefit consumers (its predecessor explicitly aimed to protect small and medium-sized retailers). The consultation process before a new large store can be opened will therefore focus on issues of traffic, rubbish and recycling, noise, and other issues relating to the environment. At the same time, the responsibility for granting permission for new large stores to be opened will be transferred from central government (MITI) to local government. The consultation period of one year remains the same, but the size of store to which this applies has been increased from 500 m² to 1000 m². It is not possible at the time of writing to assess the impact of this new law, but in so far as it hands responsibility for permitting or forbidding development of new stores to local government, it would seem that the new law will continue to offer the potential for local, small retailers to block specific projects through lobbying local government officials, albeit on the grounds of environmental impact rather than the impact on their smaller competitors. How this will work out in practice seems likely to depend on local authorities and their relationships with retailers, both large and small, in their area.

## Employment structure and career development in the retail sector

One of the peculiarities of the retail sector compared with other sectors of the economy in Japan is its large number of 'part-time' employees. In 1996, of all the part-time workers in Japan[9] 47.2 per cent were employed in wholesale and retail compared with 20.5 per cent in manufacturing, 23.4 per cent in services, and only negligible percentages in other sectors of the economy (Japan Institute of Labour 1998a: 26).[10] Viewed from the perspective of relative percentages of part-time and full-time workers in a given industry, again wholesale and retail come top, with the percentage of part-time workers in this sector reaching 27.8 per cent in 1996, exactly double the figure for services and nearly three times that for manufacturing (Japan Institute of Labour 1998a: 26). The percentage of the workforce in retail and wholesale employed as part-timers has shown a marked rise since the mid-1970s, from 5.6 per cent in 1975, when the chain store boom was just getting under way, to 18.1 per cent in 1990, and 27.8 per cent in 1996, in the wake of widespread restructuring in this sector in the post-bubble economy. Increases in part-time staff have also taken place in other sectors of the economy since the 1970s, notably in manufacturing and in services, but these increases have been less dramatic than those experienced in the retail sector, as shown in Table 2.1.

Focusing on the chain store sector specifically, the rise in the proportion of part-time staff over the same period has been even more marked than for wholesale and retail as a whole. The number of part-timers rose rapidly from 29.5 per cent of the workforce in 1975 to around 40 per cent in 1980 and stayed at that level until 1991, when the proportion began to rise again and reached 57.6 per cent in 1998. Much of this increase has been achieved at the expense of female regular staff, whose numbers fell as a percentage of the total workforce from 33.4 per cent in 1975 to 15.8 per cent in 1998. A smaller fall was experienced by male regular staff over the same period, from 37.1 per cent to 26.6 per cent of the workforce in the chain store sector (Figure 2.1).[11]

The use of a high proportion of part-timers has been one way in which the chain stores have sought to cut costs, especially in times of economic difficulty,

*Table 2.1* Part-timers as a percentage of the total workforce, by industry

| | Part-timers' share in total employees (%) | | | | | |
| --- | --- | --- | --- | --- | --- | --- |
| | *1975* | *1980* | *1985* | *1990* | *1995* | *1996* |
| Wholesale and retail | 5.6 | 11.2 | 14.6 | 18.1 | 25.3 | 27.8 |
| Manufacturing | 2.7 | 5.3 | 8.5 | 10.1 | 10.5 | 10.0 |
| Services | 2.9 | 5.3 | 7.2 | 10.0 | 12.4 | 13.9 |
| Finance and insurance | 0.5 | 0.7 | 1.7 | 5.4 | 4.6 | 4.6 |
| Real estate | 0.4 | 1.6 | 4.0 | 7.3 | 17.7 | 3.5 |
| Transport and communication | 0.4 | 1.0 | 2.9 | 2.7 | 6.1 | 7.2 |
| Mining | 0.6 | 0.2 | 0.4 | 0.4 | 2.1 | 2.6 |
| Electricity, gas, and water supply | 0.3 | 0.1 | 0.4 | 0.9 | 1.9 | 1.8 |

Source: Adapted from Japan Institute of Labour 1998a: 26.

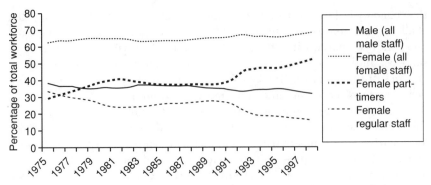

*Figure 2.1* Changes in the composition of the workforce in Japanese chain stores 1975–98. Figures from the Japan Chain Store Association 1998.

as can be seen during the economic slowdown of the second half of the 1970s after the oil shock of 1973, and again in the post-bubble economy of the 1990s. In fact, the term part-timer is a misnomer, as these employees often work thirty or more hours a week. Rather, the best way to understand this category of employee is in opposition to the other category of employee, the regular employees (*seishain*). The point at issue is not so much the hours worked as the status within the company. Whereas regular employees draw a monthly salary, receive sickness benefits, contribute to the company pension scheme, and are protected from redundancy by their membership in the company union, 'part-timers' receive few or none of these benefits and are paid at an hourly rate that in most cases ensures them a considerably lower take-home pay at the end of the month than is the case for regular employees. So what decides which employee is allocated to which category on entry to the company?

As noted in Chapter 1, 'lifetime employment' is, or has been until recently, an influential norm in large Japanese companies. In practical terms, this refers to the preference for recruiting regular employees from new high-school or university graduates. For these recruits, in the case of men the official expectation is that they will remain with the company until retirement, although in contrast women may only be expected to remain for a few years, possibly until marriage or the birth of her first child. Although it is possible to become a regular employee in some companies at a later point after a period of employment with another company, this path is both more unusual and more difficult, and it has even been given a special term: *chūto saiyō* or mid-career recruitment. Mid-career recruitment is essential for companies that have only recently been established, or that are experiencing a period of rapid growth, and was therefore widely practised by the chain stores during their period of expansion, but once a company is established, it tends to revert to the norm of recruiting only new graduates as regular employees.[12]

In any event, mid-career recruits who join the company as regular employees are almost invariably men. For the many women who rejoin the workforce after a break, for example to marry and/or to have children, the status of part-timer tends to be the only option available. It is also one taken up by far more women than men: a 1997 survey of the Japanese labour force found that 14.4 per cent of the workforce as a whole had part-timer status, but whereas this status covered 29.8 per cent of employed women it included only 1.2 per cent of employed men (Japan Institute of Labour 1998a: 25).

In many ways the status of part-timer has developed symbiotically with the re-entry of older women into the workforce in large numbers from the 1960s onwards (Brinton 1993: 10). Many of these women have tended historically to have few marketable skills, and thus they form a pool of relatively unskilled, cheap labour. Furthermore, for married women, the tax system in Japan gives incentives to take work that is paid below the threshold at which they would have to start paying tax, and thus enables employers to hire them at relatively low wages. And although the hours they work may often not be very much shorter than those worked by regular employees, even a small difference in the timing of shifts can be significant from the point of view of a married woman with children who has to get her family ready for school in the morning and to shop and cook for them at night. In Nagasakiya, for example, part-timers tended to work from 9.45 a.m. to 4.45 p.m. and many took Sundays off. In contrast, a female regular employee might work an 11 a.m. to 7 p.m. shift and also work Sundays with days off during the week – a far less convenient timetable for a woman who needs to consider childcare. For a woman with a family in Japan, therefore, the part-time option is in many cases preferable, despite the low wages.

On the other hand, the system of low-paid part-time working is open to criticism in Japan (as in many other countries) in that it is largely predicated on the misleading notion that part-time workers are married women working for pin-money: their income is secondary to the household, and their husband is the main breadwinner. This view has also been somewhat uncritically accepted by some academic commentators on Japan, as can be seen in Larke's comment on part-time women workers in retail:

> they do these jobs to fill their time and to top up the family budget. Some use this work as a source of pocket money.
>
> (Larke 1994: 29)

In fact, for many women, including some who head households, this income is indispensable for the survival of their families. In any case, it is argued by some (including a number of part-timers themselves) that they should receive an equal wage for equal work, regardless of their family circumstances. This is an area of controversy that will be returned to in Chapter 7.

The other main category of non-regular worker are the temporary staff, or *arubaito*, (from the German *arbeit*). These are, in the main, young people; sometimes they are students, or, particularly since the economic downturn, recent high-school graduates working on temporary contracts of employment.

This category shows a much more even gender split and accounts for 6.9 per cent of the workforce as a whole, 5.2 per cent of employed men and 7.5 per cent of employed women (Japan Institute of Labour 1998a: 25). Student *arubaito* often work for a few hours in the evenings, when chain stores are often short-staffed as the part-timers go home at the end of their shift, at weekends, or in school holidays. Recent school leavers who take an *arubaito* position, on the other hand, may work long hours six or more days a week. They are a floating element of the workforce, who receive no company benefits, have no job security, and receive little or no training. In chain stores they often do the simplest, most physically tiring work: moving goods round the store for the men, and shelf-filling and cleaning for the women.

In chain stores, then, the workforce consists of male regular workers, with almost all the older men in managerial positions, and the visible sales staff in the branches, a majority of whom are female. The women employees can again be divided into the regular workers, most of whom are single women under thirty years, and the part-timers, most of whom are older women who are married with children of school age or above. In addition there is a floating temporary workforce of *arubaito*, both male and female.

A further distinction in the workforce that underpins this structure is the sub-classification of regular employees into two tracks: a career track in which employees are subject to transfer anywhere in Japan or abroad (often termed *sōgō shoku*) and a non-career track in which employees are recruited to join a particular branch, or geographical area, and are not subject to transfer. Employees on the non-career track are not eligible for promotion beyond a fairly junior level. This tracking system is widespread among large companies in all sectors of Japan's economy, and has provided an effective unofficial gender-sorting mechanism since the implementation of the Equal Opportunities Law in 1986. Whereas most male employees enter the career track, most female employees are placed on the non-career track. However, this may be done ostensibly on the basis of factors other than gender, such as level of education. This often amounts to gender segregation by the back door, for many companies recruit male graduates from the four-year universities and female graduates from two-year junior colleges or high school.[13] Often, the reasons for discrimination against female university graduates is summarised and justified with reference to the expected life-course of the women:[14] the ideal age for marriage is supposed to be twenty-five for women, and it is expected that all women will marry and if possible will then have children. They are expected to resign from their company at the latest by the birth of their first child. It is therefore argued that it is in the employer's best interests to use women in relatively unskilled work, requiring little investment in training, and to hire them as young as possible in order to maximise the period of their employment by the company.[15]

In general terms, it is the male regular employees who are considered (at least from a management perspective) as the long-term core of the workforce in chain stores, as is the situation in other types of companies in Japan.

Whereas male employees are destined for long-term employment and managerial positions in due course, female employees tend to remain at low levels in the company doing jobs that are perceived as being relatively unskilled. As individuals, female shop staff tend to be seen as both dispensable and interchangeable to some degree; hence the general trend to reduce the number of regular female staff while increasing the number of cheaper female part-timers. The female staff in chain stores also contrast with the male staff in their heterogeneity: divided by generation and employment status, and with relatively high mobility between employers, there are many potential sources of tension in this section of the workforce, as will be seen in the more detailed description of employment in Nagasakiya in Chapter 5.

## Nagasakiya

Among the chain stores, by the late 1980s Nagasakiya was generally considered (and ranked in comparative sales and profitability tables) as distinctly second rate. This had not always been the case. Founded in 1948, Nagasakiya is one of the oldest of the chain stores. The first store was opened outside Hiratsuka station in one of the more distant suburbs of Tokyo by Iwata Kohachi the eldest son of a futon shop owner, and his wife.[16] Initially, it was a small family business selling futons and everyday clothing, but as it prospered more branches were opened and the range of business expanded.

By 1962 Nagasakiya had become a chain store with ten branches, and in 1963 it moved its headquarters to the present location in Nihonbashi in central Tokyo. The chain continued to expand during the 1960s and 1970s, and it established a number of subsidiary companies, including a clothing manufacturing company supplying low-priced merchandise to Nagasakiya stores. Throughout this period Nagasakiya was one of the top-ranking chain stores, outranking Daiei and Itoyokado both in size and in market share. In 1968 Nagasakiya became one of only three chain stores to be listed on the first section of the Tokyo stock exchange (Daiei, now the biggest chain store group in Japan, did not achieve this distinction until 1973, and Itoyokado not until 1974).

In the 1970s and 1980s, Nagasakiya followed the general trend among chains stores in diversifying its operations, setting up a series of linked companies, including specialist shops, franchise operations, travel and leisure companies, in-store family restaurants, and a chain of convenience stores. By 1991 the Nagasakiya group had 115 branches throughout Japan and two branches overseas, as well as over fifty subsidiary companies, including a chain of convenience stores, a chain of discount shops, a chain of speciality children's clothes shops, and a travel agency.

In the 1980s the company again followed more general trends in the sector to offer a range of services encompassing leisure and educational services as well as retail. In 1988 Nagasakiya announced its 'New Nagasakiya' plan, in which the company stated it wanted to provide not only clothes, food, and household necessities, but also 'play, sports, study, health and beauty' (Nagasakiya brochure for new recruits 1991). One of the major developments in this new plan was the opening of an indoor amusement centre in Hokkaido, called 'Fantasy Dome', in July 1990. Company brochures in the early 1990s also claimed to offer educational opportunities for new staff, such as English conversation classes, although staff in the Koganei branch, where I worked, had never heard of this option actually being available.

Despite its expansion and diversification, however, Nagasakiya experienced a steady loss of prestige and market share relative to its competitors throughout the 1980s. While Daiei and Itoyokado pursued a strategy of expansion through take-overs and mergers with other chain stores, Nagasakiya tried to grow as a single entity. Also, while other chain stores relied on food for a large proportion of their sales, the Nagasakiya stores did not include food as part of their main business until 1989.[17] Even at the end of the 1990s, by no means all Nagasakiya branches had a food section, although in a number of cases a part of a Nagasakiya branch was rented to a rival chain which provided the food section. By deciding to concentrate on selling clothes, Nagasakiya, in the view of many of its managers, had become weaker than its rivals in that it was less likely to draw in people who were simply doing their daily shopping.

Other factors contributing to Nagasakiya's decline were problems in senior management and the company's failure to create an attractive image. While other supermarket chains succeeded in re-branding themselves or in developing speciality lines (most notably Seiyu's *Mujirushi ryōhin* – no brand goods – line, which has also been successfully exported) to appeal to a younger market, Nagasakiya retained a middle-aged, unfashionable image.

As far as senior management was concerned, Nagasakiya remained a family-run firm until 1992, with the founder in charge of the company until 1988, when control passed to his son. According to some middle managers, the founder had had an authoritarian 'one-man, top-down' style of management. As long as he remained in charge, men in middle- and junior-management posts felt that they had no voice in the running of the company, and they were generally nervous about giving their opinions. It was strongly implied to me that the founder had made a number of bad decisions on the way the company should develop, and that he was largely to blame for the way in which Nagasakiya had fallen behind its rivals.

The first big crisis for Nagasakiya came in the 1980s, when the group was restructured as part of its diversification programme, resulting in the large-scale reallocation of staff among the newly formed subsidiaries. As a result of this, the figures for full-time employees show a marked annual fall for the years between 1982 and 1987.[18] This generated a certain amount of discontent among those staff who were reallocated, many against their will, and the 1986 company union survey[19] showed unprecedented levels of criticism of the company and senior management. In 1988 the founder retired from active management, becoming president of the Nagasakiya group, and passed on the post of managing director to his son. This was also the occasion for the launch of the 'New Nagasakiya' campaign already referred to (p. 23), one of the features of which was ostensibly a shift away from a management style dominated by one person to a philosophy of greater consultation with employees and a focus on the organisation rather than on its leader.

At the same time, there was a concerted attempt to improve Nagasakiya's image, with the adoption of a new company song composed by a then popular singer, a new motto, and a new statement of company vision.[20] Nagasakiya began selling food in 1989, and staff numbers again began to rise. In April 1991 there were 4,770 full-time staff, of whom 2,400 were men and 2,370 women. A further 5,560 part-time staff appeared on the company records.[21]

The 1990s, however, saw a succession of further problems again send Nagasakiya into crisis. A large fire in a branch of Nagasakiya in western Japan in the spring of 1990 in which fifteen people died further dented the chain's reputation. In 1992 compensation claims from the relatives of victims were settled, and in the same year company operations slid into the red for the first time. The founding family resigned *en masse* in October 1992, vacating the posts of president, managing director and another senior management post held by the son-in-law of the founder. The public statement said that by taking this action the family accepted responsibility for the decline in the company's fortunes. Their one concern, according to the statement, had been to ensure that compensation claims relating to the fire were settled before they resigned, and now that this had been done it was better for the company to go ahead under new management. A senior employee of the group was promptly appointed managing director, and the company's bank was approached with a request to provide the next company president.

The company's problems continued as the effects of Japan's recession began to take hold more generally in the retail sector. Under pressure from falling consumption on the one hand and increasingly fierce competition among the chain stores on the other, Nagasakiya found its problems compounded by the demands of servicing loans incurred during the company's attempts to expand in the bubble economy of the late 1980s. A restructuring programme was begun, involving selling off (often at a loss) both land and shares held by the company, as well as disposing of unprofitable subsidiary companies (and also a highly successful subsidiary chain of convenience stores, Sunkus) in an effort to consolidate the company business. Unprofitable branches in the core chain store business were also disposed of, and by 1998 the total number of Nagasakiya branches had fallen from the 1991 figure of 115 to ninety-eight.

At the same time, the company embarked on a programme of staff reduction. This was in part a necessary accompaniment to the reduction in the scope of operations, but it also served as an opportunity for reducing the proportion of more expensive employees, especially in the core chain store business. Two hundred and fifty of the older male employees were offered large bonuses to take early retirement in 1995, and another 200 were transferred to subsidiary companies, thus substantially cutting the average

age of Nagasakiya employees and the wage bill in the until then primarily seniority-based wage system. The numbers of staff in the head office of the company were also reduced. Recruitment of new full-time staff was scaled down, with the number of new female full-time staff in particular being drastically cut back. The total number of female full-time staff was allowed to shrink gradually through natural wastage, and their positions were filled where necessary by cheaper part-timers. By 1999, the number of full-time staff had fallen to 2,714 (1,553 men, 1,161 women) compared with 4,770 (2,400 men, 2,370 women) in 1991, but the number of part-timers had risen slightly from 5,560 to 6,023.[22] In percentage terms, this means that part-time staff, excluding those on short-term temporary contracts, climbed from around 54 per cent to nearly 69 per cent of the workforce over this period, whereas the total workforce dropped by a little over 15 per cent. At the time of writing, however, it appeared that none of these attempts to rescue the store had succeeded, and that the Nagasakiya group was heading inexorably towards collapse.

## Employment in Nagasakiya

In general terms, employment in Nagasakiya has followed the overall pattern for chain stores, with employees divided into regular and non-regular, career and non-career track, although it has its own particular twist on the latter division. Regular employees in Nagasakiya are divided up into three categories: national, zone, and home. National employees correspond to the career track and may be transferred anywhere in Japan. Zone employees may be transferred anywhere within a particular area, and home employees are recruited to one specific branch and are not subject to transfer. Most male regular employees are on a national contract, which means that they are subject to periodic transfers anywhere within Japan, sometimes entailing long periods of separation from their families.[23] Unmarried men under thirty generally live in company dormitories, and older married men either live in a house that they have purchased with help from the company or in company accommodation. Having once established a family in one location, they do not generally move the family when they are next transferred, and they may only see their wives and children rarely.

The national contract is not the only one available to men: although it is rare to find a male 'home' employee – this status is generally reserved for female regular employees – there were, at the time I did my fieldwork in 1991, a number of men who had opted for zone status, invariably for family reasons, generally ill-health of one or more family members. However, such a choice had serious implications for the career of the man concerned, imposing a relatively low ceiling on promotion prospects.[24]

The career paths of male regular employees have changed over time, with mid-career recruitment during the chain's period of establishment and expansion giving way to a policy of recruiting only new graduates, but in recent years even this recruitment has been drastically scaled down in response to the economic downturn. Given the policy of offering early retirement and relocating older male employees to subsidiary companies during the recent restructuring of the company, actual patterns of employment for male employees have often diverged widely from the norm of lifetime employment, although in 1999 this was still widely held as an ideal by the company managers, to which they hoped the company would return as economic conditions improved.

The transfer system, combined with the working hours of the retail sector (stores in Japan are open on Sunday, when most non-retail employees have the day off) tends to lead to most male employees' lives becoming very much centred on the company over time. For them, socialising tends to mean drinking with fellow company members (generally male), and their long-term bonds are with Nagasakiya rather than with a particular neighbourhood, in contrast with the experience of women employees. One manager in his forties whom I asked about his social life replied, 'Yes, all my friends are fellow employees. With our work schedule, working on Sundays, it's hard for us to see people who work for other companies. And anyway, we eat from the same rice pot' (i.e. the same company pays their salaries).

As with many companies in Japan, there is no official discrimination between male and female employees on the basis of gender in Nagasakiya, but a highly effective unofficial system exists through the sorting of new recruits into two categories depending on whether they are university or high-school graduates. University graduates are placed in the national contract scheme whereas high-school graduates are given 'home' employee status, with correspondingly fewer promotion chances. In practice, this division follows gender lines. During the period from 1964 to 1989, male employees were recruited exclusively from universities,[25] and, although recruitment of male high-school graduates resumed in 1989,[26] it is still true that the vast majority of male employees are university graduates. As far as women employees are concerned, I only came across one female university graduate employee at Nagasakiya during my fieldwork – all the rest were high-school graduates.

Nagasakiya personnel officers were reticent about the paucity of female university graduates in the company, simply remarking that perhaps such women were not interested in applying. However, it is likely that this lack of interest may have reflected a combination of the knowledge among women university students in Japan of the difficulties they are likely to face on entering any large corporation on favourable terms and more specifically a knowledge of Nagasakiya's poor record in employing women in senior positions. It is also possible that the company in past years had pursued an unofficial policy of discouraging such applicants and was unwilling to admit it to a female university-based researcher. Finally, it should be noted that there are, in any event, fewer female than male university graduates in Japan, owing in a large part to the poor employment prospects women face on graduation.[27]

In contrast to their male colleagues, female employees, even those who are full company members, find their lives less bounded by the company, both normatively and in practice. Long-term commitment is neither expected nor, in most cases, given, and since female employees are employed under the home contract their promotion prospects are in any case limited. Official company policy urges them to stay for at least three years and urges them to do their best to reach the rank of section chief. But this constitutes the effective ceiling to their career advancement – in the whole Nagasakiya chain by 1992 only three women had been promoted as far as floor manager, and none beyond that rank. In line with general practice in Japanese companies as outlined above, women regular employees are expected to leave, if not on marriage then by the time they become pregnant with their first child. Provisions did exist for women to take maternity leave and resume work later, but to take advantage of this would run counter to both company and social norms, in addition to posing not inconsiderable problems in arranging childcare given the shifts worked by regular employees, which often continued until 7 p.m., past the hours (roughly 8.30 a.m. to 6.00 p.m.) during which nursery care (*hoikuen*) for under fives is generally available in Japan.[28] Outside these times, it is difficult for women to arrange childcare as in Japan there are few private individuals who will provide such care, and also because many people disapprove of children being cared for by someone who is not related to them, by kinship, neighbourhood, or some other social tie. In practice, the most commonly used option is to ask a grandmother, but this is dependent on a grandmother living nearby, by no means always the case in contemporary urban Japan, where many people live at some distance from their natal families.

The management representation of the typical employment pattern of female regular employee at Nagasakiya, as expressed to me in interviews, was a brief period of employment at junior level, followed by resignation in order to marry or to have children. However, this was somewhat at variance both with the results of the company union survey on this issue and with the accounts given to me by the young women with whom I worked. In the company union survey of 1991, fewer than one-third of the women full-time employees stated that they wished to stop work on marriage or on the birth of their first child. On the other hand, this did not mean that they saw themselves as 'career women'. Only 18.9 per cent expressed a wish to continue for a long time, whereas 17.4 per cent said they wanted to stop soon but not to get married. The remainder (about half the sample) were 'don't knows', possibly reflecting a reluctance either to commit themselves or to disclose their intentions, even anonymously, to the company.[29]

From more detailed interviews conducted with the women regular employees at the branch where I worked, it would seem that many of them had their own life-course agenda, in which Nagasakiya was an initial staging post and marriage seen as an ultimate goal, but with other goals to be pursued between the two. These alternative agendas, and their implications for the emergence of a stage of independent young adulthood in the lives of Japanese women, are considered further in Chapter 7.

The other side of female employment within Nagasakiya is the employment of middle-aged women as part-timers. Broadly speaking, the pattern of employment for part-timers in Nagasakiya follows that described for retail as a whole, but at the time of my fieldwork in 1991 there were also two important sub-categories of part-timer: *junshain* and *teijishain*. *Junshain* can be translated as junior company member. These employees receive the advantage of health insurance and twice-yearly bonuses in return for a slightly lower hourly rate of pay than that of ordinary part-timers. *Teijishain*, literally meaning fixed-term employee, was a status open to part-timers with at least one year's service who passed a special exam. In addition to the benefits received by *junshain*, *teijishain* status conferred membership in the company union, a privilege only open to this category of part-timer. Since one of the main functions of the union is to resist any of its members being dismissed, this status was also thought to confer greater job security than that attached to other part-time positions.

Neither *junshain* nor *teijishain* status was generally differentiated by staff when talking about their own or another's position in the company. A more salient division in terms of the way part-time staff viewed themselves was that of 'veteran' (*beteran*) versus the rest. The 'veterans' were those who had worked with the company for a long time – in some cases ten years or more. Although as 'part-timers' they were denied the opportunity for promotion to a managerial rank, often these women effectively undertook managerial responsibilities, running sections of the store, and were appointed as mentors to supervise and train new regular female staff. They correspond to what Nakamura (1990) has termed 'core part-time workers' (*kikan gata pāto*).[30] On the other hand, there was a floating pool of part-timers who stayed only for a short time and tended to do simpler, more routine work, often under the supervision of a 'veteran'. Although the formal job status of these two types of part-timer was in many cases the same (although sometimes a veteran attained the rank of, for example, *teijishain*), the veterans themselves, at least, saw them as distinct categories and were sometimes impatient with what they saw as ordinary part-timers' lack of commitment. Other research suggests that this type of division among part-timers in retail may be widespread, and it calls into question the characterisation of regular workers as the core workforce with part-timers on the periphery (Mitsuyama 1991; Honda 1993; Wakisaka 1997). This is a debate that will be returned to in more detail in Chapters 7 and 9.

The other kind of non-regular worker, the *arubaito*, comes at the bottom of the Nagasakiya hierarchy. These workers, as described above (pp. 21–2), are either casual student labour or recent school leavers effectively working full time. In the climate of the late 1990s, many of these may have become *arubaito* simply because there was no other job available, but in more prosperous times before the economic downturn there were also a number who had chosen this work pattern in preference to the more restricted (though more secure) working conditions of the regular employees.

To talk about company employees as a general group is, therefore, in the Nagasakiya case at least, highly problematic. Indeed, the company itself recognises the diversity of its staff in the various categories to which they are allocated. The main dividing lines that are used by the company to classify employees are those of gender, education, and part-time/full-time status. If official employment status is left to one side, an alternative way of viewing the divisions within the company is along the lines of gender, generation, and place of origin (rural or urban). For any branch in the Tokyo area, the female regular employees are mainly young, from rural backgrounds; the part-timers are female, middle-aged, and generally from the city; the temporary staff (*arubaito*) are young, urban, and may be either male or female; but only the male regular employees span the generations and the rural–urban divide.

However, even these dividing lines are not as simple as they at first appear. To take only the example of gender as a classificatory device, not all male employees resemble each other, even if they are of an analogous level of education and generation and enjoy full-time employment status. Further differentials are introduced by such factors as whether or not they are mid-term recruits, whether they have opted for a zone or a national contract, and how successful they have been in the promotion stakes. Any notion of a typical male employee receives a further blow from the male *arubaito*, whose work strategies seem radically different from that of the stereotypical Japanese salary man. Equally, as we shall see in Chapter 7, regular female employees fail to follow neatly the stereotype of working until marriage and child-bearing persuade them to leave the workforce; in practice, they follow a range of trajectories in which work, social pressures, and marriage and child-bearing intersect in complex ways. And even within the category of part-timer there is greater diversity than at first appears, with veteran part-timers working alongside a shifting pool of short-term, part-time labour.

One might reasonably ask at this point, what, if anything, joins these different employees together? What made them choose Nagasakiya as their employer? What does the notion of Nagasakiya as a company mean to them, and how do they perceive their role within it? And how have they been affected by the decline in Nagasakiya's fortunes? As a first step to answering these questions the next chapter investigates the process of recruitment. But before moving on to look at recruitment, the next section looks more closely at the Koganei branch of Nagasakiya in western Tokyo, in which I did my fieldwork, my position in the branch as a part-time temporary employee, and the ways in which that has affected the research presented in the remainder of this book.

## The context: Nagasakiya, Koganei branch

The Koganei branch of Nagasakiya, in which I worked as a sales assistant between 1990 and 1991, is located in a suburb in the west of Tokyo, about a thirty-minute train ride from Shinjuku. Koganei is a fairly mixed area, with substantial private houses interspersed with low-cost municipal housing, privately owned apartment blocks, and more dilapidated private houses. North of the station, the area was largely farmland until about the 1960s, when a period of rapid construction began. Today, little farmland is left, and the main distinguishing feature of the area is its enormous park, reputed to be one of the three best places in Tokyo for viewing cherry blossoms.

Construction of shops in the area was first dominated by small family businesses, but in the early 1970s the first large chain store, Seiyu, was built immediately in front of the north exit of the station, followed three years later by the construction of the Nagasakiya store, a mere fifty yards or so down the street from its rival. Initially, small, local shops, especially clothing shops, campaigned against the opening of the two chain stores, but twenty years on there was little evidence of lingering bad feeling, with local shop owners' families shopping regularly in the large stores, and sometimes socialising with the employees.

The Koganei branch of Nagasakiya has seven floors and a basement, with a total sales area of 10,000 m². It is therefore slightly larger than the average Nagasakiya branch (6,000 m²) and has nearly twice the sales area of its neighbour, Seiyu. It is, by some way, the largest chain store in the area, and this advantage of size, combined with the fact that in the case of this branch the company owns both the land and the building outright, unencumbered by loans, helped the Koganei branch to survive while other neighbouring branches of Nagasakiya closed during the 1990s.

In appearance, Nagasakiya is fairly typical of large Japanese chain stores. Window displays are forgone in favour of a larger sales area, with the space outside the front of the store taken up by customers' bicycles and stands selling an ever-shifting selection of low-priced goods on special offer. It is always very congested outside the store, especially at the side, where only a narrow alley separates it from the *pachinko* parlour next door,[31] and the store periodically gets into trouble with the fire department because of the customers' bicycles blocking the street.[32]

Inside the store, the customer's eyes are immediately drawn to numerous stands displaying cut-price goods (Figure 2.2), and the day's special offers are further reinforced by announcements on the public address system. This also provides a stream of background music, often songs recorded specially for Nagasakiya, in which the store's name is repeated again and again in the chorus.

The Koganei branch sells a wide range of goods, including household necessities, furniture, and toys as well as clothes, Nagasakiya's original speciality, with each floor roughly themed to bring together similar goods. White linoleum flooring and cheap-looking display units combined with the ubiquitous cut-price stands help to create a bargain basement atmosphere. However, some luxury goods such as imported designer brand leather handbags, gold jewellery, and fur coats are also available. As is common with

*Figure 2.2* Stands in front of the Koganei branch of Nagasakiya displaying cut-price
    goods

chain stores, the goods sold are aimed chiefly at the middle-aged housewife
market (identified by in-house research as Nagasakiya's main customers).
From the point of view of the younger generation of Japanese, including most
of the store's young employees, the goods on sale lack fashionable appeal,
and most of the younger employees therefore prefer to do their shopping
elsewhere, despite the employee discount that is available to them.

## From customer to employee: becoming a part-timer at Nagasakiya

The part-time staff at Nagasakiya are drawn largely from the same base as
the store's customers: women who live within easy walking or cycling distance
of the store. Some are introduced to the store by friends already working
there, and others may apply in response to advertisements placed in the store
(or in the local press). At the time that I did my fieldwork in 1990–1, there
was a labour shortage in Japan and, in Tokyo especially, such jobs were easy
to find.

In some ways, my life at that time was not dissimilar from that of other
part-timers in the store. I was married with a small child and living in Koganei,
a five-minute cycle ride from the store. My husband commuted to work in
central Tokyo, working late every night, and I looked after our one-year-old
daughter and took care of our small flat. The reasons that made Nagasakiya
an attractive local employer to other married women with children living
locally also applied to me: it was close to home, and the hours were flexible
and could be combined with childcare (on obtaining a job at Nagasakiya my
daughter rapidly got a place at the local nursery on the basis of my being a

working mother). It had also been politely suggested to me by department stores which I had originally approached as possible field sites that for someone like me – perhaps referring to my age (thirty-one) and less than perfect command of formal Japanese – a local chain store might be a more suitable employer than a department store.

Like a number of other part-timers at the store, my job – officially an *arubaito*, or temporary member of staff, but with the uniform usually worn only by part-timers and regular members of staff – was eventually arranged with the help of an introduction. In my case this was from an influential local businessman and property owner, Mr Sekiguchi, to whom I had been introduced via a network of local and foreign housewives. Mr Sekiguchi knew the manager of the local branch of Nagasakiya, and he introduced me to him as a visiting researcher who wanted to experience work in a Japanese chain store.

The fact that my entry to Nagasakiya was arranged in this way, through a local network of contacts, had some important implications for the research I was able to do. First, my view of the store remained firmly locally based, and I had only limited contacts with the store's central organisation until a return visit in 1999, five years after my family and I had moved to England. On this occasion, Mr Sekiguchi arranged for me to talk to a senior manager at the head office about the changes in Nagasakiya since I had ceased to work there. The manager whom I interviewed appeared somewhat surprised to learn of my earlier fieldwork, thus confirming my feeling at the time that my access to the store had been arranged without official higher-level approval.

My perspective throughout my fieldwork was thus constrained both by being localised and by being that of a junior female employee. I had no chance to observe the way in which the company was managed at the most senior level, or the way in which important decisions were reached. On the other hand, I was able to participate in the everyday working and social life of the company without restrictions, other than those imposed by my status as a female part-time employee, and to talk to whomever I wished about whatever I chose. This contrasted with my return visit in 1999, when most of my previous senior contacts had left, including the store manager who had initially made the research possible. On this occasion, I was restricted, as far as currently employed members of the company were concerned, to conducting pre-arranged interviews in the formal setting of the branch office. As I already knew most of these employees from many years before, we were able to chat in a relatively relaxed way. However, there was still some feeling of constraint in this formal setting, and my feeling is that had I conducted my research on this formalised basis initially there is much material I would have missed.

Other factors affecting my research were my age, gender, and family situation, as well as my betwixt and between status as a foreigner married into a Japanese family. As a married woman with a one-year-old child, I had to juggle demands of family and work in much the same way as other female part-timers, and, as the wife of a Japanese man, I was also subject to the same sorts of social norms and expectations as other Japanese women. At the time of my initial research, I was in my early thirties and was classified as a middle-aged woman in Japanese terms, one of the 'auntie' or *oba-san* generation. This meant that certain types of behaviour were seen as inappropriate for me – more particularly so as my husband is Japanese, and I was therefore expected by the Nagasakiya employees to conform to Japanese norms of behaviour. For example, there was a limit to the extent to which I could participate in drinking parties, an important type of socialising in Japan. All-male drinking parties were out, and when, in the course of an evening's outing, it came time for the women to return home and the men to carry on drinking alone, I had to go home too. Much of the informal world of the male employees was therefore barred to me.

If the perspective taken here is therefore partial, it is also one shared to a great extent by other part-time women employees of the same generation within the company. As Jenkins (1994) has argued, there is, in any case, no such thing as a neutral, disengaged perspective in fieldwork. The vast majority of published material on large Japanese companies to date concerns the experience of male employees, so there is in any case a need for a more careful consideration of the working lives of women, and women part-timers in particular, in large companies. I have, however, tried to supplement this part-timers' perspective by interviews with a range of employees, and also by participating in some events and courses intended for regular employees, including recruitment seminars and the training course described in Chapter 4.

In terms of the way in which I was perceived by other employees, I was initially introduced as a researcher attached to Tokyo University, and I was clearly under the patronage of the manager of the store. This contributed to a degree of reserve in the way in which other employees responded to me in the first months of my employment. However, my other identity as local housewife and mother helped to break down barriers, as did my curiosity value as a foreigner and speaker of English – a language many of the staff wanted to learn. Also, as I continued to work alongside other employees, doing exactly the same work as other part-time staff, it seemed that I gradually came to be viewed as less of an outsider.

Over the months that we worked together, I found a shift took place in the kind of statements other employees would make to me, with a gradual increase in willingness to express their misgivings or criticisms of the company becoming evident as they got more used to having me around. It thus seemed clear to me that a range of representations of the company were evoked depending on context and on who is asking the questions, with more normative accounts reserved for the public face of the company and people seen as outsiders. In this respect, an important turning point in my research was after I took part in the training course for new full-time recruits, six months after joining as a part-timer (this was purely for the purposes of research –

normally no part-timer would be allowed to do this course). On returning from the course I found that other full-timers began to talk to me more, and I started to be invited to company events and parties. Eventually I came to be regarded with a certain amusement, and would be greeted by groups of employees with comments such as: 'Watch out, it's Matsunaga-san coming to interview you', 'Be sure you tell her the truth now', 'Matsunaga-san, stop taking notes!'

I gathered later that few people expected me to stay as long as I did – eleven months – leaving, as it turned out, one month after the branch manager who had first allowed me to work there was transferred. At the second stage of his leaving party, when we had adjourned to a karaoke bar and most people appeared pleasantly inebriated, he announced to me that he had never thought I would last, and that I was the only foreigner ever to have worked that long in the store. He said he thought most foreigners did not have the right spirit to last in the job and somewhat emotionally added that he hoped I would always continue working there.

Although to some extent this remark merely reflects the mood of that particular evening, and in Japan one is not supposed to admit to remembering remarks made while drunk in any case, the manager's comment does seem to me to have some implications worth noting. First of all, it underlines the importance attached to endurance, sticking it out, a quality that the company sought to encourage (at that time at least) especially in new female recruits, a category which tended to have a high turnover. Also, although in my particular case the manager may well have been simply being polite, many other part-time female staff I know have also been strongly encouraged to remain with the company by senior male managers, and treated (at least on certain occasions) as valued quasi-members of Nagasakiya. This tendency has persisted even in the post-bubble economy, with the long periods of service of certain part-time female staff becoming even more striking in the light of the early retirement or transfer to subsidiary companies of so many of the senior male staff. Again, it tends to underline the complexity of employment relations at Nagasakiya, a theme which will be returned to in the discussion that follows.

# 3  Recruitment

## Recruitment and the labour market in the 1990s

The process of recruitment to Nagasakiya, as to all large Japanese retail outlets, varies considerably depending on the type of employee being recruited. As can be seen in the account of my own experience of joining Nagasakiya as a temporary employee in the previous chapter, the employment of non-regular staff is very much a local affair organised by local branch managers. Recruitment of non-regular staff may take place at any time of year, depending on the needs of the store, and it may be done by personal introduction or by advertising in the store or locally. Staff recruited for these kinds of vacancies also tend to live locally and to be familiar with the store itself, often as customers, before they begin work.

The situation for the recruitment of regular employees is very different. It is organised centrally, by the head office of the company, and takes place nationwide. For high-school graduates the practice is to recruit through their high schools, as is generally the case for large companies in Japan,[1] but for university graduates there is a more complex process of informal contacts with students, as well as a more public series of talks or seminars organised by individual companies for prospective recruits.

Recruitment of regular employees notionally follows a fixed timetable, and voluntary agreements between the employers' association, Nikkeiren and the schools and universities exist to regulate this procedure. For high-school graduates, individual applications may be made to companies from 1 July, teachers' recommendations may be submitted from 5 September, and company entrance examinations may be held from 16 September. Until 1991, the rule for university graduates was that contacts between the company and new recruits could be made from 1 August, with firm offers of employment issued from 1 October for entry the following April. This was relaxed in 1991 to allow companies to begin recruiting university graduates from 1 July. In practice, however, informal job placement of university graduates begins far earlier, with most job offers for management track employees already made well in advance of the official deadline (Rebick 1998: 20–2).

In many cases, including that of Nagasakiya, new recruits are officially selected by an examination (in the case of Nagasakiya including an IQ test and a test designed to assess character) followed by an interview. However, Rebick (1998: 22) suggests that the examinations may be designed more in order to give an impression of fair and objective hiring rather than as an actual means of selecting recruits. This suggestion is supported by comments made to me by a recruitment officer at one of the more prestigious chain stores, who explained that her company decided whether or not to take someone on the basis of their performance at the interview, whether they were friendly and well spoken, and on the basis of the ranking of the university they attended, with the exam being merely a formality.

The principle of ranking, both of educational institutions and of companies, is important in understanding recruitment in Japan. A large number of publications exist giving the comparative rankings of universities on the one hand and companies on the other, and this type of information is widely disseminated. In general terms, top-ranking institutions will seek to recruit from top-ranking universities, whereas lower-ranking institutions have to content themselves with graduates from equivalently ranked universities. However, as Rebick (1998) shows, this matching of graduates with companies of equivalent rank to their universities is never a perfect fit and will vary depending on economic conditions. In times of relative economic prosperity, for example, the top-ranking companies may not be able to fill all their vacancies with graduates from prestigious universities, and they may thus have to also recruit from lower-ranking universities. However, in some cases lower-ranking companies may also try to find ways of attracting graduates from high-ranking universities in order to improve their own prestige.

Viewed from the perspective of Nagasakiya, a middle-ranking company in a low-prestige sector of the economy, the ranking system means that in general the company had little hope of attracting graduates from top-ranking universities. The problem of attracting male university graduate recruits for the management track became particularly acute during the early 1990s, when Japan was experiencing a shortage of new graduates relative to job openings. This led to fierce competition among lower-ranked companies in the retail sector and elsewhere for the available recruits. In this climate, the emphasis was less on the recruits trying to present themselves in a favourable light to their potential employers and more on companies repackaging themselves to create a more attractive image for the potential recruits.

At the same time, there were also fewer high-school graduates entering the job market, owing to a combination of the declining birth rate and an increasing trend for students to enter some form of tertiary education.[2] This posed a particular problem for companies in sectors (such as retail) that were heavily dependent on high-school graduates. Probably the worst hit sectors were those popularly characterised in Japan as the three Ks, *kitanai, kitsui, kiken,* (dirty, tiring, and dangerous), such as the building trade,[3] but a survey released by the Labour Ministry in December 1991 showed that personnel shortages were also reported by 53 per cent of manufacturing firms; 45 per cent of wholesalers, retailers, and eating establishments; and 58 per cent of service industries (*Daily Yomiuri*, 11 December 1991).

High schools targeted by recruitment officers tend to be of two types: vocational high schools or lower-ranked ordinary high schools (graduates of higher-ranking ordinary high schools tend to go on to further education). Japan's vocational high schools are classified into six types depending on the kind of courses they offer: industrial (offering subjects such as mechanics and electronics), agricultural, fisheries, commercial, home economics, and nursing. Companies targeting the vocational high schools will select a high school teaching subjects appropriate to the company's needs; for example, manufacturing companies tend to target industrial high schools.

Companies in the retail sector look for recruits from the lower-ranking ordinary high schools or the commercial high schools. However, as many companies from various sectors were targeting these schools in the late 1980s and early 1990s, competition for recruits was quite intense, especially in the metropolitan areas of Japan, where a large number of companies were concentrated. In rural areas there were far fewer locally based employers, and the job openings to applications ratio in the outlying areas of Japan was therefore not as favourable, even during Japan's bubble economy, as it was in the main urban centres and surrounding districts.[4]

In this context, and given that the higher-ranking companies all recruited in the Tokyo area, one solution for lower-ranking companies with a recruitment problem was to recruit their high-school graduates from areas outside Tokyo, and preferably outside Kanto (the larger geographical area within which Tokyo is located). This was the pattern followed by Nagasakiya, where the vast majority of female regular employees at that time were drawn from outlying areas of Japan, particularly Tohoku in the north east and Kyushu in the west, with the percentage of non-local staff among the female regular employees at the Tokyo branches of the chain exceeding 90 per cent.

With this type of recruitment one motivation for joining the company may often have been a desire to leave home and move to the city, as I found for a large number of Nagasakiya's female regular employees. In such cases, the company was attractive to the new recruits not for its own intrinsic qualities but because it could offer access to an independent urban lifestyle enjoyed by young adults in the time between joining the workforce and getting married.

In addition to recruiting from rural areas, in the early 1990s many companies suffering from the labour squeeze increased the numbers of part-time employees and introduced year-round hiring (*Japan Times*, 3 May 1991). There were also some moves to try to retain female employees beyond the marriage and child-bearing watershed, but with limited success. However, the preference for hiring new graduate labour persisted, and the main response of most companies was to try and make themselves appear more attractive to potential recruits still in school or further education.

One common strategy was to improve the fringe benefits offered; for example, by offering new recruits single-room 'dormitories' that were identical to private apartment blocks of self-contained studio flats, but at heavily subsidised rents and for the exclusive use of unmarried employees of the company.[5] This was a very attractive benefit even for Tokyo residents wishing to leave home, and still more so for recruits from the countryside. Rents for private accommodation in Tokyo are prohibitively high, particularly since 'key money'[6] and a damage deposit are required, in addition to rent in advance. Altogether, anything from three to five months' rent or more may be required up front before the tenant can move in. In addition, there is the cost of furnishing the flat, as apartments in Japan are rented unfurnished, and, in more modern buildings, the tenants may also have to bear the cost of installing an electric heating and air conditioning system.[7] For young people from poor families in rural areas, becoming a regular employee of a Tokyo-based company and thus qualifying for heavily subsidised company accommodation, with generally a minimum of essential equipment such as heating and a washing machine provided by the company, can be an attractive means to an end. In any case, for both rural and urban-based recruits, the quality of dormitory accommodation offered by a prospective employer was an important consideration at that time.

A less tangible area that companies sought to address in order to resolve their recruitment difficulties was that of corporate image. The deputy director of a Tokyo-based company that researches into social trends in Japan, Hakuhodo Institute of Life and Living, commented in 1991 that:

> It is becoming increasingly important for businesses to create good images from the point of view of securing manpower. Music and sports used to be popular tools, using high-tech to create amusement facilities to lure young people is a new trend.
>
> (H. Sekizawa, quoted in *Asahi Evening News*, 16 June 1991).

The same article that quotes Sekizawa refers to three companies, Fujita Corp. (a construction company), Toyota, and Matsushita, which had attempted to improve their image by constructing virtual-reality-type amusement centres at their offices in Tokyo, with all the attractions open to the public free of charge. These centres had subsequently become popular dating venues for young people and were also well received by employees with young families, who liked being able to bring their children for a day out at their workplace. Another common way in which companies sought to improve their image, widely reported in the press at the turn of the decade, was by commissioning a famous designer to redesign the company uniform in a more modern style, or sometimes a choice of styles.

A plethora of articles and books appeared in the late 1980s and early 1990s addressing the question of what it is that the new recruits seek in an employer, and what sort of image would appeal to the current generation of school/college leavers. League tables were also produced ranking the most popular employers, often producing different results from the more established rankings by turnover or profitability.[8] Implicit in these publications was a view of the potential recruit as consumer, shopping around to find the company that would best suit him or her in terms of style and image as well as the prestige of the company and the benefits on offer.

Newspaper articles bewailed the changing attitudes of the new generation of recruits, noting that these young employees increasingly sought to impose conditions on what sort of work they were willing to do within the company, rather than, as in former years, accepting whatever post the company allocated to them. Survey findings were regularly published purporting to measure the extent to which new recruits put their personal life before their company, generating articles with titles such as '40 per cent of New Recruits Refuse Overtime Work in Order to Have Dates' (*Asahi Evening News*, 16 July 1991). And the new chairman of Nikkeiren went on record in May 1991 as attributing the labour shortage to the 'fact that people here just don't want to work anymore' (*Mainichi Shinbun*, 21 May 1991).

Tobin (1992b: 23) sums up the view expressed in the media as depicting this new generation, the *shinjinrui*, as 'disrespectful, individualistic, selfish, uncommitted, and materialistic'. However, in Tobin's view, the last of these characteristics, that of being 'materialistic' is the defining trait of the *shinjinrui*: he sees them as a generation driven by consumption, who construct their own identity and lifestyle in terms of the goods they buy, the places at which they shop, and the type of leisure interests they pursue. In this scheme of things, the company for which one works is no longer the defining aspect of identity, as it was claimed to be for the previous generation by Nakane (1970).

Novels, dramas, and other products of popular culture from Japan's boom years often depicted young people for whom work was a means to an end, providing a pay cheque, friends, and an opportunity to achieve an urban lifestyle in which leisure pursuits are prominent. The subordination of work and company affiliation to consumption and leisure was highlighted by the popularity of the *arubaito* (temporary employee) as a character in television dramas aimed at the youth market.[9] Often one of the leading characters might be a young man who had chosen not to be a regular employee, instead opting for *arubaito* status work for the freedom it bestows. This revisioning of the role of *arubaito* is evident in a term recently coined for this type of employee, *furiitā* from the English for free. During the early 1990s this type of free, uncommitted lifestyle became trendy, if not necessarily to follow oneself, then possibly to admire from a distance.

With this consumer-orientated youth market in mind, the trend in Japan in the early 1990s was to repackage companies to make them more attractive consumer products, offering not only employment, but also, ideally, a fashionable image and lifestyle. At the same time, numerous publications were produced assessing the relative merits of different companies, enumerating their defects and suggesting how they should change. For example, in *Yoi Kaisha* (*Good Company*), a best-selling publication of the *Nikkei shinbun* (*Japan Economic Journal*) first published in 1989, the authors argue that Japanese companies need to change from 'strong companies' (*tsuyoi kaisha*), driven by a desire to increase market share, to being 'good companies' (*yoi kaisha*). Whereas strong companies have a closed image, with a corporate culture of *'ganbarisumu'* (giving it all you've got), 'goodness' (English word used in the text) is defined as a combination of traits. A good company must have a character that is at the same time universal (*fuhensei*) and individual (*dokujisei*); universal here meaning internationalist in outlook,[10] and individual meaning having its own particular character that differentiates it from its fellows. Most importantly, a good company, according to this analysis, is one that creates a happy atmosphere and motivates its employees by trying to see things from their point of view (Nikkei Business 1989: 9–23).

Individual companies attempted to revamp their image during this period by calling in corporate identity specialists to produce new logotypes and corporate brochures aimed at new recruits. In the creation of a new corporate identity, the designers would work from a list of key words embodying the image that the company wished to project. Some of the most popular words that recurred in this context were *kokusaika* (internationalisation) *kosei* (individuality) or *dokujisei* (individuality, originality), *wakawakashisa* (youthfulness), and *yasashisa* (kindness, gentleness).[11] Individuality here refers to the individuality of the company compared with its rivals, but in corporate recruitment literature of this period the theme of the company responding to the diverse needs of its employees as individuals also receives emphasis, contrasting sharply with English-language depictions of Japanese companies as primarily group orientated. Foreign loan words such as *dainamiku* (dynamic), *akutibu* (active), and *charenji* (from challenge, but used to mean exert yourself) are also prominent, again emphasising the twin themes of internationalism and youthfulness.[12]

By the late 1990s, in contrast, the change in economic conditions meant recruitment generally had slowed, as many companies cut back on recruitment of new graduates as a way of reducing overall staffing, and in some cases (as in retail) shifted to a greater reliance on part-time and temporary employees. University graduates, especially from low-ranking institutions, were experiencing increasing difficulty in finding jobs, and in 1998 the number of employed university graduates fell to its lowest level for forty-eight years, at just 65.6 per cent (Naganawa 1999: 1). For high-school graduates too, the situation had altered, with less demand from large companies in sectors that had previously employed school leavers. Instead, the relative balance shifted in favour of smaller companies, who by the late 1990s were able to recruit school leavers more easily, with the percentage of high-school graduates finding jobs in firms with fewer than 500 employees rising to over 60 per cent by 1995, compared with around 50 per cent in 1991 (Naganawa 1999: 5). However, at the same time, the proportion of high-school graduates continuing to tertiary education has continued to rise and the total number of high-school students to fall, so that unemployment among high-school graduates is not, at present, a major problem in Japan.

Against this background, the ways in which companies have sought to present themselves to new recruits has also shifted. In the remainder of this chapter I examine this shift as shown in the recruitment brochures produced by Nagasakiya for high-school graduates and for university graduates entering the company in 1992 – these were distributed in 1991, just before Japan entered recession – compared with those produced in 1999 in the context of the post-bubble economy. I also compare the ways in which Nagasakiya has sought to present itself to high-school recruits and to university recruits, and the implications of this for the ways in which the relationship of these two types of recruit with the company are envisaged.

## Repackaging Nagasakiya: recruitment in the period of labour shortage

Recruitment brochures produced by companies in Japan tend to be of two types: those aimed at high-school graduates, and those aimed at university graduates. The style and content of these two types of brochure tend to vary widely, reflecting, in Nagasakiya's case, the fact that the high-school brochure is aimed largely at young women, who are not expected to stay with the company very long, whereas the university brochure is aimed largely at male recruits, who, it is anticipated, will form the managerial core of the company in the future.

The Nagasakiya 1992 girls' high-school recruitment brochure is designed in the same format as a girls' fashion magazine (Figure 3.1). The brochure is indeed described in English as, 'Magazine for High-school Students', although the Japanese in the right-hand corner reads '1992 company entrance information'. An international image is suggested both by the use of English and by the title of the brochure, the Italian greeting 'Ciao'. The text reads like a paradigm of contemporary youth concerns with the following headlines (going from right to left): 'Work to suit your style!' (*jibunrashiku shigoto shiyō!*); 'In Nagasakiya you can have fulfilling private time too!' (*Nagasakiya nara, puraibeto taimu mo jujitsu dekiru*); 'Document! The people of Nagasakiya and their work' (*dokyumento! Nagasakiya no hitobito to shigoto*); 'Detailed check. Nagasakiya is this kind of company' (*komakaku chekku. Nagasakiya wa konna kaisha desu*).

Inside, the brochure continues in the same vein, still with a fashion-magazine-type layout, and lots of colourful photographic illustrations, mostly showing young, smiling, Nagasakiya employees surrounded by montages of the various goods the chain sells. Throughout the brochure there is a strong emphasis on individuality, with frequent use of words such as *jibun* (self) *hitorihitori* (one by one, each person) and *kosei* (individuality, personality). The discourse is predominantly that of consumption, with work and the company presented as a consumer product, something you choose because it fits your personality and lifestyle.

*Figure 3.1* The Nagasakiya 1992 girls' high-school recruitment brochure

For example, the introduction pictures a young female employee in uniform and text written in an informal, spoken style of Japanese. This begins:

> Each person has a different personality. That's why I think having your own sense of self, your own style, is important. Just like you express yourself through fashion, you want to express yourself in work, too.[13]

Other points highlighted in this introduction as features that made

Nagasakiya a desirable workplace were contact with people, the cheerful atmosphere of the workplace, the uniforms designed by a well-known fashion designer, and the kindness of more senior employees (*senpai shain*).[14] But the point most emphasised, running throughout this section, was that at Nagasakiya employees could do work that was *jibunrashii*, a difficult word to translate, but which derives from the word *jibun*, self, and has the meaning of suiting or expressing one's self; it is very often used in the sense of a person's individual sense of style – whether fashion or lifestyle.

This focus on how Nagasakiya can help its individual employees to express themselves, and make work an expression of their lifestyle, continues throughout the brochure. First, there are short interviews with employees (five women and one man), revolving around the theme of how they found various aspects of the work difficult at first but have now overcome these difficulties. One particular aspect focused on for several of the women was nervousness with customers, with the comment that once customers get to recognise the new employee and speak to her themselves when they come into the store, the employee begins to feel happier about dealing with them and can begin to find satisfaction in being a sales adviser. Other topics discussed in the interviews include comments on the company dormitory (all favourable), leisure, or 'private time',[15] and plans for the future; the two women who spoke about their future plans said they wanted to do further study of some sort.

Leisure activities offered through Nagasakiya were also prominently featured. One section showed the company's leisure ventures, including an amusement park in Hokkaido, the Fantasy Dome, and another showed young employees pursuing some of the company-sponsored leisure activities. These included photographs of employees on company tours to the US, pursuing English lessons, and an outside view of the company's most recently constructed dormitory block. A section on company trips (short holidays organised annually for regular employees) was headlined: 'Company trips appeal to a different you!' (literally, 'a different self' – again, the word *jibun* is used) and went on to outline the attractions of these trips: singing karaoke on the bus, partying in the hotel, and getting a chance to mix with fellow employees you do not see in your daily work. The image conveyed is that of a fun get-together for young regular employees, with the more senior male university graduates and female high-school graduates getting a chance to mix and get to know each other – always one of the attractions of company events.

Information about the organisation of the company and its history was confined to a double spread at the back of the brochure. Themes that are perhaps more familiar in the literature on Japanese companies, such as the importance of working together and of trying one's best, were relatively downplayed, and even where they appeared, in a brief statement by the managing director at the end of the brochure, they were linked with a reiteration of the importance of *kosei*, individuality, or personality, with an invitation to the potential new recruits to do their best together with the happy individuals who would be their friends and colleagues at Nagasakiya (*Nagasakiya no koseiteki de tanoshii nakama to isshoni ganbatte ikimasenka*).

The brochure for university graduates in 1992 presented a different image. The presentation of the brochure was more sober – a plain white cover with the English words 'New Nagasakiya Mind Book' emblazoned in red and black across the centre and a Japanese subtitle reading 'Feel the New Nagasakiya'. In terms of content, the brochure contained much more text, written in a less colloquial style, appropriate to the more educated audience at whom it was aimed. However, this was balanced to some extent by numerous colourful photographs inside the brochure, featuring Nagasakiya's leisure ventures and showing young employees, so there was once again an attempt to emphasise the company's youthful character and involvement in leisure activities. The centre spread, for example, featured the managing director casually dressed, sitting in a film director's chair surrounded by young employees in relaxed poses, and a caption saying, 'With you, I want to take a "feel good" direction'. 'Direction' is written as *direkushon*, a foreign loan word that suggests in Japanese too a double meaning of orientation and film direction, thus again evoking a leisure-orientated image calculated to appeal to the youth market.

The opening pages of this brochure were devoted to reflection on the general changes in the retail sector, followed by an outline of Nagasakiya's corporate philosophy and future plans and the Nagasakiya group's organisation. The importance of individuality (*kosei*) was still highlighted, but the emphasis was on reflecting on one's own individuality in order to understand the varying needs of the customers as individuals. The catch phrase here was 'the feel-good factor' (*kimochi yoi koto*), which, the brochure explained, referred to any activity that might make customers feel good – whether related to leisure, health, or any other area – and Nagasakiya's goal of identifying and expanding into these areas. The leisure side of Nagasakiya's business was particularly highlighted, with references to the company's indoor amusement park and to several musical events it had recently sponsored.

There was also an emphasis on taking responsibility, with the metaphor of film director used as a unifying theme for the brochure, both visually (with the use of the image of a director's chair and clapperboard) and in the text.[16] The message here, directed at the employees Nagasakiya sees as its potential future managers, was that the company was looking for 'directors' in the sense of people who can contribute their own ideas and personal perspectives to help Nagasakiya to expand into new areas of service provision.

Like the high-school brochure, this brochure contained short interviews with current employees, but in this case they were confined to one double spread towards the end of the brochure, with a title introducing the employees pictured – ten men and three women, ranging in age from late teens to early thirties – as 'directors' (*direkutātachi*) of the individualised (*koseitekina*) feel-good factor. The topics covered also differed somewhat from those in the high-school brochure, including a question on what they thought of the company, and what work they hoped they would be doing in ten years' time, as well as questions on leisure interests. Most of the work-related aspirations stated here concerned promotion to a more senior level, or a more specialised kind of job within Nagasakiya, both for the men and for the women interviewed. The subject of promotion and career progression was addressed in more detail in the next section of the brochure. Here, again, there is a contrast with the high-school brochure, which did not address these topics at all.

In a mirror image of the high-school brochure, in this brochure leisure activities offered under the auspices of the company were relegated to a small section at the end. It is here, too, that the brochure most resembles the discourse of the high-school brochure in sections explaining the importance Nagasakiya attaches to the individuality of its employees and their 'private time'. Words such as *jibun* (self) and *kosei* (individuality) occur frequently here. However, this stress on the self is explained in terms of service to customers and usefulness to the company. For example, the statement that Nagasakiya has some of the most generous holiday arrangements of any company in the retail sector is preceded by the following explanation of why the company gives its employees so much 'private time'.

> If you feel good in yourself, you will be able to make the customers feel good. Nagasakiya does not want so-called 'company people' (*kaisha ningen*). We think people who have a strong sense of self (*jibun to iu mono o shikkari motte iru hito*) can pull Nagasakiya forward.

Overall, comparing these two recruitment brochures, produced during a period of affluence and labour shortage, there are clear areas of overlap in the kind of language and imagery used, but there are also some important differences. For both the high school and the university graduate market Nagasakiya seems at some pains to portray itself as youthful and sympathetic to the needs of its employees for leisure. Indeed, there is an attempt to link this with the company's own business area as a provider of both retail and leisure services. There is also a strong emphasis, particularly in the high-school brochure, on the concrete benefits employment at Nagasakiya can offer – comfortable dormitory accommodation in single rooms and a wide range of subsidised leisure activities being some of the most noteworthy.

The importance of self and individuality within the company also forms a constant theme, but one that is dealt with in somewhat different ways in the two brochures. Around the concept of *jibun* – the part which is the self – a complex discourse is developed that emphasises for the high-school graduates *jibunrashisa*, something being suitable for one's self, fitting one's sense of style, whereas for the university graduates having a strong *jibun*, a strong sense of self, is contrasted with being a *kaisha ningen*, a company person, enveloped (as in Nakane 1970) by the company. However, in the latter case this sense of self is highlighted as something of value to the company, as a quality which will enable them to relate better to the consumers the company serves.

## Recruitment in the recession: Nagasakiya recruitment brochures in 1999

By 1999 Nagasakiya's recruitment brochures had changed their appearance considerably. Looking first at the high-school brochure, the brochure as a whole was much smaller, and it no longer mimicked the layout of a fashion magazine. Interviews with employees still took a prominent place, but these were now divided into two sections, one with female employees, and one with male employees in the food section. This reflects the fact that high-school recruitment by this time targeted male employees for Nagasakiya's food section (the only section to recruit male high-school graduates)[17] as much if not more than the female recruits who had previously formed the main focus of Nagasakiya's high-school recruitment drive. The statement from the managing director had been moved forward to take pride of place at the front of the brochure, and the section on leisure activities available through the company had been condensed, and sections referring to possible trips abroad and English conversation lessons had been removed. There were also some changes in the wording in this section, with the paragraph concerning company trips re-worded to explain that the purpose of company trips is to facilitate communication among employees, and thus to encourage 'teamwork',[18] an explanation that contrasts sharply with the portrayal of company trips in the 1992 brochure described above. There was also a new section outlining possible career progression through the company.[19]

The introduction to the 1999 high-school brochure refers to self (*jibun*) only once, and then in a different vein to its predecessor. In this version, potential recruits were told, 'through work you will surely find a new self' (*shigoto o tōshite, kitto anata wa atarashii jibun ni deau*). In the interviews with employees, too, the importance of the self or the individual is reframed, with the emphasis placed on using one's individual abilities to work more effectively and thus find satisfaction. One example of this, echoed in other interviews, is the following comment by a female employee:

> When I choose things by myself to show to the customers I feel happy. If my own sense of style appeals to the customers, I really get a lift out of it.

Compared with the 1992 brochure, less space is devoted in the interviews to the employees' leisure pursuits and future dreams, although we do learn that one of the women pictured likes taking part in karaoke with her friends in her spare time, and that her dream is to get married, and that the other woman interviewed hopes to make more use of Nagasakiya's leisure facilities for employees and dreams of living abroad one day. The men, on the other hand, hope for promotion in the future.[20] As far as leisure is concerned, one man mentions window shopping (which can, in any case, be construed as a sort of informal research for work, which employees are encouraged to do in Nagasakiya in order to check out the store's competitors) while the other makes no mention of any leisure pursuits at all.

If the 1999 high-school recruitment brochure showed a shift away from the company as a style statement approach of 1992 towards a more work-centred, low-key image; this shift was even more apparent in the brochure produced for university graduates. The cover of the brochure showed a thought bubble superimposed with the single statement: *Nagasakiya jū wanen nayamimashita*, which can be roughly translated as 'Nagasakiya: ten years' soul-searching'. *Nayamu* also has the meaning of suffering and immediately directs the reader's attention to the problems Nagasakiya, like many Japanese companies, has been suffering during the recession. On opening the brochure, this continues 'And we have answers'. This leads in to a series of five interviews with senior management in Nagasakiya, which deal with the problems the company has faced in recent years and their views on the causes of these problems and the ways in which they aim to resolve them. The use of black and white photography and the serious expressions of a number of these top executives give an impression in marked contrast to the bright colours and film director imagery of the 1992 university graduate brochure. The general theme of the reflections presented here is that Nagasakiya in the past has been characterised by top-down management, poor communication, too many older employees, and an atmosphere in which young junior employees in the store's branches were unable to develop or to communicate their ideas to the senior management. In this climate, Nagasakiya had failed to capitalise on these younger employees' knowledge of consumer trends and had missed out on consumer booms. According to these interviews, in particular the last one with the managing director, Nagasakiya was now changing into a more open and youthful company in which employees could express their ideas to senior management.

Colour is re-introduced in the following pages of the brochure, which provide extended interviews with two recent recruits, one man and one woman, both university graduates. In both interviews the recruits reflect at length on their work, the knowledge, and the skills that they have needed to acquire in order to perform effectively, and the importance of co-operating with the different sorts of employees around them, including senior regular employees, part-timers, and temporary staff. Neither interview makes any mention of leisure pursuits; indeed, the only mention of time off from work occurs in the interview with the woman employee, when she recalls her realisation, in her second year of employment, that she still did not know enough to run the product ranges (toddlers' clothes and clothes for older children) to which she had been allocated effectively. She reflects that this is because she has relied too much on her co-workers,[21] and that she must try harder to acquire the knowledge she needs. Subsequently, she starts taking notes assiduously, and approaching her work in a more 'positive' (*sekkyokuteki*) way.

> Even on her days off, she goes to look round in rival stores, and when she is walking in the street she pays attention to the fashions worn by children out with their families. She's shaken off her dependency on other people.[22]

Here, we have a remarkable shift from the insistence in 1992 that 'private time' is important, and that leisure is important in order for employees to feel good in themselves and to serve the company better. In 1999 it would seem that work, in an echo of much earlier writing about Japanese companies, has once more spread to claim employees' time outside the workplace. In view of this, it is perhaps not surprising that in this brochure mention of leisure activities sponsored by the company is confined to a small section at the back of the brochure, with no illustrations.

## Boom and bust for company as lifestyle: corporate imagery and recruitment in the 1990s

Comparing these two sets of brochures, the first produced during the bubble economy and the second during the recession, a number of contrasts can be drawn. First, in both sets of brochures there is a clear difference in the way in which Nagasakiya seeks to project itself to potential recruits depending on whether they are high-school or university graduates. The university graduates will provide the next generation of managers for the company. The company expects both a higher degree of knowledge about the company and a higher degree of commitment from this category of employee. Brochures for university students give far more information about Nagasakiya's corporate organisation and future plans. They also seek to stress the opportunities for promotion and career development within the company, an aspect that is entirely absent from the high-school recruitment brochure of 1992 (aimed primarily at women), and remains relatively under-emphasised in the 1999 brochure (aimed at both female and male recruits). There is also more emphasis on mastering the skills of the job and less on leisure in the brochures for university graduates than in those for high-school graduates.

However, alongside this difference, there is also a clear shift in the way in which Nagasakiya seeks to present itself in 1999 compared with 1992. In the interim, Nagasakiya had changed in a number of ways, one important change being the replacement of the founding family of Nagasakiya in the senior managerial positions. The managing director of Nagasakiya in 1999, Inoue Tamio, rose through the ranks of the company and was regarded by senior management as one of their own in a way that had not been true of the previous managing director, who owed his position to the fact that he was the son of the founder. From this vantage point, Inoue could afford to criticise past management policies as being 'top-down' in style, and he was also well-placed to project the image of a new Nagasakiya, with greater participation by all levels of employee.

But more than the change of personnel at the top, the changes in the presentation and content of the recruitment brochures of 1999 would seem to reflect the change in the economic climate. In 1992 the company was presented as a means of self-expression, an aspect of a new lifestyle that would respond to individual aspirations and value leisure and 'private time', whereas in 1999 the discourse has shifted to a more conservative one in which fulfilment is to be found through work. This is particularly evident in the high-school recruitment brochure. In simple terms, although the labour shortage and competition between companies for recruits led to an emphasis on what the company could offer its new recruits in the recruitment literature of the early 1990s, by the end of the decade the emphasis had returned to what the company expected of its new recruits.

This is not, however, merely a matter of an oscillation between individual-centred and group-centred approaches, depending on economic circumstances. The self is not submerged or enveloped by the group in the image of the company and working life projected in the 1999 brochures, rather it is something to be encountered through work and in the interaction with customers. The idea of the self, or *jibun*, that is implied in the two cases is different, but important in both. Whereas in 1992 the self appears (especially in the high-school brochures) as consumer, preoccupied with fashion and individual style, the self implied by the later brochures is that familiar from more conservative discourses in Japan of achieving maturity, becoming a full human being (*ichininmae*), in this context through work (a term used in the 1999 brochures, but absent from the 1992 brochures).[23]

There remains the question of the impact of these brochures on those at whom they were directed. For this, I only have data for recruits from the bubble years. As far as university graduates were concerned, many I interviewed largely discounted both the brochure and the recruitment seminar some of them had attended, except as sources of information on details such as working conditions and company benefits, such as dormitories. The reasons given for applying to/joining Nagasakiya by applicants and recent recruits to whom I spoke included 'I applied to Daiei but I failed their exam'; 'I'm attending a new university, and we don't have any contacts with companies. So I want to go somewhere where they don't have *gakubatsu*.[24] But I'm applying to Jusco, Seiyu, and Itoyokado too'; 'My elder brother lives at home with his wife and children. It's really crowded and I just had to move out. Nagasakiya has the best dormitories – everybody gets a single room'; 'Well actually I didn't have much choice. In the year I graduated not so many people were being taken on by the large stores as now, and this was the only place I could get into'.

Among the high-school graduates, however, a number had been impressed by the brochures they had seen (those of the years leading up to 1992, I was told, closely resembled the 1992 brochure described above) and particularly by the pictured dormitory building. In previous years, before the new dormitory near the Koganei branch was built, this had occasioned some disillusionment among the new arrivals from the countryside when they first saw what was to be their living quarters. One woman commented:

> They lied. You write that down in your thesis, Matsunaga-san, they lied.
> In the brochure the dormitories looked beautiful, but when we got there

they were so old and dirty some people left immediately. Now they have built the new dormitory it's better, but then ...

In the years of relative prosperity at the beginning of the 1990s, then, it would seem that Nagasakiya was to some extent the victim of its own success in portraying itself as an attractive consumer product, with some new recruits acutely disappointed by the disjuncture between the glossy packaging and what they found on arrival at the company. It seems unlikely that such problems would arise in the harsher climate of the turn of the century, where jobs for regular employees have become much scarcer, and companies do not need to try as hard to attract new recruits – if indeed they are still recruiting at all. But in the boom years with which this book is primarily concerned, the transition to company employee also involved a shift in the way in which Nagasakiya and company–employee relations within Nagasakiya were presented and experienced. This shift was particularly dramatic in the case of female high-school recruits, for whom the company as lifestyle statement message was most stressed in the brochure material, and on whom brochures seem to have had most impact. The next two chapters explore this transition and the changing ways in which the company is imaged through an examination of the training course and induction programme for new women high-school graduate recruits in 1991.

# 4 Member of Nagasakiya, member of society

## Company entrance and narratives of adulthood

The provision of in-company training is the norm for large Japanese companies. In addition to on-the-job training, in 1995 over 96 per cent of companies with over 1,000 employees provided off-the-job training (Japan Institute of Labour 1998a: 66). Off-the-job training may be provided at various stages of the employees' careers, but the area that attracts most attention, and absorbs the largest part of the company budget, is generally the induction training given to new recruits (Dore and Sako 1989: 83).

The explanation usually offered for the preference for in-company training is that it is a logical concomitant of the lifetime employment system.[1] Large companies in Japan prefer to recruit new graduates, and they are therefore recruiting for potential rather than for specific skills. Furthermore, male recruits, at least, are recruited as 'generalists' rather than 'specialists' (White and Trevor 1983) and may be expected to do a number of different jobs within the company in the course of their careers. Throughout, the company provides all necessary training, secure in the knowledge that the investment thus made in their employees will not end up being lost to a rival company (Nakamura 1988). This argument has been further refined by Koike (1988), who suggests that where the skills required for the job have a high degree of specificity to the enterprise concerned, it makes no economic sense to recruit workers trained elsewhere, and, equally, the training received within the enterprise is not externally marketable.

Implicit to this view of company training is an apparently obvious assumption: training is equivalent to the transmission of skills. A different perspective, however, is offered by Rohlen (1970, 1973, 1974) on the basis of two periods of fieldwork, one carried out in Osaka at a large engineering company in 1965 and the second at a bank in western Japan in 1969. Rohlen suggests that induction courses may best be understood as rites of passage, showing the characteristic tripartite structure described by Van Gennep (1960) of separation, transition, and incorporation:

> Separation being emphasized by travel to a remote dormitory and isolation there, change to uniforms, loss of money, and introduction to unfamiliar routines and the like. Transition occurs throughout the month

as the individual is forced to adjust to the new and demanding situation by changing his perceptions, attitudes and behavior to group-centered company norms. The concluding ceremonies, where business suits are again worn and tension is released through beer drinking, a rugby game against the instructors and a campfire sing, serve to conclude the incorporation process and begin the process of return to everyday life.

(Rohlen 1970: 188)

In support of Rohlen's view of induction training as, at least in part,[2] a rite of passage, a number of points can be made. First, induction training is the rule in all large Japanese companies, whatever the level of skill required of the trainees. In Nagasakiya, for example, a number of managers commented to me that the work of a sales assistant is distinctive in that it requires almost no skill, and indeed little or no training is offered to new part-time or temporary sales staff, who are expected to learn on the job for the most part.[3] Nonetheless, all the new full-time recruits to Nagasakiya attended the residential training course that will be described in this chapter.

Second, induction training courses in Japan commonly follow the pattern described by Rohlen (1970) of initial isolation in a company training centre, which may be in a remote location, followed by training that targets attitude and general behaviour as much as specific skills; the training is concluded by a ceremony marking the recruits' formal acceptance into the company. Nagasakiya's induction training also followed this pattern, with the recruits first sent from their homes to the company training centre, and then after completion of the training they were formally accepted into the company at an entrance ceremony. Each stage of this process was marked not only by spatial movement but also by other features such as change of dress, rules of behaviour, and change of formal status, as will be described in further detail below.

The most controversial aspect of Rohlen's account is probably that which concerns the content of the training programme. Rohlen (1973) argues that this aims to instil 'group centered company norms', a process he terms *seishin kyōiku*, or 'spiritual education'. He gives examples of the way in which this type of training is pursued, spanning not only lectures on what is expected of employees at this company but also activities that are less familiar to a Western European or American reader, such as Zen meditation or military drills.

The extent to which this type of training was, or is, the norm in Japanese companies is questionable. Certainly, it has received much publicity outside Japan, but this is probably in large measure because it appears exotic, and therefore interesting, to a Western audience. Such publicity has not always been welcome in Japan, where such practices have a negative image for many, redolent of old-fashioned, pre-war, right-wing ideas. By the early 1990s, there were few companies in the chain store sector using such methods, although one notable exception was the chain Yaohan, which relied on spiritual education programmes run by a new religious movement, Seicho-no-Ie, with which the store's management was closely associated (Matsunaga 2000). But on the whole, given the nationalist right-wing connotations of *seishin kyōiku*, this type of training was viewed as old-fashioned even when Rohlen conducted his fieldwork, and Rohlen himself estimates that probably only about one-third of Japanese companies used *seishin kyōiku* in 1973 (Rohlen 1973: 1542). This proportion had dropped to around one-quarter by 1980 according to figures quoted by Inohara (1990).

This decline in the use of the term *seishin kyōiku* and in the use of activities such as Zen meditation or military drills in Japanese company training does not, however, mean that companies are no longer concerned with modifying the attitudes of their recruits, rather this concern is likely to be expressed in different ways. A term frequently heard today in Japan as an alternative to *seishin* is *kokoro*, meaning heart/mind/spirit, which is free of the right-wing connotations of *seishin*, and was the term preferred at Nagasakiya. This was also the term used in Nagasakiya's recruitment seminars in 1991, when a recruitment officer commented on the importance of transforming the employees' *kokoro* and stated that the training programme aimed to change the recruits' way of thinking.

It can therefore be argued that in general terms, Rohlen's (1973) model of the overall structure and aims of induction training in Japan is still applicable, although the specific content of training courses may vary. And it would also seem that to characterise such training as purely concerned with the transmission of skills would be to neglect its wider social significance. If we accept the broad outlines of Rohlen's analysis there is a strong case for viewing induction training in a large Japanese company as a rite of passage.

The question may then be posed: a rite of passage from what to what? The transition emphasised repeatedly in the Nagasakiya training course was that from *gakusei* (student) to *shakaijin* (member of society). *Shakaijin* may also be translated as adult, but its connotations are rather wider, and it is not defined solely by age or physical maturity. Alternative terms exist in Japanese for denoting adult in the sense of having reached the legal age of majority *(seijin)* or adult in a physical and developmental sense *(otona)*. *Shakaijin*, on the other hand, indicates a status where the person is recognised as a full member of society. This also implies a positioning within a web of social relationships, with this positioning being the means through which full membership of society is achieved. In contemporary Japan there are two distinct contexts in which this repositioning as full member of society occurs: that of employment, where membership of the company mediates membership of the wider society, and that of marriage, where taking up one's prescribed adult role within the household becomes the index of full social membership (Edwards 1989: 116–27). In both cases, the transition to *shakaijin* is stressed, and in both cases becoming a *shakaijin* is a stage in the maturing process, with a further marker of maturity, becoming a whole person, or *ichininmae*, yet to be achieved (Kondo 1990: 235).

The company training course and subsequent induction ceremony for new recruits can therefore be conceived of as mediating a dual transition: that from student to employee and that from childhood to adulthood. An examination of this process thus provides an insight not only into the ways in which company–employee relations are framed but also into constructions of adulthood and maturity in Japan.

## Induction training: the Nagasakiya case

I participated in one of four training courses held in March 1991 for new female high-school graduate recruits to Nagasakiya. All these courses lasted six days and were broadly identical – the reason for dividing these recruits into four groups was simply that the training centre was not large enough to hold all of them at the same time. Two other courses were also held: one for male high-school graduates and one for graduates of tertiary education, the majority of whom were men, although in 1991 there were also six women on this course.

Nagasakiya offered me the choice of attending either the course for female high-school graduates or the one for graduates of tertiary education. I chose the former because this type of recruit was, at that time, in the majority in the Nagasakiya group as a whole, and in 1991 provided six new regular employees for the branch at which I was employed, as against two (one man and one woman) from the university graduates' course. I was told that the latter course differed mainly in that the participants were considered to be more adult (*shakaijin*), and it was therefore not necessary to be as strict with them, 'You just tell them to do something and they get on with it'. Also, their higher level of education meant that a faster pace was possible on the technical training side, particularly the part involving arithmetical calculations. The course for male high-school graduates had broadly the same content as that for their female counterparts, but it was less popular with the trainers, who complained about the participants' wild behaviour, particularly at night, when they tended to smuggle alcohol into the dormitories and get riotously drunk.[4]

There were 120 participants on the course I attended; they came from all parts of Japan, stretching from Hokkaido in the north to Okinawa in the south. In addition, there were six male trainers, who stayed for the entire course, and four female trainers, who arrived on the third day. The course took place in Hiratsuka, in Kanagawa prefecture to the south-west of Tokyo. This was the location of Nagasakiya's first store and also of the company's training centre, located about half an hour's walk from Hiratsuka station.

The trainees were all lodged in the training centre dormitories, as were four of the male trainers. Two of the male trainers stayed in a hotel near the station on a rota basis, a privilege to which they very much looked forward, as they complained that the dormitories were uncomfortable and overcrowded. Lack of space and a concern for my comfort were the reasons given for placing me in a hotel rather than the dormitory, and in fact I was unusually fortunate to have a very large and comfortable room to myself at the company's expense; the female trainers also stayed in a hotel but had to share rooms. For the sake of my research, I would have preferred to stay in the dormitory with the other trainees, but it did not seem possible to push this particular issue.

My status on the course was therefore somewhat peculiar; although I participated in all course activities on equal terms with the trainees, in generation and in the way I was treated I seemed to have more in common with the trainers. This ambiguity in my status worked against me in some ways, since the trainees tended either to avoid me or to treat me with exaggerated respect, but on the other hand I was able to establish a good rapport with the trainers and thus, perhaps, to see the training process from more than one point of view. I was also, unfortunately, unable to attend the first day of the training course; the company deemed this unnecessary as, according to the manager responsible, it only consisted of checking that everyone who was supposed to had turned up and giving them a medical examination. As with the question of dormitory accommodation, I was in no position to insist. My account of the first day is therefore based on interviews with the training manager and with some of the trainees, and on my own observations of the first day of the subsequent course, which overlapped with the course I attended.

### Day 1

The trainees began to arrive in the late morning on the first day, all wearing smart suits, many in appropriately pastel colours for spring. The first task of the training staff was to check that all those registered to attend had arrived – often new recruits change their minds between accepting an offer of employment and the beginning of the training course. This time only three had dropped out, leaving 120 to attend the course. Since the trainees come from all over Japan, they arrived slowly in twos and threes and there was a lot of hanging around in the ground floor canteen before the orientation meeting began at 3.00 p.m. This was an opportunity for them to get to know each other and also to size up Nagasakiya's training centre, which in most cases seems to have made an unfavourable impression. One recruit told me much later:

> When I arrived I was shocked, it was so dirty and shabby. I just wanted to go straight home again. Everybody felt the same way.

The orientation talk lasted about forty-five minutes and concentrated on explaining to them how the course would be organised: the daily schedule and rules to be observed during the course. All trainees were given a timetable (see Appendix 2), a list of rules for the course (see Appendix 3), and company textbooks for new recruits, covering company history, philosophy, and organisation, as well as dress and etiquette codes and more technical matters such as gift-wrapping and basic calculations and paperwork. After the orientation course, the trainees were given a medical, and at 6.00 p.m. they had dinner in the centre's canteen. No activities were scheduled for the evening, giving them time to settle in and get acquainted with their room mates before lights out at 11.30 p.m.

## Day 2

The next morning began with a wake-up call at 7.30 a.m., followed by breakfast. From now until the end of the course the pastel suits were put away, with all the trainees dressed in tracksuits, mostly the ones they used at high school. Roll call was at 9.00 a.m., followed by a talk by the personnel manager at 9.20 a.m. I arrived shortly before 10.00 a.m. and went straight to the lecture room, where everyone was waiting for the next talk, an introductory talk on the company, to begin. I have transcribed my first impressions, as recorded in my fieldnotes, below.

> Training centre – shabby, grubby, dilapidated modern building, located in equally shabby suburb/corner of urban sprawl spreading out from Tokyo. Very unimpressive. Quite far from the station.
>
> Arrived shortly before 10.00 a.m., met by Mr Iwakura, went to sit in on talk. Murmurs of *gaijin, gaijin* (foreigner, foreigner). People I sat next to immediately walked off ... During the break after the talk most people flopped forward onto the benches, everyone looked very tired. Tried to engage the girl sitting next to me in conversation, but she was very monosyllabic. This is going to be an uphill struggle.

At the beginning of this introductory talk, and all the others for the rest of the course, the trainer giving the talk called on one trainee to lead the formal greetings. These followed much the same pattern as in Japanese schools: the designated trainee stood up, at the same time saying *'kiritsu, rei'* (stand up, bow), while the other trainees stood up and bowed in unison, then all saying together *'onegaishimasu'* (please). The leader then said *'chakuseki'* (sit down), and everyone took their seats. The importance of correct greetings was emphasised throughout the course, and in the introductory talk we were told that greetings were the first thing we had to learn, 'Even if you can't do anything else, you must be able to greet customers in a lively manner with a smiling face'.

Aside from stressing the importance of greetings, the trainer giving this talk was at pains to emphasise the change in the trainees' status from *gakusei* (students) to *shakaijin* (adults, members of society). Here there were clear parallels with Rohlen's (1974) account of the introductory talk at the bank training course he attended in which it was explained that:

Our aim is to build you up as people so you can grow on your own once you leave here. That's the reason we have tough (*kibishii*) training. All of you are entering society for the first time. Co-operative living is different from the kind of living you knew in your school days.

Your study here will also be different. In public schools, all you had to do was study for examinations. Whether you got along with your fellow classmates or not was not very important. Here, we have co-operative living as our style of life.

(Rohlen 1974: 200–1)

On the Nagasakiya course, we were told:

Until now you have been students. Now you are members of society (*shakaijin*), and you receive a salary ... But your life has changed in other ways too. Before, maybe you had your own room, or shared with just one or two brothers and sisters. Now you have to stay in a dormitory. There may be eight other people in the room ... Here, it's group living.

As a corollary of this change, they were also told they would now have to be more responsible:

When you were at school, your teachers probably told you again and again to do something. Here you have three chances – we will only tell you twice.

Having made these basic points, the trainer moved on to give a brief outline of the Nagasakiya group: its size, the scope of its business, the way in which Nagasakiya, as a chain store, differs from the department stores, and finally the 'vision' of Nagasakiya and the company's mottoes. At the end of this talk, we were told that for the rest of the training we would be divided up into six base groups (*han*), each comprising twenty trainees (this division into groups is also common practice in Japanese schools and would therefore have been a familiar method of organisation for the recruits). For videos and lectures we would continue to all gather together in the main lecture hall, but for the remainder of the course each group was allocated its own small room and trainer.

When the trainer had finished speaking, he again called on a trainee to lead the greetings, which followed the same pattern of standing up and bowing, this time with everyone saying in chorus, 'Thank you very much'. As soon as the trainer had left the room, most of the trainees flopped forward onto their benches, apparently with the intention of using the twenty-minute break for a quick nap.

After the break, lectures continued with two talks: the first on wages, health, and company welfare, and the second on a special Nagasakiya in-house insurance scheme. By the end of the second talk, despite valiant efforts by the speaker to involve his audience through asking them questions and cracking jokes, the trainees seemed to have had enough and started fidgeting and chatting among themselves. The lunch break seemed to come as a relief to all concerned, and the trainees trooped off down to the canteen, duly turning and bowing at those remaining in the room on their way out and saying '*shitsureishimasu*' (excuse me), as course etiquette demanded.

After lunch we returned to the lecture hall for a video on 'workplace manners' (including timekeeping and rules designed to prevent theft by employees) and the correct appearance of Nagasakiya's female employees: hair neatly tied back if long, discreet make-up, no jewellery except for one plain ring and a pair of small ear studs, uniform correctly buttoned, low shoes. Introducing this video the trainer again commented on the recruits' change of status from students to adults, but this time stressing the continuity between school and company life:

> You might think rules are something from high school. Why am I working at a company if I still have to obey rules? But now you're getting a salary.

After the video, the appearance rules were gone over again, this time from the new entrants' textbooks.[5] The trainees read in turn from the textbook, mostly inaudibly, with many hesitations over the reading of characters and periodic pauses when the trainer told them to underline some especially important point. On the subject of wearing make-up, the trainer repeatedly reminded them that Nagasakiya was not a night club and make-up must be subdued. He also commented on their hair, which in most cases was long and loose, with many very long fringes in evidence. The main reason given for the strictness of the appearance code was that inappropriate make-up or jewellery might upset the '*oba-san*' (literally auntie, used to refer to middle-aged women) customers.

We then moved on to the next section of the textbook, covering an area described as 'manners at work'. The most important points here were timekeeping, the 'five minutes etiquette', i.e. you should always be five minutes early for everything (also included in the rules for the course), and the rule prohibiting bringing valuables to work. Both of these rules were justified in terms of trying not to inconvenience fellow employees:

> If you bring valuables, or a large sum of money to work and it gets stolen it will cause bad feeling ... If you are five minutes late back from lunch, and then the next person also takes an extra five minutes and so on, in the end the last person to go will have no lunch break left at all. So please think about the people you work with.

The distinction between work time and private time was also gone over here, with the trainer again pointing out that we get paid while we are at work, and it is therefore not the place to chat to friends about what was seen on television the previous night.

At this point the trainer broke off his talk, and, returning to the issue of appearance, abruptly told all of us to tie up our hair and remove our jewellery, 'Now, immediately', and to keep it that way for the rest of the course. My fieldnotes record:

> Incredulity from the audience as it sputtered reluctantly into life. Looked at each other, muttered, did nothing about it. All trainers lined up at front, two went down the room handing out black hair fasteners to those with long, loose hair, or showy hair fasteners. Very reluctant to comply on hair. Looked round, paused, finally mostly complied. Then checked by senior trainer, those who still hadn't complied were told to.

Addressing the shocked, but now noticeably more awake, audience again, the trainer commented:

> The difference between school rules and work rules is that if you break the rules at school you can get away with it, but at work you can't. You see, the rules are stricter than they were at school. And you thought, I'm an adult (*shakaijin*), I'm free.

After a short break, another video and lecture slot concluded the large group session for the day. The video dealt with appropriate facial expressions, body language, and greetings when dealing with customers: first by showing how not to do it (film of a sullen, unsmiling sales assistant failing to greet an approaching customer, and then using abrupt and insufficiently formal language towards the customer), and then by showing how it should be done. The correct way was then broken down, component by component, showing the correct smile, how to bow and what angles are appropriate to different situations, and the basic greetings to be used with customers. This video occasioned a lot of giggling in the audience, particularly in the sections showing how not to deal with customers and the part where the sales assistant pulled up the corners of her mouth to set her smile at the correct angle. As before, the lecture covered much the same ground as the video, but this time from the course textbook, with some additional elaborations, for example a gloss on the meaning of the greetings used when a customer enters the store (these are standard throughout Japan):

> On customer entering store: *Irasshaimase* (literally welcome) I'm grateful you chose this store.

> On customer leaving store: *Arigatō gozaimashita* (literally thank you very much) Thank you very much, the money you spend here pays my salary.

By the end of this talk several people were snoozing, and a few were sound asleep; this is, apparently, common on these courses. One of the trainers had warned me that the afternoon session on the first day had a lot of videos and was pretty boring, and said that I could slip out if I wanted to.

After another break, we broke up into our base groups and moved to one of the smaller upstairs classrooms for the last session of the day. This was devoted to games, giving the trainees a chance to relax a bit, but with the important underlying aim of encouraging them to get to know the other people in their group. The trainer for our base group was Uenoyama-san, a sporty looking man in his early thirties with a brisk but friendly and cheerful manner. Like all the male trainers, and the trainees themselves, he wore a tracksuit throughout the course.

First of all we had a name-memorising game, where we all had to learn each other's names, and then we divided into smaller groups of five or six to play more games, including a kind of bingo played with *kanji* (characters used in written Japanese), and games involving guessing each other's favourite pop star, film star, and car. These games became quite animated, and the pop star, film star, and car games in particular gave the recruits the chance to talk to each other about a topic in which they were all interested.

After the games Uenoyama-san announced which section of the store each of us had been allocated to, with the comment that it might not be what we had hoped for, but we shouldn't think '*yada*' (yuck).[6] We were then dismissed for dinner, after which I returned to my hotel, and the trainees set off to wander around the area near the training centre for a while before the 9.30 p.m. curfew.

### *Day 3*

The next day I arrived at the training centre at 8.30 a.m., and after a brief breakfast, joined the other members of my base group in the main lecture room. They had been up since 7.00 a.m., in order to wash, attend roll call and do exercises before breakfast. The base group was then divided into three, with the Koganei branch, a group of six trainees plus myself, forming one of these smaller groups. We were told that we would be responsible for cleaning the lecture hall on a rota basis, starting this morning with the Koganei group. Again, this echoes routines familiar from school in Japan, where students take it in turn to clean classrooms. However, my fieldnotes record:

> Reactions to being told to clean ranged from unenthusiastic to appalled. Did it reluctantly, two did not do it at all, went and chatted with their friends in other groups instead. Those not on cleaning duty stood around watching and laughing.

At 9.15 a.m. the whole base group assembled in our home classroom to complete various bits of paperwork and go over the tests that had been distributed to all new recruits before the course. There were two of these, one issued in December and one in February, to be completed with the help of information sent out by Nagasakiya to the new recruits. The December test was concerned with Nagasakiya's corporate philosophy, and the February test dealt with the principles to be followed in order to get on well with fellow employees. Going over the tests, our trainer, Uenoyama-san, talked about company philosophy and corporate identity and gave the trainees some background about the company symbol mark and song. He also emphasised the importance of getting on with other people at work:

> You will find there are many different kinds of people at work. It's not like school, where you choose your own friends because you have something in common, you have the same interests. And you're all the same age.[7] You'll have to work with people you have nothing in common with, there are a lot of *oba-san* too [groans from the trainees] ... try to find out about their hobbies, see their good points.

Finally, he stressed the importance of teamwork and told the trainees to think about the effect on other people of any failure on their part to carry out their allotted work.

The remainder of the morning was taken up by learning how to do gift-wrapping – a service provided by all large Japanese stores. The main surprise for me here was the detailed instruction given on the symbolism of different types of *noshi* – special Japanese paper with bows drawn on it in different colours and tied in different ways. Since this paper is quite commonly used, I had thought that the recruits would be aware of what the different bows represented, but they were apparently just as ignorant in this respect as I was.[8]

After lunch came a two-hour session on fire awareness and training, beginning with a talk given by the manager responsible for the Kansai (western Japan) branches of Nagasakiya. He explained that he was in charge of this aspect of training because it was in one of the branches in his area that a serious and well-publicised fire had occurred the previous year, killing several people. The main burden of his talk was that every member of staff should take responsibility personally for knowing what to do in case of fire, since, he pointed out, if a fire were to break out it would make no difference if you were a new recruit or not – customers would still turn to you for help.

This talk was followed by a video showing what to do in case of fire, including newsreel of two fires at large, well-known stores (but none of the Nagasakiya fire), and fire prevention. Finally, we all trooped out to the parking area in front of the training centre for practice in our base groups at using fire hoses and fire extinguishers.

As it was a bitterly cold day, it came as a relief to get back inside again for the final session of the afternoon, which was billed as the basics of dealing with customers. For this session all the male trainers were replaced by female 'sales adviser (SA) trainers', of whom I had had a sneak preview when I sat in the trainers' staffroom killing time in the breaks between sessions. The SA trainers, as they were referred to, varied in age from early twenties to late forties. When they arrived, they all looked quite different in dress style, make-up, and general manner, but by the beginning of this session they were transformed into the image of the perfect sales assistant, uniformed and groomed accordingly, in sharp contrast to the much more casual-looking male trainers.

The SA trainer for our base group was Koyanagi-san, one of the older women, very elegant and poised even in her casual wear, and had an unwavering smile. After introducing herself, she told us that she wanted to begin by hearing a three-minute speech from each of the trainees, telling her something about themselves, their families, and their schools. We were given five minutes to prepare.

The first trainee called on was Nakamura-san, a young woman who seemed exceptionally quiet even when she was not confronted with a large audience. She managed a twenty-second speech by the trainer's watch, and thereafter merely giggled, despite being forced to remain standing for the full three minutes. The trainer took this unpromising start calmly, simply telling her that it would not go down well at the store at which she was to work if she was so quiet. Koyanagi-san then said she would reduce the length of the speeches to one minute for that day, but that she expected everyone to make a five-minute speech the following day. She then asked Nakamura-san to speak for another forty seconds. She remained standing but continued to giggle without speaking. Finally she was allowed to sit down.

Next, was Araumi-san, who had formed a close friendship with Nakamura-san and shared the same rather withdrawn character. Araumi-san also failed to speak for a full minute, managing only forty seconds. The others improved somewhat, mostly managing the minute, but very shy and giggly. All the speeches followed the same pattern, 'I have two sisters, my bloodtype is O,[9] I come from Niigata ... oh dear, what shall I do ....' One unusually long and self-confident speech made the rest of the audience giggle even more.

Koyanagi-san watched calmly and without comment, except to tell them how long they had spoken, until they had all had their turn. She then told them that they should remember two things, first to keep a smiling face at all times and second to speak clearly.

> Please remember to look bright and cheerful. Remember your mother's face when she came to greet you at the door when you returned home from school. If she wasn't smiling you wondered what was wrong.
>
> Most of you were speaking quietly, and some of you were mumbling. If you do that at work no one will hear you or understand you.

We then moved on to the next part of the session, elocution, with Koyanagi-san drawing a chart to show how Japanese vowel sounds are produced and then getting us to recite the Japanese syllabary in chorus, concentrating particularly on getting everyone to open their mouths wide enough to enunciate clearly.

After this, Koyanagi-san tackled our non-smiling faces, by drawing a smiling face on the board. She said that it had eyes like bananas and a mouth like a melon. She then asked one of the trainees what her favourite food was, and, failing to get an answer, asked another one the same question. The second girl finally replied after conferring with a friend. Very slowly, she got answers from most of the group. She then told us all to think about our favourite food, and how we feel after eating it, and smile. We then had to smile at each other in pairs, checking our partner's face to see if she had a sufficiently bright smile. No one took this very seriously, although there was quite a lot of involuntary smiling as everyone was giggling. Concluding this practice by telling us that a smiling face is very important when dealing with customers, especially when we cannot comply with a customer's request, as they are more likely to accept 'I'm sorry that's not possible' when it is said with a smile, Koyanagi-san allowed us a ten-minute break.

After the break came more elocution practice, this time concentrating on intonation and voice projection, aiming particularly to erase certain intonation patterns that are characteristic of high-school girls but deemed inappropriate to polite young sales assistants. Koyanagi-san also gave an impressive demonstration of the different sorts of greetings appropriate to different workplaces, from the bellow of the fishmonger to the soft voice of a hospital nurse, situating the Nagasakiya greeting somewhere between the two. Finally, we learned the prescribed ways of standing, walking, and bending down to pick things up, and the different angles of bow appropriate to different work situations. We also spent quite a long time practising the correct bow for greeting customers at the beginning of the day. As with the *noshi* session, I was surprised by the ineptitude of the trainees, given that bowing is such an everyday feature of Japanese life. Few could bow with a straight back, simply flopping forward awkwardly, and this required a lot of practice before Koyanagi-san considered us passable.

After this session I had dinner with a group of the trainees for the first time, and I was able to find out something about their reactions to the course. They all said that they were tired, and that they found the course harder than being at high school. The talks made them sleepy, and their feet and backs hurt after the physical exercises. No one evinced any enthusiasm.

Later, I had a second dinner with the trainers, and I was surprised to hear from them that the reticence and apparent shyness of the recruits was quite usual. One of the most outgoing of the women trainers said that she had been extremely shy when she joined, but that her ten years working at Nagasakiya had changed her, especially her experience working as a political campaigner (under duress) for a candidate fielded in the Koganei area with the support of the Nagasakiya company union. After that, she said, no one could be shy again. One of the male trainers said that he was of the opinion that perhaps only 10 per cent of the current batch of trainees would ever be of much use to the company, but that was true of all these (implicitly, female high-school graduate) groups – this batch was no better or worse than the norm. Conversation then strayed to more personal matters as the trainers took advantage of all being brought together from the branches at which they usually worked to catch up on each other's news before the women turned in for an early night and the men went on to do some serious drinking.

## Day 4

The next morning at 9.00 a.m. we were back in the classroom with Koyanagi-san, preparing five-minute speeches to give to the rest of the base group. To help us, Koyanagi-san suggested topics we might cover in our speeches; for example, why did you choose this company? What section did you hope for? Those who had friends prepared together, the others sat in silence.

When they came to give their speeches the trainees all did better than they had done on the previous day, but there was still a lot of mumbling and giggling, rendering some of what they said completely inaudible. The most common reasons given for wanting to join were that Nagasakiya's recruitment material looked good, that there were one-room dormitories, and that it was easy to get into. Other reasons given included salary, holidays, teacher's or *senpai's* (senior's) advice. Only two of the group mentioned having visited the store for shopping and liking it.

A number of the trainees commented on how exhausting they found the course, but perhaps the most surprising speeches came from the two who had been so tongue-tied the previous day, Nakamura-san and Araumi-san. They both said that they found the training strict, that they did not have enough free time, and that they thought the course did not suit them. Araumi-san wound up the session by saying she wanted to go home.

Koyanagi-san seemed quite unperturbed by all this, smiled, and said that she supposed everyone joined for similar reasons:

> I joined because the salary was good. I went to the Osaka branch, and in my intake there were ten university graduate men and ten high-school graduate women. My husband was one of the ten men. We got married, we've had four children, and my husband has been transferred four times. I follow him when he is transferred. So, you may join for one reason, but what you end up getting from the company may be quite different. You never know what the future will bring.

This seemed quite an astute speech, as it both identified Koyanagi-san with the trainees in terms of attitude towards the company (at least on joining) and held out a view of a rosy future including a successful marriage and children (still very much the social norm for Japanese women) under the auspices of the company. For once, Koyanagi-san held the entire group's attention, and there was no giggling.

After the speeches we had more practice in elocution and bowing, culminating in a paired role play on taking goods and money from the customer and then giving back the change. This was followed by further gift-wrapping practice before we broke for lunch. After lunch we had a technical lecture on dealing with credit cards and other necessary paperwork, and we then spent the rest of the afternoon in a sports session described in our timetables as 'Do! Sports'.

For 'Do! Sports' all the base group trooped off together in a straggly crocodile to a sports hall about a fifteen-minute walk from the training centre. Once there, we assembled in lines and did aerobics, following two guest instructors standing at the front. The general response to this was very unenthusiastic. We then chose which of two types of ball game we wished to play and competed in our base groups, with half of each base group in one competition and half in the other. This went in rounds up to a grand play off, and most people seemed to enjoy it and really tried hard. There was little interference by the trainers, who simply refereed and kept the score, and two of our base group, Nakamura-san and Araumi-san, managed to sneak off undetected (at least by the trainers) and did not participate at all.

After the finals, and formal announcements of how well the different base groups had done, we returned to the training centre and broke for dinner, assembling again in our separate base groups at 7.00 p.m. for an open question time with our supervisor. Most of the questions concerned the dormitories: their layout; the curfew, and whether it was strict or not; and whether they could have friends to stay or not. This prompted the supervisor to ask if they meant male or female friends, to giggles all round, immediately leading on to another trainee asking whether there would be any male employees living in the dormitories. Finally, the supervisor gave us our schedule for our first week as regular Nagasakiya employees after completing the training course, and handed out materials to prepare for the next day's training. At 8.00 p.m. we were free for the evening, and the other trainees wandered off window shopping around the centre, and I returned to my hotel.

### Day 5

The last full day of the course was mainly devoted to technical training: basic arithmetic necessary for sales, the images conveyed by different colour combinations and how to create effective displays of clothing using these, and specialist training for the section to which we had been allocated. The colour sense session was tested immediately afterwards, and there was also a competition in which we all created our own colour combinations and were then judged by our fellow students.

By this point in the course the trainees were all looking very tired – two failed to turn up for the morning session, according to their friends they had caught cold and were staying in bed. And in a break in the afternoon session eighteen of the twenty members of our base group flopped forward onto their desks and went straight to sleep. As it was raining, the course organisers decided to cancel the scheduled evening trip to the local branch of Nagasakiya, giving us all a welcome free evening.

### Day 6

The final day began with a test of how much we had understood of the course. This was not very strictly supervised, giving plenty of opportunity for conferring, and we then marked it ourselves. After the break, our trainer briefed us on the branches we were destined for, store organisation, salary, holidays, and career prospects.

One notable point in this briefing was a warning about possible problems with the part-timers.

> You're regular employees, so you'll get a higher salary than the part-timers, even though they have more experience than you do, and they're older. So they may resent you and bully you. Please watch out. Just say 'yes, yes' like sweet little girls when they say something to you.

And on promotion, 'Try to make it to section chief. You can do it in four years' (greeted by sniggers, meaning 'we're not going to stay that long').

> Try to bear it for three years. Think: if you can do three days you can do thirty days. If you can do thirty days, you can do three months. If you can do three months, you can do three years.[10]

Finally, the trainer emphasised the importance of gratitude, and asked the trainees to write to their teachers and thank them for everything they had done, and to telephone their parents when they arrived at their designated store. We then had a break before assembling in the main lecture hall at 11.30 a.m. to sing the company song. This was by way of practice for the graduation ceremony, which would be held for all the new entrants all together the following week. Schedules for the ceremony, company handbooks, and song sheets were handed out to the trainees, who were now all in a relaxed mood, chatting and laughing in informal groups. The song itself was sung rather half-heartedly, with the trainees drowned out by the tape recorder that was put on to accompany us. The head trainer then summed up the main message of the course: remember to give lively greetings.

After lunch, everyone went off to the dormitories to pack, and changed out of the tracksuits they had been wearing throughout the course, replacing them with the formal pastel coloured suits they had worn on arrival. We then assembled again in the main hall with our bags, waiting to be picked up by representatives from our respective branches and driven to our future workplace and home (which in most cases the recruits had never seen before). Everybody was chatting happily, and many seemed sorry it was over in so far as they would have to say goodbye to friends they had made who were going to different branches. There was also a lot of excited speculation on who would pick them up (inevitably a male employee) and whether he would be handsome or not.

As things turned out, the Koganei group were treated to no less than two young male escorts, as there were too many of us to fit in one car (the men sent to collect us had to drive their own cars down for the occasion). This caused quite a stir when the trainees first spotted them, followed by shy silence for most of the long drive back to Koganei. The two young men were very friendly and did their best to chat to the women, taking us all out first for coffee and then for a tour of Yokohama and the Yokohama Bay bridge on the way back.

## Arrival

We got to the branch late, delayed by traffic, just after the store had closed. We drove into the goods entrance and went up to the office floor in the very dirty and shabby elevator reserved for staff use, where a welcoming committee was waiting, consisting of the deputy branch manager, floor managers, and one female member of the office staff in her late twenties introduced as *dai-senpai* (roughly translated, very important senior colleague). The corridors on the way to the office were lined with posters welcoming the new arrivals, one for each new recruit, showing a drawing of her and messages to her from the other regular staff working on her floor (none of whom had previously met her).

The women were then given their new Nagasakiya uniforms and formally introduced to their floor managers by the deputy store manager, who also said a few words welcoming them to the company. The two young men allocated to take care of them then took them all off for dinner before taking them to the company dormitory, while I was buttonholed by various members of staff who had been hanging around in the hopes of seeing the new intake and asked what they were like.

My direct involvement with their grand entry to the Koganei branch was interrupted rather abruptly at this point, for now the course was over and we were all back in Koganei the general expectation seemed to be that I should hurry home to my husband and child; in any case, the trainees were looking rather tired, and perhaps they needed a quiet evening without the presence of a nosy visiting anthropologist. The formal ceremonies welcoming the new recruits to the company only took place a few days later, as the new recruits were given two days off to rest and settle into the dormitories. The first of these was a short ceremony welcoming the new recruits to the branch, with another neighbourhood ceremony organised shortly afterwards to welcome new recruits to locally based companies to the Koganei area. There were also a series of informal parties staged to welcome them at the branch, all of which involved a considerable amount of drinking, singing, and joking. These were probably the most enjoyable part of the welcoming process from the point of view of the recruits. However, from the company's point of view the main event was the entry ceremony to the company as a whole, which took place on completion of all the training programmes for that year, bringing together all of the new regular employees of 1991.

## The entrance ceremony

The entrance ceremony took place in Hiratsuka civic centre not far from the company training centre, a week after the completion of the training course in which I had participated. The new recruits assembled at 12.30 p.m., necessitating an early start or even an overnight stay for those who had completed their training earlier and were travelling from the more distant areas of Japan. Male and female alike were dressed in suits: dark colours for the men and spring pastels for the women. Once at the centre, we registered with reception, and we were each given a booklet setting out the order of events for the day and listing all the new recruits, divided by branch. Also included were the company motto and the text of the company song, and several blank pages that we were later told to use to make notes on the speeches given by the president and managing director of the company. After this, we went to the main hall, where we were seated by branch and geographical area. The recruits were also divided by gender, with the men at the front of the hall.[11] The atmosphere was initially quite animated, as the recruits took advantage of the opportunity to chat with other recruits who had attended the same training course but had been allocated to different branches. However, the chatting was soon curtailed, when we were drilled by the training managers on our bowing; in the actual ceremony, shortly to commence, we would be called on to stand up and bow in greeting to the company president and managing director.

At 1 p.m., the ceremony began. The curtain concealing the stage at the front of the hall was raised, revealing a podium flanked by two benches, on which senior company officials were seated, with a backdrop consisting of the Japanese flag on one side and the company flag on the other; these in turn were framed by banners. The topmost banner read 'Entry Ceremony to Nagasakiya Ltd., Heisei year 3',[12] and the banners on either side showed the Nagasakiya company mottoes. One of these banners showed the 'management vision': 'to be loved by the customer, and to aim to be a diversified general merchant', and the other showed the three slogans that summarised Nagasakiya's corporate aims:

Expand – network of kindness
Join together – network of trust
Extend – network of competitiveness

There was also a small stand for announcements on one side of the stage, and this was now mounted by one of the training managers, who announced the day's order of events and introduced the company's president and managing director, who were seated at the right-hand side of the podium.

The first event was formal greetings from the new recruits to the company president and managing director. For this, the names of the geographical areas into which the store's branches are divided were called in turn, at which both male and female recruits from that area all rose, and one male and one female representative mounted the stage to greet the managing director, who was now standing at the podium. They each received a certificate from him stating that they were now employees of Nagasakiya, which he handed to them bowing, and saying, *'ganbatte kudasai'* (please do your best). The representatives answered, *'hai, ganbarimasu'* (yes, we'll do our best), and then all the recruits from that area bowed in unison. As each recruit received his or her certificate all the officials on the stage clapped, except for the company president, who simply took notes. One girl slipped and fell on her way to the platform, prompting an outbreak of gasps and giggles, with mutters of *'kawaisō'* (poor thing).

After the greetings were over, we all resumed our seats to listen to speeches by the company president and managing director. The company president, Iwata Kohachi, spoke first. He began by telling us that we were now *shakaijin*, and we had to change our way of thinking from that of *gakusei* (students) to *shakaijin* (adults and members of society). He then introduced himself, explaining that he was the founder of the Nagasakiya group. He told us his age – sixty-eight years and ten months – and said he supposed he was probably about ten years older than the new recruits' fathers. He then went on to give us an outline of his own and Nagasakiya's history.[13]

> I started out when I was twenty-three, with very little money. The first store I opened was right here; it was a clothing store called Oasis. Now the chain has 10,737 employees. Isn't it amazing how things have grown? Do you know why Nagasakiya is called a chain store? It's because a chain[14] has lots of links, and Nagasakiya has lots of stores.
>
> Maybe I will only be able to meet you once or twice a year, so please listen to what I am going to tell you. I've written a book about my life, it has 360 pages and it's become a best-seller. I wasn't very good at school, I failed university entrance and was a *rōnin*[15] for three years. I don't try to hide this because I think people's failures are interesting. Please read my book, then maybe you can understand Nagasakiya a little better.

Drawing on these experiences, he told us that there were three key points we should remember: first not to approach life in a self-indulgent way; second that suffering while young led to happiness later on; and third that there was no such thing as being lucky. He concluded his speech by urging us all to put our whole energy into living.

This was followed by a speech by the managing director, a post at that time occupied by the founder's son. Like his father, he told us his age – forty-four – and said that he was probably about the same age as the new recruits' fathers. He emphasised the importance of gratitude: that we should be grateful to our parents; our teachers; our seniors; and our siblings, both older and younger. He then stressed once more the distinction between *shakaijin* and *gakusei* touched on by his father in the previous speech.[16]

From today, you are all *shakaijin*. The life of a *shakaijin* and the life of a student are fundamentally different. From today you have become *shakaijin*. And you have also become *Nagasakiyajin* (Nagasakiya people).[17] From now on, you must always take notes of what your superiors tell you, you will find that otherwise you will forget. As *shakaijin*, this is common sense. What have you all written in your notebooks on page four?[18] Now turn back to page three. Did you write anything? Maybe it doesn't matter now, but it will matter in a year's time.

This galvanised a number of the audience into picking up their pencils and starting to take notes in the space provided in our booklets. Having thus ensured himself of our full attention, he then announced the numbers of new recruits this year, high-school and university graduates, male and female, before returning to the theme of the differences between *shakaijin* and students.

As students, you had many rights (*kenri*), and few duties (*gimu*).[19] But now you are receiving a salary. As *shakaijin*, you have many duties and few rights. As a student, whatever you achieved was a result of knowledge plus action. However, as *shakaijin* action becomes much more important, so what you achieve is the result of knowledge times action. Knowledge in and of itself is far less important as a *shakaijin* than at school, you must above all learn how to use your knowledge, how to put it into practice. For a *shakaijin*, knowledge should be reflected in actions.

Do you know how much the company will pay you if you stay until the age of sixty? If you are a man, probably about 200 million yen. Some people repay the company with 100 million yen, some with 50 million yen. These people will not do well in the company. Think about it.

He then moved on to a consideration of the character training that would be required of us in our new role.[20]

You must not be guided by your personal likes and dislikes. You won't be able to do your job if you make these distinctions. There will be customers you like, and others you don't; tasks you like, and others you don't. When you're a student it's alright to only try hard at things you like, but it's not alright now that you are *shakaijin*.

You must take responsibility for your own self-discipline.[21]

Up until yesterday, you received guidance from your parents and teachers. Now everyone thinks of you as a *shakaijin*, so you must take responsibility for your own actions. You will get little or no guidance from others, so be grateful to those who do give you guidance.

Make good use of your time and money. You have 115 days' holiday a year, and your salary is between ¥100,000 and ¥200,000 a month.[22] How are you going to use this? If you spend your time watching television you are wasting your lives – think what else you could do with the time, for example you could use it to study something. And concerning money, some people get themselves into debt, which causes a lot of problems. Please be careful about this.

Learn your job as quickly as possible. Ask your superiors about anything you don't understand. How should you learn your job? This is a very important point, so I shall go into it in some detail. Think about learning to drive: if you sit in the back seat, you'll never learn. It's the same at work. You have to try to do it yourself. When you ask questions about something, make a note of the answers. Sometimes you will try to do something and fail. That's OK, but don't fail twice. If you fail twice it's OK, but don't fail three times. If you fail three times it's OK, but don't fail any more. One of my favourite manga[23] is about a girl who keeps failing in her attempts to become a stewardess, but never gives up. Don't be afraid of failure.

He then moved on to a consideration of male and female employees within the Nagasakiya group. He commented that men and women were equal but different, and said that he therefore proposed to talk about them separately. On women, he pointed out that there are many women employed in retail, and that a number of different career paths were available to them within Nagasakiya. He said he hoped they would progress within the company and told them that they could achieve a responsible position within the Nagasakiya group.

Turning his attention to the male recruits, he considered the question of how they could make it to the top posts within the company.

There are only a small number of top posts available. So how do people make it to the top? The first essential quality is strong leadership: the kind of attitude that says 'I'll do it, leave it to me.' Second, you have to like people – this is fundamental to retail. Third, you should have a cheerful, optimistic disposition. I know you all drink sake and beer. If you think when you've drunk half your beer, 'Oh, I've still got half a bottle left', that's a good way of thinking. In the same way at work, there are two sorts of people, those who think, 'I've finished half my work now, I'll do my best for just a bit longer'; and those who think, 'Still half left to do ...'

In the concluding part of his speech, the managing director told us always to remember that our salaries came from the money spent in the stores by the customers, and that if we offended the customers in some way and they ceased to come to the store, this would inevitably affect our pay. He then noted that over the past two days 1,170,000 people had entered companies (in Japan) as new recruits, 130,000 of them in the retail sector. Of those, we 650 had chosen Nagasakiya. To us, he addressed a special message, something to remember:

Where does happiness come from? It does not come from the north (*kita*), it does not come from the east (*higashi*), it does not come from the west (*nishi*). It comes from *minami*. This is not *minami* meaning south, but *minami* written with the characters for *mina* (everyone) and *shin*, or *mi* (body).

With this slightly enigmatic comment, presumably referring to the importance of mutual co-operation, the managing director left the podium, and we proceeded with the programme of events.

The next event was the formal introduction of the remaining dignitaries on the stage and then a brief answering speech by a representative of the recruits, affirming that we had now become *shakaijin*, and that we pledged our best efforts to the company. After this, we all rose and sang the company song in chorus – although it was sung fairly half-heartedly and punctuated by giggles in the group in which I was standing.

After a fifteen-minute break, in which the recruits resumed their unfinished conversations with friends from other branches, swapping impressions of the work so far, the dormitories, the sections to which they had been allocated, the ceremony continued with another long (forty minute) talk, which seemed to test the patience of the audience, judging from the background of fidgeting, chatting, and mutters of *tsumaranai* (boring) that became increasingly audible as the talk progressed. Some of the recruits quite openly went to sleep at this point, but the majority of those sitting near me who appeared at first glance to be industriously taking notes were in fact, as a closer look revealed, merely doodling.

The speaker began by congratulating us all on our entry to the company and saying how much he envied us all, as he remembered the day that he had joined. Much of the speech reinforced points already made by the managing director, for example on the importance of gratitude, but in a more verbose and informal style, liberally illustrated with anecdotes of the speaker's own experiences as a new employee at the company, and drawing on a wide range of ideas from both Japan and the West, covering areas as diverse as *un* (fate) and biorhythms. He spent a considerable time discussing basic character differences among each year's batch of new recruits, dividing them into two main categories, the enthusiastic, active type (*ii kandōsha*) and the 'cool'[24] type. Many of his anecdotes served to illustrate why it was better to be enthusiastic and active. Finally, this speaker alone addressed the women in the audience directly, telling us that the company wanted not just our labour, but our ideas – the female way of thinking. As an example of this, he cited some female entrepreneurs who started a successful delivery service specialising in small items. In the same way, he told us, we should all try to develop our own individual small themes, as the sum of many small things can create something worthwhile.

With the conclusion of this speech the curtain was lowered again, and we were free to disperse. No other entertainment was laid on, and there was no area where we could freely mingle and catch up with each other's news. In addition, nearly everyone faced a long journey back to the area in which their branch was located, although the fact that we would all have the day off the following day was taken advantage of by some to return to their parents' home for a brief visit. In any event, we all headed for the train station, most people now looking tired and glad to get away.

## Induction to adulthood: a world of contested meanings

In reflecting on the Nagasakiya training course and the entry ceremony that followed it, I found two points particularly striking. First, in their presentation of the process of becoming a Nagasakiya employee, both the training and the entry ceremony seemed to contrast in some interesting ways with the picture painted by Nagasakiya recruitment materials of the period. This is particularly noticeable in the case of the female high-school employees. For example, it may be recalled that the introduction in the 1992 high-school recruitment brochure spoke of the importance of finding 'work to suit you' (*jibunrashiku shigoto*), a notion that seems in contradiction with the company announcement on the training course that recruits would have to accept whatever section they were allocated to, even if it was not the one for which they had hoped, or the statement in the induction ceremony that new recruits should not be guided by their personal likes and dislikes. At the same time, there was a concomitant shift from an emphasis on company benefits and leisure activities to an emphasis on obligations to fellow employees and to the company.

Second, and arising from the first point, there seem to be competing discourses of adulthood at stake. The official view of the adult member of society, or *shakaijin*, as elaborated by trainers and company executives in Nagasakiya, in the context of the training course and entrance ceremony, is a person who recognises and fulfils his or her responsibilities, who is sensitive to relationships with others, who respects and shows gratitude to seniors, and repays the company for the salary he/she receives (and the customers whom the company serves) by hard work. Both the training course and the induction ceremony stressed the importance of co-operating with others and suppressing personal likes and dislikes when necessary. The language used also equated complaint, or expressing dislike, with immaturity, for example on the training programme the word *yada* (yuck) was used by the trainer to indicate expressing dislike or complaint, a word used by children and young women, with a childish feel contrasting implicitly with the status of *shakaijin*. In sum, it could be said that *shakaijin* status is attained through becoming part of a significant social unit – in this case the company – and accepting one's role within it. It is through this acceptance that one gains membership to the wider society.

This view of the significance of becoming a *shakaijin*, and its mediation by social institutions such as the company, reflects a pervasive (if somewhat conservative) discourse of adulthood in Japanese society, and is already well documented, both by Rohlen (1974: 37–8), in the context of large companies, and by Edwards (1989: 116–17), in the context of gaining *shakaijin* status through marriage. In taking on the role of transforming students into *shakaijin*, the company constitutes itself as agent and guardian of this discourse of adulthood, and of the view it implies of the relationship between individual and society.

Although only the male recruits are expected to stay with the company long term, in so far as the training and induction ceremony address the transformation of recruits to *shakaijin* and not simply to company employees, this is a process equally relevant to male and female recruits. The company's authority when performing this role is not dependent on a long-term commitment between company and employee, but rather on the fact that it is the first employer of these until-now *gakusei* and their point of entry to the outside world.

It is noteworthy in this context that Japanese views of the process of maturation emphasise the importance of a period of separation from the sheltered life of the home, and that this is often applied to women as well as to men. Both Tobin (1992a) and Kondo (1990) cite a number of proverbs making this point, for example 'If you love your child, send him to the wide world' and 'To become a (mature) person one must eat a stranger's rice' (Tobin 1992a: 26; Kondo 1990: 236). In Nagasakiya one of the women section managers told me that her parents had initially sent her to Nagasakiya in Tokyo from her home on a farm in the western island of Kyushu rather than to a branch in a nearby city in order to build her character before (they hoped) returning home to marry.[25]

Becoming a *shakaijin* can thus be seen as a particularly emphasised milestone in a more gradual process of gaining maturity as a social being in Japan. Many continuities are evident between the discourse surrounding entry to the company and that associated with progress through the school system in Japan. The induction ceremony, for example, showed clear similarities with school entrance ceremonies – a fact that may in part account for the rather bored and unimpressed response of many of the participants. Greetings, a succession of speeches welcoming the new entrants and emphasising their newly acquired duties and responsibilities, and a song are as much features of entry to educational institutions in Japan from pre-school onwards as they are of entry to companies.[26] Notions of the importance of duty and responsibility, gratitude to parents and teachers, and co-operating in groups are ideals inculcated in children at kindergarten (Tobin 1992a; Hendry 1986). The shift from a life dominated by rights *(kenri)* to one dominated by duties *(gimu)*, evoked in Nagasakiya's induction day speeches, is also one of the objectives of education at pre-school level – coincidentally I attended a speech on this topic by the head of my daughter's new pre-school shortly after the induction ceremony at Nagasakiya. In this context, the recollection of one recruit concerning one of the speeches at a locally organised welcome event for new entrants is entirely comprehensible, 'He just said the usual things'.

Herein lies an irony: although the Nagasakiya training course stressed the transition from school student to member of society, most of the features taken as defining the status of member of society are very familiar from the school setting. This irony was recognised by trainers in their comments to trainees that becoming a member of society was not about gaining freedom but about accepting more restrictions. In this sense, the transition to adulthood implied in the officially sanctioned view of becoming a *shakaijin* seems to be based on process and the gradual increase in responsibility and restriction running from pre-school entry through to taking up employment and marriage, rather than on a radical transition between two quite different states.

However, the Nagasakiya case suggests that there is also an alternative discourse of adulthood, defined in terms of lifestyle, consumption, and freedom from parental restrictions. This may be of particular relevance to the female high-school recruits focused on here.

Long-term promotion prospects for women within Nagasakiya are poor, and their employment at the store is seen both by the majority of female recruits themselves and by their employers as temporary, even though they are recruited as regular employees. As Ogasawara (1998) has pointed out in her study of office ladies in Japan, this apparently unfavourable position in the workplace can in some ways, paradoxically, give young women working as regular employees more power than their male colleagues to resist or ignore their seniors. Put simply, they have less to lose and therefore are relatively freer to pursue their own agendas.

At the same time, young women regular employees were then and remain one of the highest-spending consumer groups in Japan, and a group heavily targeted by advertisers and the leisure industry. Unmarried women working as regular employees tend to have a high disposable income, as they live either in subsidised company accommodation or with their families, and they rarely have to contribute to their family living costs. Nor are they expected to save for future costs of marriage and setting up home, unlike their male counterparts. They are a section of the population to a great extent defined within Japanese society in terms of consumption. This alternative definition of young adulthood for women in terms of consumption was implicitly recognised by Nagasakiya in its high-school recruitment brochures for women produced in the early 1990s, with their fashion magazine style of design.

For those women entering the company in 1991, in particular those who had requested allocation to a branch in Tokyo, far from their native homes,[27] joining Nagasakiya was a means of accessing the independent urban lifestyle of which they had seen so much in television dramas. Their work was a means to an end located in leisure and consumption, and their salary a means of acquiring the indispensable material adjuncts of their desired lifestyle. In this context, they had little or no interest in the information that was offered them on the company and its philosophy, either in the training course or in the induction ceremony, and few could recall it later. Of more interest was the establishment of friendships with other young employees, comparing interests and tastes, exchanging information on current trends, and discussing what type of up-to-the-minute consumer electronic goods they would purchase for their longed-for one-room company apartments.[28] In the training course, when allowed to ask their own questions, the much publicised dormitories and rules governing curfew and guests came top of the recruits' concerns.

In practice, the aspirations of these new recruits were tacitly recognised during the training course, as trainers tried in the more successful sessions to capture the interest of the new recruits by references to popular media figures, favourite cars or music, and workplace romance. In the ceremony for new recruits, too, the last speaker attempted (though largely failed) to engage their attention with references to topics of popular interest such as blood type and character, as well as the use of numerous anecdotes.

Despite these efforts, for much of the training programme, and during the induction ceremony itself, the female recruits made plain their boredom and lack of involvement by fidgeting, giggling, dozing, and simply not doing what they were asked. Later, some of them recalled nervousness during the training course, mainly at being, for the first time in their lives, brought together with other young people from all over Japan. As many of them were from distant, rural areas, they had been used to speaking in their local dialect and were particularly nervous about speaking in standard Japanese in front of a large group. However, there was also an element of passive resistance or non-co-operation on the part of some of the women, who used the limited resources at their disposal sometimes quite effectively to undermine or disrupt parts of the training programme (for example through giggling or silence). This is reminiscent of Scott's (1985) discussion of resistance by relatively powerless groups, or, more recently, Ogasawara's account of the ways in which office ladies in Japan can deploy behaviour stereotyped as 'feminine' such as gossip to undermine the authority of male managers (Ogasawara 1998: 70–98).

Many of the female recruits to Nagasakiya in my intake recalled reactions of disappointment and disillusionment during their training. The training centre shocked them by its shabby, dilapidated appearance after the glossy, modern impression conveyed by the recruitment brochure. Nor had they expected the course to be so strict, rule-bound, and tiring. Most of them complained of exhaustion during the course, and many of the rules, such as those concerning hairstyle, were widely resented and resisted. They had expected more freedom, not the imposition of restrictions that would be more strictly enforced than in high school.

They responded to this disappointment in various ways. Two, Nakamura-san and Araumi-san, acquired a certain notoriety by leaving the company immediately on completion of the training course, only pausing at their new workplace long enough to redirect their luggage. This was, apparently, not the first time such a thing had happened. Others were uncooperative to varying degrees during the training course, but appeared to settle on arrival at the branch and to enjoy the social life and new friendships that the company offered. Of those I knew, none hoped for a career within the company, and none was employed by Nagasakiya by 1999.

In the very different economic climate prevailing at the turn of the century, it may be that those lucky enough to find a position as a regular employee can no longer afford to be as cavalier as Nakamura-san and Araumi-san in the early 1990s. However, there is little evidence to suggest that young women entering Nagasakiya in the late nineties are more likely to remain long term than were their counterparts a few years previously – certainly the impression of those I spoke to when I visited in 1999 was that little had changed in this regard.

All this is not to say that joining Nagasakiya was an unimportant event for its young female recruits. But it is an event that has a different sort of significance for them, on the whole, than that projected in the official company discourse of becoming a *shakaijin*. These are issues that are returned to in Chapters 7 and 8, in which the questions of gender in the workplace and the role of the company in the lives of its employees are examined in more detail. But first, Chapters 5 and 6 examine everyday working life in Nagasakiya, and the various group events sponsored by the company in the early 1990s.

# 5   Harmony and consensus?

Employee relations in the
workplace

## Daily work at Nagasakiya, Koganei branch

In 1991, daily work in the branches of Nagasakiya was organised mainly at the section level.[1] All the sections on one floor were under the supervision of a single floor manager, and employees of all sections gathered together every morning for a meeting of all the employees on that floor. Each section was composed of a number of part-timers (usually two or three), one or two regular employees, and sometimes one or two temporary staff. Typically, each section had five or six members and was usually, though not always, headed by a section chief (*bumonchō*). The section chief was always a regular employee, and so the post might not be filled if there were no regular employees available with sufficient experience. In such a case, the section would usually be unofficially headed by a senior part-timer. Unlike the official section chief, these unofficial heads received no compensation in their salary for the increased responsibilities their job entailed.

Within the section, one of the regular employees might be a new recruit, or *shinnyūsei*, still undergoing on-the-job training. When this was the case, the new recruit was allocated a trainer, or *shidō pātonā* (guiding partner), who was generally the official or unofficial head of the section. In addition to running the section, this person then took on the responsibility of training the new recruit in the daily work of the section over the first six months of his or her employment. Watching and imitating one's trainer was an important part of learning to do the job, and the trainer would gradually allocate more and more responsibility to the new recruit according to a centrally established timetable of training. Regular meetings of all the trainers together with the manager in charge of training were held to discuss the progress of the new recruits and the best way of dealing with any problems that might arise.

Aside from the various sections of Nagasakiya proper, each floor also contained one or more small shops that rented space from the store. Some of these were, in fact, subsidiary companies of Nagasakiya, and when this was the case their staff would also join in the morning meetings. The appearance of the staff at morning meetings was therefore quite mixed: male regular employees in sober suits, female regular employees and part-timers, indistinguishable except for age, in Nagasakiya uniforms, temporary staff in casual clothes and aprons (pink for women, blue for men), and employees of subsidiary companies in their own company's uniform.

The working day began with the morning meeting or *chōrei*, which was taken by the floor manager if he was working that day, or otherwise by one of section chiefs or a male regular employee.[2] This meeting was held at 9.45 a.m., just before the store's opening at 10.00 a.m., and it always followed a set pattern. The public address system, broadcast throughout the store, asked the staff if they were ready and announced that the morning meeting would commence shortly. Everyone then assembled on their floors around a sort of mobile notice-board, wheeled out of the manager's office for the meeting.

The meeting began with the person in charge greeting all those assembled. This greeting was returned by the other employees with a slight bow. Then a register was taken, and the names of those who were absent or were on a later shift were also read out. Then the meeting leader went through a list of points he or she had previously written up on a chart, and the other employees took notes in company notebooks provided for this purpose.

The first point was always who would represent the floor at the store entrance when employees lined up to greet the customers at the store's opening (any female employee below the rank of section manager), and who was to do other jobs such as operate the cash register and turn on the electricity. Other topics varied – often the staff were reminded of special offers in the store that day or the current monthly campaign (each store had a theme for a campaign every month, for example cleanness or greetings). Special store events were also noted, for example the anniversary of the store's opening, when prize draws took place and free gifts were distributed to customers. The most common item on the agenda was probably sales targets and sales achieved. These were broken down section by section, and sections that were not reaching their targets were urged to try harder. Reasons for not achieving targets might also be discussed; for example, warm weather reducing sales of winter clothing (which on at least one occasion led on to quite an animated discussion after the meeting about the greenhouse effect).

Sometimes the meeting leader conducted a random test of the staff on questions such as the day's sales target for each section (except for temporary staff, everyone was expected to know this for their own section – the information was available in a large book kept next to the cash register). Staff not producing the correct answer were then reprimanded and urged to make sure that they knew in future. Whether or not such a test was held and the general tone of the meeting varied considerably depending on who was conducting it. On the floor where I was employed, the floor manager took a very relaxed attitude to the meetings, generally starting them late and rarely quizzing the staff. In contrast, one of the section chiefs (a young woman) was very strict, started meetings early, reprimanded the inevitable stragglers, and tested everyone regularly on sales targets. It seemed that within broad guidelines, the way in which a meeting was conducted was very much up to the person leading it.

The meeting was concluded by a group practice of the five basic expressions used towards customers: *irasshaimase* (welcome), *osore irimasu ga* (sorry, but …), *shōshō omachi kudasaimase* (please wait a moment), *omatase itashimashita* (sorry to keep you waiting), *arigatō gozaimashita. Mata okoshi kudasaimase* (thank you. Please come again). For this, one employee stood in front of the others and said each expression, followed by a bow. The other employees repeated in chorus, also bowing. One reason for practising these expressions daily was to practise the correct formal Japanese for dealing with customers. However, as many of those attending the meetings had many years' experience, and all were able to use these expressions without difficulty, the practice also struck me as having a ritual aspect, as an affirmation of our common status as employees of the store. Practice was concluded by the practice leader saying, *Mō ichinichi ganbarimashō* (let's do our best for another day), to which the others replied in chorus, *Hai, ganbarimasu* (Yes, we'll do our best).

After the practice, the floor representative went to the entrance of the store, where a representative from each floor together with the branch manager and deputy branch manager stood in a line. Other employees did some last minute tidying of their section before going to the edge of their section as the loud speakers began the pre-opening announcements. These were always the same and asked the staff if they had completed the preparations for the store's opening, exhorting them to do their best for another day. The company song was then broadcast, and all the employees listened in silence. After the song had finished, the doors were opened to customers, and all the staff bowed to the customers and said '*irasshaimase*' as they came in. The bowing at the store entrance/section edges continued for five minutes, after which the staff at the entrance dispersed, and everyone set about their daily work. Thereafter, staff only bowed to greet customers as they approached their own section.

The first morning task was to tidy and clean the section, which also involved restocking the shelves. After that, the pattern varied somewhat depending on the day of the week. The busiest days were Mondays and Thursdays, because the deadline for ordering new stock was Monday afternoon, and the stock was delivered and put on the shelves on Thursdays. Lunch breaks were one hour, work then resuming until leaving time, which could be any time up to 7.00 p.m., when the store closed, depending on the category of employee and the shift she was working. In general, the part-timers started early and had finished by 4.45 p.m., whereas the regular employees often worked a later shift, staying until the store closed. This was because of the family commitments of the part-timers, and resulted in the store being particularly short-staffed after 5.00 p.m., the busiest time of day. Temporary staff were therefore used in the evenings to try to solve this problem. It also resulted in very long days for those of the regular employees with managerial responsibilities, who had to take it in turns to supervise the opening of the store, arriving by about 9.15 a.m. and often not leaving until 7.30 or 8.00 p.m., when the last duties of the day were completed.

At the end of the day, the total takings for each section were calculated, and the daily report for each section was filed in a large folder kept near the cash register. This noted any particular features of sales that day, for example 'typhoon, good sales of umbrellas and rainwear', and the total sales achieved for that day and for the month so far. The percentage of the daily sales target achieved was also noted. The report was usually filled in by the regular employees of the section, partly because by closing time most of the part-timers had gone home, and those remaining were generally a mix of regular employees and temporary staff. The temporary staff were not, at that time, trained to do jobs considered complex, such as the filling in of reports.

All employees were expected to observe certain basic rules: first to be punctual (a check is kept on this through the use of a clock-on clock-off system); second to respect the company code for employees' appearance; and third to be punctilious about greeting customers and keeping a bright smiling face at all times. These rules were not, however, consistently observed; in practice, employees did leave collar buttons undone, tied up their hair with the wrong colour of ribbons, and failed to smile at customers, and managers often turned a blind eye to these details.[3]

Discipline, and the organisation of work within a section was largely left up to the section chief, who rarely needed to intervene actively. The more experienced staff all knew exactly what had to be done, and each tended to take charge of a particular line of goods within the section as far as ordering was concerned. Only the temporary staff and new recruits – whether regular staff or part-timers – really needed to be told what to do. Otherwise, everyone got on with the work with remarkably little chatting or time-wasting. To understand why this should be so, it is helpful to look at the internal organisation of the sections in further detail.

## Hierarchy and group harmony: the Nagasakiya case

The sections into which the workforce at the Nagasakiya branches were divided were, in 1991 at least, heterogeneous in terms of employment status and generation, and sometimes gender, although there were so many women employed at the lower levels of Nagasakiya that a number of the sections were composed solely of female employees. This heterogeneity had important consequences for the way in which the daily work was conducted, and also for the interpersonal relations between section members. This section considers the implications of this heterogeneity for notions of hierarchy and harmony as applied to groups in Japanese society.

Nakane (1970) has argued that heterogeneity is characteristic of groups in Japan, and that in order to unify such groups, the members of which have few or no common attributes[4] to bind them together, an 'emotional' sense of 'group consciousness' is encouraged (Nakane 1970: 10). She further argues that in the absence of 'horizontal' ties of the type that link people with the same attributes, groups in Japan tend to be characterised by hierarchical, 'vertical' interpersonal relations.[5] How far does this view of Japanese social

*Figure 5.1* A section chief at the Koganei branch of Nagasakiya

groups, as characterised by an emotional sense of group consciousness and bound together by vertical relations between their members, describe the Nagasakiya case?

To take the question of 'vertical' relations first; the problem, in the Nagasakiya context, with characterising a relationship between two employees as vertical is that there are a number of criteria according to which individuals may be ranked, and these frequently overlap and even contradict each other. The main criteria for ranking are position within the company (for example section chief or ordinary employee), employment status (especially, regular employee or part-timer), level of education (university or high-school graduate), length of service, age, and gender. The last two are not officially criteria of ranking, but they are important on an unofficial level. In practice, gender is officially subsumed, as is often the case in Japan, in the category level of education – almost all the university graduates are men, and most of the high-school graduates are women. However, for those whose gender and level of education are not congruent, gender can be seen to play an important role, with male high-school graduates encouraged to take on more responsibilities than is the case for their female counterparts, and conversely the only female university graduate whom I met in the course of my fieldwork was treated in apparently identical fashion to the female high-school graduates.

It is this type of lack of congruence between principles of ranking that both necessitates further explanation and provides a way in to understanding the internal dynamics of the sections and of the company as a whole. For example, how would we characterise the relationship between a part-timer in her fifties with fifteen years' experience and a regular employee with one year's experience? Or the same part-timer with a female section chief whom she had trained ten years previously? Or a female section chief, and high-school graduate, with a male university graduate, notionally placed under her supervision? All these relationships are potentially highly ambiguous, and all are cases I encountered in my fieldwork. Nor are they unusual – in the case of part-timer–regular employee relationships in particular, the ranking criteria of age and length of service on the one hand and employment status on the other are frequently, even generally, at odds. It is no coincidence that this relationship was the one most frequently referred to as problematic, both by senior management and by the employees involved. In the following sections of this chapter, two of the most frequent types of conflict between different principles of ranking are explored with reference to actual examples at the Koganei branch: first where ranking by gender was in conflict with formal status ranking, and second where employment status was in conflict with ranking by age and length of service.

## Gender and authority: problems on the first floor of the Koganei branch

The first floor of the Koganei branch, where I worked in 1991, was fairly typical of the store as a whole in terms of its mix of employees. There were two section chiefs, both women, Arakawa-san, whose story is given in more detail in Chapter 7, and Nishiguchi-san. Arakawa-san was a well-liked and outgoing member of staff, married to another Nagasakiya employee who worked in the head office. A high-school graduate from a farming family in Kyushu, she had joined the company at the age of eighteen and had, at the time of my fieldwork, spent fourteen years at the Koganei branch, reaching the grade of section chief seven years previously. Nishiguchi-san was a good friend of Arakawa-san, but some four years younger and still unmarried. Two sections on the floor had no official section chief and were, in practical terms, run by experienced part-timers who received neither extra pay nor higher status in recognition of the responsibilities they assumed.

Of the other regular employees on the first floor, four were women, one of whom had joined in 1990, with the other three (one of whom was a university graduate) all new entrants in 1991. There were only two full-time male employees on the floor: Kobayashi-san (whose story is given in more detail in Chapter 8), who had also joined in 1990, and the floor manager, Tanaka-san. Both were university graduates.

The floor manager took a fairly relaxed attitude to his job, intervening very little in the day-to-day running of the floor, to the chagrin of some of the employees, who would have liked to see him take a more active role; for example, to reallocate staff between sections in periods when one section was particularly busy while another had little to do, or to intervene with the buyers on occasions when sections felt that they were being given inappropriate or poor-quality goods to sell. Such problems were taken seriously by staff owing to the pressure of sales targets and were difficult to resolve in the case of the two sections without official section chiefs, because nobody had the formal authority to deal with this sort of issue.

Tanaka-san often seemed distracted when these sorts of problems were brought to his attention, and to compound the frustrations of the part-time staff on the floor he was not infrequently absent, taking extra leave in addition to his allocated two days a week. I eventually discovered that he had a chronically ill daughter, and his absences were often in order to accompany her to hospital. He had opted out of the standard male career ladder and had opted to be a 'zone' employee, remaining within one geographical area of Japan, but relinquishing the chance of further promotion in order to be close to his family and to help care for his daughter.

However, despite the fact that he had not himself followed the normative path for male employees, Tanaka-san had firm views on gender roles in the workplace, as became particularly evident in his treatment of Kobayashi-san, the other male employee on the floor. Although Kobayashi-san was a timid and generally unenthusiastic and ineffectual employee, from the manager's point of view he was destined for a managerial position because of his gender. Tanaka-san was aware of Kobayashi-san's poor ability to communicate with other staff, and even on one occasion expressed his frustration to me, explaining that he would like to feel that other employees could turn to Kobayashi-san with any problems or queries when he, Tanaka-san, was absent. This surprised me, as in the formal hierarchy the two (female) section chiefs were the next step down from Tanaka-san, and I would have expected them, rather than the inexperienced Kobayashi-san, to be called on in the manager's absence. I said this to Tanaka-san, but he replied that 'it's because Kobayashi is a man ...'

Probing indirectly to discover what Arakawa-san felt about this situation, since Kobayashi-san was in her section, and, notionally, her subordinate, I was surprised to find a total lack of resentment. From Arakawa-san's point of view, it was perfectly normal to promote men over the heads of women with greater experience. She noted that when the section chief system was first introduced, all the men in her intake were promoted to this rank first, followed by the women. She described this as 'natural'. It may be relevant to note here that Arakawa-san came from a rural area of Kyushu, a part of Japan renowned for the clear differentiation between male and female roles, and for a kind of male gender model thought of as strong and dominant, generally referred to as *Kyūshū danji*, literally Kyushu man. Arakawa-san may, therefore, have been predisposed to see male and female roles in all spheres of life as being quite separate, with positions of leadership falling to men.

Nishiguchi-san, the other section chief, a dynamic and very efficient woman, also appeared to take it for granted that male employees would be given greater responsibilities than women and promoted to a higher rank. She pointed out in this connection the difficulty for a young woman such as herself to give orders to the part-timers, who were notionally subordinates but in fact much older than she was. Orders received from men would, on the other hand, be much more likely to be followed. She also offered the opinion that men were more likely to be able to pass the necessary exams to reach the higher levels of the company, owing to their superior education.[6]

In general terms then, masculinity was seen as conferring automatic authority. Where women were placed in positions directly superior to men, this was seen as a temporary situation, as they assisted in training new male employees up to a level where they would be able to take on a managerial role. Within this frame, criticisms of male staff, by either male or female employees, tended to be couched in terms of their failure to exercise the authority expected of them, as can be seen in the cases of both the floor manager and Kobayashi-san.

For female staff the position was different. Divided into two categories, the part-timers, who were almost all senior to the regular employees in terms of age, and many of whom were also senior in terms of experience, and the regular employees who, although younger and often less experienced, were senior in terms of formal rank; the issue of who had authority over whom was highly ambiguous.

## Generation versus formal ranking: ambiguities in the female workforce

The relationship between women employed as regular employees and the women part-timers was probably the most apt to be problematic of all the different employee relationships within the company. Both female, both low status, both thought of as lacking a long-term commitment to the company, these two categories of employee were differentiated by age, pay, and employment status. Although generally twenty years or so younger than the part-timers, the regular employees received a higher salary[7] and were notionally senior in the company hierarchy. This was despite the fact that many part-timers could boast far longer terms of service within Nagasakiya. Also, the regular employees had job security and could look forward to promotion to the rank of section chief if they remained with the company long enough, a position beyond the reach of the part-timers.[8]

These differences were commented on as unfair, and they were resented by many part-timers, who compared themselves directly with the female regular employees in a way that neither group did with the male regular employees. However, there was no official forum in which they could air their grievances, since, as noted in Chapter 2, company union membership was restricted to regular employees and a very small subdivision of the part-timers, the *teijishain*. One woman told me that a group of them had got together a few years previously and tried to set up a special union for part-timers, but that this had been blocked by the company, and subsequently an excuse was found to dismiss the ringleaders.

Most part-timers, however, were not so articulate in their criticisms of the company, saying that the differences in wages and promotion prospects between themselves and the female regular employees were unfair, but unavoidable, and not specific to Nagasakiya. The reaction of Kimura-san, the senior part-timer in the section where I worked, was fairly typical in this respect – she simply shrugged her shoulders when asked about this point, saying, 'It's like that in all Japanese companies. It can't be helped'. This view was shared, to some extent, by company union officials. When I asked the deputy leader of the company union why they did not do more for the part-time employees, he responded that this was not a problem Nagasakiya could tackle on its own, as the treatment of part-timers was fairly standard in all chain stores. For one chain store unilaterally to improve the wages of its part-timers would therefore increase costs and decrease profitability relative to the store's competitors. That was something no store could afford to do on its own, so it would have to be an industry-wide initiative. Such initiatives were difficult to realise because no industry-wide union existed, although discussions did take place among the various company unions in the sector. However, he did point out that Nagasakiya had recently admitted the *teijishain* to the company union, and said that this was highly unusual in the retail sector, and this showed that the union was doing what it could for the part-time employees.

In any event, deprived of the means to complain directly to management, and, in many cases, accepting the status quo as inevitable and beyond management's control, the resentment of the part-timers often focused itself on the young women working as regular employees.[9] This led, in some cases, to something akin to bullying, a problem of which company management was well aware, and about which new trainees were warned during the initial training course. But more often, the resentment surfaced in muttered, and indirect, complaints to other part-timers, along the lines of:

> This cleaning work is hard on people my age, you have to bend down all the time. It would be better if the younger people did it …

Or,

> You spend so much time teaching them how to do the job, and they're just about learning to do it properly when they leave, and you have to start all over again with a new one. They make some excuse like 'my parents are ill', but I don't believe it, leaving your job because your husband or your children are ill is one thing, but your parents?

Or,

> The trouble is they're so young, they can't cope with human relations
> (*ningen kankei*). If somebody says something that upsets me, I just control
> myself and carry on. That one who left, she couldn't do that.

The implication behind all these remarks is that these young women are in
some sense immature and irresponsible, unable to do their jobs effectively,
and in the end they create more work for the part-timers, for example by
leaving after a short length of time, and thus obliging the part-timers to
train yet another new person. Further evidence that this view was widespread
can be drawn from the company union survey, in which over a third of the
part-timers surveyed said they felt that part-timers work more conscientiously
than do the female regular employees. A little over 20 per cent also complained
that not enough respect was shown in the workplace for older people.

This attitude among the part-timers made it quite difficult for younger
female regular staff appointed as section managers to exercise authority over
them. The regular staff were very conscious of this, and most said they felt
that the only way that a woman could be effective in the still higher rank of
floor manager would be if she were considerably older than the average for
female regular employees – at least in her forties – so that the part-timers
would be more inclined to defer to her. This was indeed the case of the only
woman floor manager at the branch, Ushijima-san, who is described in more
detail in Chapter 7. This in itself acted as a deterrent to the young female
regular employees from aspiring to promotion beyond section chief, for they
would have to wait over twenty years before, in their terms, such a promotion
would become a realistic possibility.

In general terms, a distinct wariness was shown by many young women
regular staff of the part-timers with whom they worked, a wariness that served
the company well in that it acted as a constraint, tending to make the regular
staff work harder for fear of criticism from the part-timers. An example can
be drawn from the hosiery section in Nagasakiya, which comprised Kimura-
san, a *teijishain* in her fifties with fifteen years' experience, two other part-
timers with a shorter length of service, Morinaga-san, who was in her forties,
and Suzuki-san, who was in her thirties, me, and one regular employee,
Kojima-san, who was nineteen years old when I joined and had a little over
one year's experience with the company. Kimura-san acted as the unofficial
section head and had trained all of the other members of the section at various
times, and Morinaga-san was the next most senior in terms of length of service
(five years) and deputed for Kimura-san when necessary in most of the section,
but she always steered clear of that part of the section allocated to the young
regular employee.

In general, work within the section proceeded fairly smoothly, with Kojima-
san, the regular employee, getting on with the work in her part of the section
and taking her turns on the cash register with no apparent ill-will and minimal

chatting with other staff. She seemed to form rather a separate unit, allocated to the children's part of the section, whereas the part-timers all worked together on the adult part. As the floating temporary employee, I was sometimes sent off to help her, but otherwise anything to do with her area was regarded as her responsibility, no-one offered to help her, nor did she offer to help in the rest of the section. This sort of arrangement was quite typical, and it reflected company policy to train new regular staff by giving them responsibility for their own product line.

The working timetable was generally arranged so that either Kimura-san or Morinaga-san was always present, but on one particular day both were absent, and a striking change was immediately evident in Kojima-san. She took far longer than usual to get going with her work, looked sulky, and complained about how *kitsui* (exhausting) the work she had to do that day was. As we were doing the work (re-pricing) together, I suggested to her that having done a certain amount of it we leave the rest for another day. At this, Kojima-san rounded on me, and said it was all right for me, I could leave it and no-one would say anything, but if she did not do it all she would get into trouble with the two senior part-timers when they returned the next day. Despite this comment, she took advantage of various excuses to absent herself from the section for extended periods and continued to work at a snail's pace for the rest of the day; she reverted to her normal behaviour the following day, when Kimura-san and Morinaga-san were also back at work.

I found this conversation interesting because Morinaga-san had no authority of any kind over Kojima-san, and Kimura-san's authority within the section was highly informal, and derived from the fact that after fifteen years she knew her way around better than anyone else, rather than from her formal status. In fact, in terms of formal status, Kojima-san, as the only regular employee, enjoyed higher status, and also a higher salary, than anyone else in the section. However, this evidently did not prevent her from feeling that she could not slack off when the older part-timers were present, much as she might have wished to do so.

If anxiety over the reactions of the part-timers working in the same section acted as a constraint on the regular staff, what of the part-timers themselves? How did they feel about their work, and what incentives did they have to work hard given a system that gave them no hope of promotion or a significant pay increase? For this group of employees a number of factors complicated workplace relations, not least of which was the absence of job security, since in contrast to the situation for regular staff, companies in Japan are not seen as having a moral obligation to ensure the continued employment of part-timers in the workforce. This tended to act as an incentive to work as hard as possible for fear of losing one's job, and caused resentment of anyone in the section, whether part-timer or regular employee, who was seen as not pulling his or her weight. The problem here was that performance was judged not on an individual but on a section-by-section basis, with sales results of each section regularly announced in morning meetings and compared both with other sections on the same floor and with the same section in other branches of the company. Although the performance of the section would have no effect on the wages of the individual part-timer, and she was not in any case eligible for promotion, if the section performed badly over an extended period of time the floor space allocated to it might be reduced, with a consequent reduction in staff. These might in turn affect the part-timers, who feared that they would be the first to be discharged. For this reason, next to the section chiefs, the part-timers tended to be the most anxious for their own section to perform well and were correspondingly vigilant towards their fellow section members.

Furthermore, the part-timers as a group were far from being homogeneous. They varied in age from about thirty to late fifties, with a correspondingly wide range of family circumstances. Although all those I encountered were married with children, the children of the older ones were already grown, with children of their own, and their domestic duties were hence less onerous, freeing them to dedicate more time to the company, for example by working on Sundays. The older part-timers were also much less able to change jobs than were their younger counterparts, owing to a decreasing demand for female employees in Japan with increasing age, and consequently they experienced greater pressure to perform at Nagasakiya, for losing the job they held there might mean losing their place in the workforce altogether. One result of this was that the commitment to the company and the degree of effective job mobility varied a great deal within the category of part-timers, although their wages and employment conditions did not vary significantly. As noted in Chapter 2 (p. 29), this division between different sorts of part-timers was recognised by the staff themselves in the unofficial label of 'veteran', applied by part-timers to those of their number who had accumulated a long period of service with the company.

The failure of management to recognise this, from the employee perspective, important distinction among part-timers was seen as another case of unfairness by many, along with the preferential treatment received by female regular employees, and was a source of resentment. Morinaga-san commented:

> In this place, it doesn't make any difference if you work hard or not. There's no recognition for hard work, everyone is paid the same. And often they ask us to do too much. Sometimes I get really fed up and I want to stop.

Morinaga-san also said that she regularly went through advertisements for part-time workers, looking for something better. The option of changing jobs was still open to her, although it was becoming more difficult as she was in her mid-forties. But her situation was still relatively less constrained than that of her colleague and immediate senior in the section, Kimura-san.

Kimura-san made it clear that she did not continue to work out of any great love for the job *per se*, simply from necessity. At fifty-five, she was anxious about her future, particularly as her husband was unwell, her son was as yet unmarried (weddings are very costly in Japan, to both families involved), and she herself was very close to the official retirement age. And she felt she had little choice but to continue with Nagasakiya, where she had been for the past fifteen years.

> I'm not qualified for anything, and I'm not so young. And I don't want to travel. Nagasakiya is convenient, I can come here by bicycle. If I worked somewhere else, even if they paid me a better hourly rate, if you consider travelling time and fares it wouldn't be so good. And this is a good place to work if you're a housewife – you have to go out anyway to shop, so you can just pop into the food hall downstairs before you go home, which is really handy, don't you think?
>
> If I had some kind of qualification, I could do something else – if I had a driving license for example, I could do delivery work, or if I had computer or word-processor training … But I don't have any qualifications.

Kimura-san felt that she worked very hard for little recognition, and that her job was made harder owing to the absences of other staff. She complained particularly bitterly about Morinaga-san, who took her day off on delivery day, leaving the rest of the section to unload and shelve the deliveries without her. On occasion, this meant that Kimura-san had to do the job entirely by herself, as the third part-timer on the section, Suzuki-san, and I both had young children, which inevitably meant periodic absences from work owing to illnesses or school events, and the regular staff member on the section was sometimes absent for one-day conferences or training programmes. Fortunately for us, our reasons for absence were regarded by Kimura-san as valid, but she made no excuses for Morinaga-san, whose absences she appeared to attribute to sheer wilful selfishness. Kimura-san's feelings towards Morinaga-san reached a nadir when the latter absented herself for two weeks to go on holiday in Greece with her husband.

Despite all this, and her frequent criticisms of both the floor manager and the buyer, who annoyed her by appearing to ignore her suggestions about new stock for the section, Kimura-san was anxious for the section to perform well, and for her own hard work to be noticed. She explained:

> The retirement age for part-timers is fifty-seven. It's gone up, it used to be fifty-five. And for regular employees it's sixty now. But sometimes they let you continue as an *arubaito*. But the senior people keep an eye on you, they know if you are working hard or not. And if you aren't, when you ask to continue they won't let you. Also, you have to watch the sales for your section, they're compared with sales for the same sections in all the other branches.

Returning to the relationship between Morinaga-san and Kimura-san, the two were on far from cordial terms, despite their apparent similarities in generation, gender, and employment status, and the fact that they had worked closely together for the past five years. To an extent, this can be attributed to the difference in potential mobility between the two women, but I would argue that the inherent tensions in belonging to the same section and therefore being interdependent in terms of assessment by superiors and job security also play an important role. During the year I spent at Nagasakiya, I observed a number of warm friendships between part-timers, but never between part-timers employed in the same section, and it therefore seems to me that membership of the same section often acts as an obstacle to forming friendly relationships, whatever the image projected for outsiders may be.

## Ambiguities and tensions in the workplace

One of the main features of employee relations within Nagasakiya was, therefore, that different criteria of ranking tended to cross-cut each other, so that relative seniority was often somewhat ambiguous. This was a particular source of tension among female employees, where seniority calculated by age or length of service often conflicted with official status within the company hierarchy, so that the older part-timers with greater length of service were, in terms of job status, junior to less experienced young women working as regular employees. Analogous tensions are noted by Ogasawara (1998) in her study of office employees, where she found that ranking in terms of education often conflicted with ranking based on age for the female employees (Ogasawara 1998: 50–6). Ogasawara argues that it is this tension, based on an ambiguous hierarchical structure, that sows dissension among female employees and prevents them from organising more effectively to improve their position, a conclusion which seems to me to be equally applicable to the Nagasakiya case. Taking Ogasawara's findings for office employees together with the research presented here for the retail sector, it seems that it is the case in many Japanese companies that the female workforce is far more diverse in terms of age, job status, length of tenure, and educational background than is the male workforce. For this reason, simple models of vertical hierarchy developed by writers such as Nakane (1970) seem to be very male gendered and of limited applicability to Japan's growing female workforce.

Turning to the regular staff in Nagasakiya, the ways in which employee relations were structured varied significantly depending on gender. In the early 1990s, owing to the high turnover of female employees, the annual intake of regular employees was heavily biased towards female high-school graduates. One result of this was that at branch level it was likely that several women of the same intake would be allocated to the same branch, whereas perhaps only one man of that intake would be allocated to the branch. Among the men of the branch, then, all relations would tend to be 'vertical relations' of the senior–junior (*senpai–kōhai*) type, as none of the men would be from the same intake. However, among the women, 'horizontal' relations, or relations among those of equivalent level, the *dōkisei* of the same intake, were very important, with women socialising with and comparing themselves with their *dōkisei* in the same branch. Often, this comparison would be concerned with progress towards goals outside the company, such as getting married, or getting another job, so that as all the other women from the same intake left, the one or two remaining would feel increasing pressure to do likewise.[10] Here again there is a difference in that men's personal networks within the company tend to be mobilised for work-related ends, whereas female networks, among young regular women employees at least, are often concerned with progress towards the goal of leaving the company.

For the male employees, senior–junior relations were important as the predominant basis of their social networks within the company and after hours socialising and also in the linked domain of their future career trajectories within the company. Since a large proportion of these employees end up staying with the company long term, senior–junior links formed and cultivated in a man's early years at the company can be of considerable use later on. However, even for men, these are not the only relations that count. Rather, each man will build up his own personal network as he progresses through the company, including seniors, juniors, fellow entrants from the same intake, and those linked by other ties such as having attended the same university. As these men are transferred between different branches and sections of the company, their personal network spans the divisions of the company and provides an alternative means through which they can obtain favours or get things done by other sections of the company, often more quickly than if they used official channels. Conversely, those with a less extensive personal network may be disadvantaged. For example, the branch manager of Koganei, who initially acted as my patron within the company, had been working in Osaka before the Koganei posting and lacked a network in the Kanto area. He was also one of the few men of his rank not to have graduated from a four-year university, and he was therefore also unable to appeal to a school clique. For these reasons, when I wished to participate in the training programme for new entrants, the branch manager gave his approval, but told me that I would have to arrange this through my floor manager, Tanaka-san. Tanaka-san, it transpired, had a *dōkisei* who was highly placed in the training department. This *dōkisei* was also a graduate of the same university as Tanaka-san, and their wives, also ex-Nagasakiya employees, were close friends.[11] I found that thenceforward any queries about training were much better dealt with through Tanaka-san rather than through the branch manager, even though the latter was formally more senior in the company hierarchy. This case was quite typical in that I found throughout my fieldwork that the best way to set up an interview or obtain certain information was to find out who, of the employees I knew and was on good terms with, was plugged into the relevant network, and then set up the connection through that employee, irrespective of his or her position in the formal hierarchy.

Even where the regular employees are concerned, Nagasakiya thus appears less like a vertically structured pyramid of the type suggested by Nakane (1970) than a constellation of overlapping networks and cliques. This pattern of networks and cliques is reproduced among the part-timers, and again 'vertical' links are not necessarily the ones that count. In fact, age seemed very important here, with the younger *arubaito* gravitating towards the younger regular employees, and the part-timers also tended to prefer the company of other women of a similar age, generally other part-timers, but sometimes also regular employees. Interests and general personal style were also important here; one example of this being a highly visible, though small, group comprising part-timers and one regular employee around the age of thirty, some of them with small children, who tended to wear heavy make-up and smoked cigarettes. These women did not get on particularly well with their older, more conventional, colleagues, and complained of being caught in the middle between the young regular employees and the older part-timers. On their side, most of the older part-timers made no secret of their disapproval of mothers with pre-kindergarten age children who went out to work, leaving their children in day-care centres. Cigarette smoking by women and the wearing of heavy make-up were also widely regarded in Japan at that time as indicative of a degree of moral laxity.

Despite the tendency to form generation and interest-based groups, and the frequent tensions between part-timers working in the same section (pp. 91–2), there was also, perhaps surprisingly, a degree of section-based factionalism among the part-time staff. For example, in the hosiery section Kimura-san, although critical of her fellow part-timer Morinaga-san in the same section, reserved her most vitriolic comments for the part-timers working in the service section. She would get particularly annoyed with them on delivery days, when hosiery would be almost submerged by a deluge of cardboard boxes to be unpacked and shelved. On these days she would regularly point out to me that the part-timers in the service section (which sold cinema and theatre tickets and ran a delivery and postal service) were sitting behind their counter 'doing nothing'. Why, demanded Kimura-san, could one of them not come over and help us, seeing as we were clearly rushed off our feet?

In her calmer moments, though, Kimura-san furnished the explanation herself. Each section, as noted above (p. 80), has its own sales targets, and failure or success in achieving these reflects on all members of the section. But, helping members of other sections earns one no credit whatsoever. Furthermore, sections on the same floor competed with each other about who could achieve the best sales for the month. It would seem to me that in this context, there are, if anything, positive disincentives to helping out in other sections and also a certain rivalry and interpersonal tension between the sections is encouraged. This was particularly the case for the older part-timers, who felt that their future job security depended on their section's performance. Perhaps for this reason, friendships between part-timers would often span not only different sections but different floors, where they were not in competition with each other and relations could, therefore, be more relaxed. For regular employees, however, job security was not an issue in the relatively prosperous early 1990s, and I was not aware of any intersectional animosity among this category of employee.

Intersectional relations also had another side: the maintenance of the external face of section harmony. For work purposes at least, the section was the primary grouping, and followed the strong social norm that conflict should not be publicly displayed to non-group members (although private moaning to close friends is another matter). In the material presented here, all the examples of intrasectional problems are drawn from the same section, hosiery, where I was employed. I do not believe, however, that this was because the hosiery section was exceptionally conflict-ridden, but rather because, as a member of this particular group, it was acceptable for the group members to voice their complaints to me, whereas it would not have been acceptable to do so to an outsider.

It is relevant to note here that much of the 1980s literature extolling the benefits of harmony in the workplace Japanese style was written by commentators without first-hand experience of working in a Japanese company (see, for example, Pascale and Athos 1981; Ouchi 1980). In contrast, Clark (1979), in an early participant–observer study notes,

> There was frequently antipathy between a superior and a subordinate .... There were fierce rivalries between men in the same standard ranks. Two sub-section heads, two department heads, even two directors were on such bad terms that they could hardly speak to each other. A common problem was that caused by an incompetent or, worse still, a lazy member of a work-group, who gave his fellows extra work, or let the side down in its dealings with other parts of the company.
>
> Problems similar to these arise in companies everywhere, but at Marumaru the need for ostensibly good human relations caused them to be expressed in oblique and even devious ways. People were reluctant to admit that there was any competition in their own part of the organization, even though in other, less happy sections men were indeed trying to surpass each other ....
>
> The contrast between the superficial impression of determined amity and the underlying contention and resentment ... was very great. By the time I left Marumaru, departments that had once seemed to me models of 'good human relations' had been revealed to be full of animosities and spites.
>
> (Clark 1979: 204–5)

Clark (1979) tells us that the underlying tension he observe was confined to the 'immobile' employees in the company; that is, the older male regular employees with little prospect of changing their employer, and argues that relations between immobile employees in a company are inherently likely to be more strained than those between mobile employees. He suggests that this is partly because the former category do not have the option of leaving when human relations become difficult, and partly because of competition for a limited number of senior posts (Clark 1979: 180–1). However, in the Nagasakiya case, and in the case of the female office employees studied by Ogasawara (1998), tension was also present in the work relations of mobile employees. In both these cases this seems to arise partly from the heterogeneity of the female workforce, but in the Nagasakiya case tensions are exacerbated by the system of assessment on a group rather than an individual basis.

It is revealing that in each of the three studies referred to here, Clark (1979), Ogasawara (1998), and my own study, the conflicts reported are those involving the researcher's own immediate group of employees – men for Clark, female regular employees for Ogasawara, female part-timers in my own research. I think it highly likely that these differences in our findings are influenced by our gender and the fact that we were each members of a somewhat different group within the company. From an inside perspective then, conflict becomes more visible.

All this is not to say that ideals of harmony and community are unimportant, either in Japanese companies in general or in Nagasakiya in particular. But it highlights the perhaps obvious fact that harmony and a sense of community are not automatic givens in the Japanese corporate context. On the one hand, they are part of a type of representation of Japanese companies aimed at an outside audience – the public face of the company. On the other hand, they are ideals that are consciously fostered in the company, but alongside the simultaneous encouragement of internal competition and tolerance of a degree of internal conflict. As has been pointed out by Roberts (1979), it is, in any case, unhelpful to see harmony and conflict as two mutually exclusive categories. The interesting question is rather how conflict is managed. In the next chapter we turn to an examination of the group events in Nagasakiya through which the creation of a sense of community was encouraged.

# 6 Unity and fragmentation
## Group events within the company

In the preceding chapters a range of different views of Nagasakiya have been presented: the company as consumer product, the company as vehicle for adulthood and maturity, the company as arena of tension and conflict. And, in some contexts, most notably the training programme and entrance ceremony, we have also seen the ideal of the company as community, and the importance placed on co-operating with fellow employees within the company.

In the picture presented of the company so far, discourses of corporate unity have largely been associated with occasions involving the presentation of the company to the outside world (potential new recruits, the general public) and to new company members through the initial training programme and the entry ceremony. However, it would be misleading to suggest that a clear dichotomy exists between one representation directed at outsiders stressing the unity of the group, and another privileged insider representation where group unity is revealed as an illusion. Although the various schisms within the company were evident to those employed by it, in the early 1990s there was no shortage of occasions within Nagasakiya itself when corporate membership was officially affirmed and celebrated. For those looking for confirmation of the primacy of 'groupism' in Japanese organisations, on a superficial level at least examples are easy to find. In the workplace, numerous meetings were held at all levels of the company, ranging from the morning meetings discussed in Chapter 5 to quality control circles.[1] Outside the workplace too, the company year was punctuated by social events organised for the employees: sports days, union festivals, and company trips. In this chapter, examples of these group activities will be described as they took place in 1991, and the process of accommodation between corporate-centred discourses of unity and harmony and discourses of conflict and fragmentation will be examined.

Since company-organised group activities in Nagasakiya were extremely numerous, it is impossible to detail all of them here. However, they can be broken down into a number of categories. First, there were the formal meetings of staff members, with the explicit primary purpose of conveying information about the company to the employees. Under this heading came the daily morning meetings described in Chapter 5 and the monthly meetings for all members of staff. Second, there were activities that might be described as 'consultative', in that their expressed purpose was to gather employees' opinions, such as the quality control circles (pp. 103–9). Third, there were social occasions not directly connected with work, organised outside working hours. These included branch-based events, such as welcome or leaving parties, company trips, and the cherry blossom viewing party in the spring; and company-wide events, such as the sports day or the company union festival. Many of these were organised by the company union, and indeed the staging of such events was seen by the union officials as one of their primary responsibilities. A fourth category of group event stands somewhat apart from the rest in so far as it spanned both company employees and non-employees. Into this category fall the special invitation-only luxury goods sales that were staged periodically at a top-class hotel and, for the Koganei branch, the summer dance festival in which all major local companies as well as schools and other organisations fielded a dance team (Figure 6.1). In this chapter, examples of all these types of group activities are considered.

## Meetings

The everyday running of Nagasakiya in the early 1990s was punctuated by a great number of meetings – the daily morning meetings, monthly meetings for regular employees and for part-timers (held separately), quality control circles, section chief meetings, managers' meetings, trainers' meetings, trainees' meetings – the list could be extended. Although the precise content of these meetings varied widely, they can be regarded as falling into two

*Figure 6.1*  The Nagasakiya dance team at the summer dance festival in Koganei 1991

basic categories: lecture-style meetings, in which a largely mute audience were addressed by one or a succession of speakers; and meetings that were explicitly consultative in aim, demanding the participation of all those attending. The morning meetings and the monthly staff meetings are examples of the former type, and the quality control circles provide a good example of the latter type; they are considered separately below.

## Lecture-style meetings: the monthly staff meeting

The monthly meetings were held before work on the first Sunday of every month for the regular employees and during working hours on the following Monday for the part-timers, many of whom took Sunday off. Whether for regular employees or part-timers, these meetings were conducted by the branch manager, and they followed a broadly similar pattern. Those attending would assemble in the staff canteen, in a relaxed and informal atmosphere, with generally quite a lot of chatting between friends as they waited for the branch manager to arrive and start the meeting. On his arrival, everyone rose to their feet, and, after the manager had greeted them, bowed their heads and chorused *ohayō gozaimasu* (good morning). The meeting would then begin with the introduction of new branch members (either new entrants or newly transferred to the branch) and announcements of transfers away from the branch. Only the arrivals of regular employees or those part-timers classed as *teijishain*[2] were noted in this way – the ordinary part-timers arrived and left again without the marker of an official announcement at a general staff meeting.[3] In the case of the regular employee meetings, the new employees would go to the front of the room to be introduced in person, and for the part-timers' meetings new regular staff would be introduced simply by having their names read out, with only the *teijishain* introduced in person.

The second item on the agenda would generally be the announcement of results of campaigns conducted during the previous month. The manager responsible for conducting the campaign would collate the results and then give his own view of the key points. Sometimes these campaigns appeared to be concerned with soliciting the opinions of staff, for example one campaign, entitled TOUCH heart,[4] involved the distribution to all members of staff of forms on which they were invited to write down anything they felt was wrong with their section, and to suggest ways in which this could be improved. The forms were then collected by the floor managers, who added their comments before submitting them to the branch manager. They were all later displayed prominently on notice-boards in the staff canteen. A wide range of categories of criticism was given on the form, including staff appearance and behaviour, type of goods stocked, appearance of the display units, and cleanliness. Although from the visiting anthropologist's perspective it would seem that not all these items were ones for which individual staff members could be held personally responsible, the forms were generally interpreted as inviting self-criticism, and similar comments were repeated again and again – typically,

'I do not smile enough at the customers, from now on I will try to always have a smiling face'. Manager's comment: 'Please try to do so'. In one monthly regular employees' meeting, the branch manager summed up the TOUCH heart campaign by saying that the point of the campaign was that employees should try and put themselves in the customer's position. He enlisted my help to quote the bible in English, 'Do unto others as you would have them do unto you', and told the assembled staff that this was the golden rule of Christianity and also the purpose of TOUCH heart.

Other campaigns had more tangible objectives, such as signing up as many customers as possible to the newly issued Nagasakiya group store card, or keeping the store clean and tidy. For these campaigns small prizes were issued to individual or group winners, most often in the form of cash, although sometimes there were also non-cash prizes, usually consisting of luxury food items such as fresh fruit. Recipients of prizes would go to the front of the room to collect their prize from the manager, to the applause of those assembled.

After the distribution of prizes came the breakdown of the previous month's sales results and the percentage of targets achieved. This was the part of the meeting to which most emphasis was given, with exhortations to the staff to try harder if sales figures failed to come up to expectations. Reminders of store rules would also be issued periodically, whenever the branch manager felt that employees were getting lax about, for example, personal appearance or chatting when they should be working. Finally, the manager moved on to announce the overall aims for the coming month, for example cleanliness, and associated campaigns, together with any forthcoming company social events. The meeting was concluded by a joint recitation of the five basic greetings, led by a representative from one floor, with the different floors taking it in turns to lead the greetings month by month.

As with the morning meetings discussed in Chapter 5, the main explicit purpose of the monthly meetings was to maintain a flow of information from senior to junior levels of the company. Much of this information, for example that concerning special sales or other events to be held at the store, was repeated at monthly meetings, daily meetings, and in the monthly schedules of store events posted up outside the floor manager's office on each floor. In this way, it became almost impossible for even the most inattentive employee to be uninformed about major forthcoming events. Consequently, central management was able to rely on employees at section level to take responsibility for matters such as ordering extra merchandise or organising special displays for occasions such as Mother's Day or the beginning of the school year in April.

In this sense, the monthly meetings, like the daily morning meetings, can be seen as part of the general dissemination of information within the company, a goal also pursued through the distribution of a plethora of company directives, schedules of coming events, reports, company magazines, and so on. This aspect of Japanese company life has been noted by Clark (1979), who also argues that 'this generous flow of information' serves to boost employee morale and increase the individual employee's sense of involvement with the company (Clark 1979: 129).

The other explicit goal of the meetings was to encourage the employees to greater efforts, through pep talks, the discussion of campaigns concerning staff attitudes, and the announcement of competition results and distribution of prizes. There is an interesting shift here from an emphasis on the wider corporate body to the divisions within that body. First, as far as competitions were concerned, although some were between individuals (such as that to sign up the most customers to the new store card), more often they were between floors or sections within floors. For the cleanliness campaign, for example, prizes were awarded to the cleanest sections. Rivalry between different elements of the company – sections or floors – was thus encouraged in the interests of improved overall performance. In this context, employees were encouraged to identify with their section or their floor rather than with the company as a whole. However, in other contexts, notably the campaigns concerning staff attitudes, the focus shifted again to the individual and his or her personal contribution to the company.

Seen in this way, the monthly staff meetings underlined the formal divisions within the company: at the base the individual employee, who is a member of ever wider, more inclusive groups, i.e. the section, the floor, the branch, and ultimately the company as a whole. At each level rivalry exists between groups on the same level, but this is subsumed by and marshalled in support of the common interests of the larger group of which they are all part. The overall picture is one of controlled and amicable competitiveness.

From another perspective, however, these meetings conveyed a different message about group membership. First, the very fact of attending one particular meeting and not another was an indicator of employee status, with the regular employees attending one meeting on Sunday mornings before work, the part-timers another held the following day during working hours, and the *arubaito*, or temporary staff, not required to attend any staff meetings at all. And whereas attendance was mandatory for the regular employees, for the part-timers it was entirely contingent on their work shifts – those who worked on Monday mornings attended, others were not required to.

The reason given for the division of the meetings by status group was simply convenience – there were too many staff for all to fit into the canteen at the same time. Many part-timers did not work on Sundays, and, conversely, the regular employees generally took days off during the week, making it difficult to find a day convenient for everyone. The *arubaito*, for their part, were considered as temporary staff, performing only routine tasks under the instruction of other employees, so it was thought unnecessary to keep them informed about wider company concerns. On occasions where it was deemed necessary to disseminate information to all staff, such as the periodic fire drills, all the staff were assembled in the store at one time and addressed as a body through the simple expedient of using a venue other than the canteen.

I was also told by one of the longer-serving staff that some years previously there had indeed been joint meetings for all the staff.

In any case, whether by accident or design, the way in which the meetings were segregated underlined the distinction between the three status groups of employee, a message that was further reinforced by the practice of announcing arrivals, departures, and transfers of regular employees and *teijishain* at the meetings, but not those of other categories of part-timer. The effect of this was that, except for those of the long-serving 'veteran' part-timers who attained the status of *teijishain*, part-timers arrived and left relatively unnoticed other than by those working on the same floor of the store. It was quite possible, and often happened, that a part-timer would not be recognised by staff in different sections of the store when she went shopping there in her ordinary clothes.

As far as new regular staff were concerned, they would be presented in person to all the other regular employees, but only to the part-timers on the floor to which they had been assigned. Thus, although a great deal of emphasis was laid on all the regular employees being known to each other, it was not considered so important that they should be known to all the part-timers. Effectively, the part-timer's sphere of interest and personal connections within the company were limited to the floor on which she worked; for the regular employees the most important group to which they could belong was not the floor or the section but the body of regular staff members, with links spreading throughout the branch and beyond.

In addition, the content of the regular employees' and part-timers' meetings, although broadly similar, was not always identical: items deemed of special concern to regular employees would often simply be omitted from the part-timers' meetings. So, for example, before the new intake of regular employees arrived in 1992, the existing regular employees spent a part of their monthly meeting preparing caricatures of each of the newcomers, with the help of photographs and other information, to hang on the walls of the staff section of the building. More importantly, before the launch of the quality control circle campaign, the regular employees used their monthly meetings to decide on the themes that the circles should tackle, a subject that was never broached with the part-timers, even though some of them were invited to participate in the campaign. Thus the separation of the two categories of employee in these meetings served to emphasise the distinction between them as (in the company management's eyes) full members of the company and those on the periphery, with the latter only selectively involved in company business.

The monthly meetings can thus be read as embodying a dual message. They emphasise the formal structure of the company, with its vertical divisions of branches, floors, and sections, especially in the competitions and announcements of sales results; however, from the point of view of meeting organisation and attendance, the horizontal strata of regular employee, part-timer, and temporary staff are the crucial ones, with members of the same section attending different meetings, or not attending meetings at all depending on their status. This difference in status also had an effect in filtering the amount of information and involvement deemed appropriate for the different categories of employee, with far greater involvement of the regular staff than of the part-timers. This distinction between regular staff and part-timers was also noticeable in other group activities in Nagasakiya, including the quality control circles.

## Consultative activities

The large number of meetings that take place in Japanese companies are often associated with a process of consultative decision-making which involves all or most of the employees and ensures a high degree of consensus among the workforce when decisions are finally taken. However, in the Nagasakiya case, even when the meeting concerned was consultative rather than lecture-like in style, there were widespread doubts among the lower-level employees about how seriously their suggestions were taken. There was also an informal consensus about subjects that were off-limits to employees making suggestions about improving corporate performance, the range of suggestions made being in practice limited to suggestions that seemed likely to be acceptable to senior management. As a very junior employee, the range of consultative meetings in which I was able to participate was strictly limited, the principal ones being the quality control circles. These are, however, a particularly interesting example, as they are a practice widely associated with 'Japanese management' – even though the idea of quality control can be traced to an American initiative.

Quality control circles were originally introduced in Japan under American influence in the early post-war period. The promotion of statistical quality control by visiting US experts in the early 1950s was followed up by the insistence of Dr Juran, a quality control expert who visited Japan on a lecture tour in 1954, that quality control should be made 'an integral part of the management function and practised throughout the firm' (Cole 1979: 136). However, the US and Japanese interpretations of this notion differed radically: in the US quality control was in practice entrusted to middle management, but in Japan ordinary employees were enlisted to form study groups called quality control circles, or QC circles. Although these circles have become most celebrated in the manufacturing industry, they exist in large companies across all sectors of the economy, and they share common features wherever they are found.

Typically, QC circles have around ten members and meet once or twice a month. Circle meetings are often held outside working hours, and they mostly last for between thirty and sixty minutes, time that may or may not be remunerated.[5] The methodology used in the circles may include quite sophisticated statistical analysis, but perhaps the most salient feature is the emphasis on brainstorming and the eliciting of contributions from all members of the circle. The topics with which they may be concerned vary widely – anything that could be construed as affecting the performance of the company as a whole can be included, ranging from product quality to employee morale. However, it would seem that the majority of circle themes can be subsumed by the category of 'themes ... directed towards the attainment of company policy, or key work unit matters' (Uy Onglacto 1988: 21).[6] Although this might appear to be an obvious point, it has important implications in so far as the QC circle is thus in the majority of cases a vehicle for the furthering of company policy; it is not an arena in which company policy can be challenged. Uy Onglacto (1988) argues that 'the QC circle serves as a useful mechanism in integrating employees in the organizational base towards the attainment of organizational goals' (Uy Onglacto 1988: 21). However, this begs the question of how these goals are formulated and by whom, and the degree to which they are shared by employees at different levels of the company. These points will be taken up in the Nagasakiya case below.

In Nagasakiya, QC circles, called 'With Circles', were organised at irregular intervals as part of periodic 'With Circle Campaigns'. One such campaign took place in the spring of 1991 while I was doing my fieldwork. In the Koganei branch separate circles were formed on each floor, with eight to ten participants in each circle, each of whom was allocated a specific role. On the first floor, where I was employed, the leader of the circle was Kobayashi-san, a relatively junior employee with only one year's experience, but, as a man, destined for a managerial role in the future. Arakawa-san, one of the two (female) section chiefs on the floor, was sub-leader, and the other section chief, Nishiguchi-san, was 'data chief'. Kojima-san, a woman on the regular staff who had joined at the same time as Kobayashi-san, was the secretary of the circle and was responsible for taking notes. Kimura-san, a senior part-timer, was charged with relaying information on the circle's activities to other non-participating employees, and another part-timer was given the role of a second 'data chief'. I was designated as responsible for 'mood',[7] which was explained to me as meaning that I was to report on the mood of the circle, and the floor manager was in charge of 'discussions'. In practice, however, I found that with the exception of the role of secretary these roles were purely nominal. No forum existed for Kimura-san to report back on the group's activities, or for me to report on mood, and in fact neither of us did more than attend and participate in meetings. And leadership of the meetings was assumed by the section chiefs rather than by the relatively inexperienced Kobayashi-san, or the manager, who preferred to keep a low profile. The final report on the circle's activities was composed by the sub-leader, Arakawa-san.

The themes to be addressed by the circles were decided at the monthly regular employees' meetings, with a different theme selected by each floor. In principle, the themes were meant to be chosen by discussion among all the regular staff from each floor, but in practice, as far as our floor was concerned, the theme was suggested by one of the section chiefs and everyone else simply assented. The theme thus selected for our floor was 'How to improve the shift system to create greater efficiency at work'. This was broken down into two objectives: how to make everybody's work easier and more enjoyable, and how to increase our speed of work. The reasons given for the choice of theme were twofold. First that the shifts were in difficulties and individual employees were unable to finish their work because many part-timers took time off on Sundays and public holidays, and because there were a lot of 'four-hour' part-timers, that is part-timers who worked for only four hours a day instead of the usual six. Second, the need to train new employees, both part-timers and full company members, had a similar effect in that it increased the workload of long-serving employees and made it difficult for them to complete their allocated daily tasks. The circle's policy was to 'listen meekly[8] to everybody's opinions', and the only rule laid down was that everyone had to express his or her opinion at least once in the course of a meeting.

During this particular With Circle campaign, the circles met a total of nine times. Four meetings, of fifteen minutes each, were held in the morning instead of the regular morning meetings. Two meetings of forty-five minutes were held on Sundays before work, and a further three meetings of ninety minutes were held after working hours. The effect of this arrangement was to limit the participation of the part-time staff, as they were only able to attend the short morning meetings, and, in some cases, the Sunday meetings. The evening meetings were attended exclusively by regular employees and were used in part to prepare data for subsequent meetings in which all circle members were able to participate. A description of one of the Sunday meetings, transcribed from my fieldnotes, may serve to convey the flavour of the proceedings.

> Sunday 28th April. All circle members assembled in one corner of the first floor, forty-five minutes before the store's opening. Theme: Why aren't the shifts efficient? Chart prepared by Kobayashi-san showed three fundamental problems: time taken in training new staff; many part-timers take days off on Sundays and public holidays; staff responsible for training new staff are too busy to explain things to trainees. Kobayashi-san went through these points briefly, then Nishiguchi-san distributed blank pieces of paper to all the circle members on which we were told to write all the further problems we thought arose from these problems. After a few minutes, these were collected by Nishiguchi-san, read out, and pinned to the chart next to the problem to which they were thought to relate. Some examples were nobody available to deal with customer queries or complaints (many part-timers take days off on Saturdays and Sundays); junior staff unable to perform some basic tasks like gift-wrapping or operating the cash register (staff responsible for training new staff are too busy).
>
> Finally, we all brainstormed solutions to the problems. Some solutions

suggested included harmonising trainers' and trainees' days off to ensure maximum on-the-job training, and getting all staff to practise gift-wrapping on empty boxes during slack periods at the store. I suggested tackling the problem of staff shortages at the weekends by paying the part-timers extra to work on Sundays. (I had been told by part-timers at Nagasakiya that the Seiyu store next door to the Koganei branch of Nagasakiya did this, and that this was one reason Nagasakiya was losing staff to Seiyu.) This suggestion was greeted with polite 'mmm' noises, but not taken up by any of the other circle members. We ran out of time while the brainstorming was still going on – to be continued.

Subsequent With Circle Meetings continued this brainstorming process, and in due course a plan of action was devised, essentially involving on-the-job training for existing employees to ensure that everyone understood how to operate the cash register and could gift-wrap quickly and neatly. In addition, the floor manager and the section chiefs undertook to ensure that all sections were staffed at all times, and it was agreed that staff should be prepared to help out in sections other than their own when necessary, consulting the store manuals for information if they were not sure about, for example, where particular goods were kept. The entire proceedings of the circle were summarised in a report, together with charts showing 'before and after' – for example, how many people could gift-wrap two handkerchiefs in a presentation box before and after the training instituted by the circle, and the average time taken to do this. This report was then submitted to head office, and an area meeting was later held to go over the results of all the With Circles. Prizes were allotted to circles that were judged by the company management to have performed particularly well, one of which was won by our circle. My suggestion about extra pay for part-timers working on Sundays was dropped from the final report; I was told that such matters were beyond the scope of the circle.

Two years later, on a return visit to the store, I asked those who had participated in this circle how they evaluated the With Circle campaign. They generally agreed that it had been effective in the short term, improving staff performance on matters such as gift-wrapping and the cash desk, but that within a short space of time things returned to the way they had been before. Assessments of why this was varied. Kobayashi-san said he thought the root of the problem in the first place was simply that the staff did not want to do troublesome jobs, such as gift-wrapping or dealing with customers in sections with which they were unfamiliar. They had made a brief effort for the duration of the campaign and then promptly gone back to their old ways. Kimura-san, on the other hand, thought that the circle failed because it did not tackle fundamental problems, such as the high turnover of staff and inadequate training. Training staff to, for example, gift-wrap had only a short-term effect because as soon as new staff arrived it had to be done all over again. She was particularly critical of the practice of putting new part-timers to work immediately with no prior training, and she suggested that they needed at least a week's training before being put to work in the store (the same as that received by the new regular employees).

The overall assessment of both Kimura-san and Kobayashi-san was that the circles had been *'tatemae'*, *'miseru dake'* (a front, just for show), an idea of top management that had never aroused any enthusiasm among the ordinary staff. They pointed to the fact that the practice of having these circles had been dropped since the change of managing director as evidence that they had never been either popular or effective, and they suggested that they had probably been a pet project of the former managing director. On asking Kobayashi-san again why matters such as the pay of part-timers had not been addressed by the circle, he told me he thought this was irrelevant, that the shortage of part-timers willing to work on Sundays was due to their family commitments and had nothing to do with money. Pressing him a little further, he reiterated that such matters were beyond the scope of the circle, which was properly only concerned with things that 'we can do' *(wareware dekiru koto)*, not things decided by the 'top people' *(ue no hito)*. He explained that in order to change things decided by the top people, different channels operated: the member of staff first talked to the floor manager, who would then take the matter up with the branch manager, who might then take it further. Sometimes this procedure worked, sometimes not.

A number of things struck me from this conversation. First, if Kobayashi-san was a typical example, the younger regular staff were very out of touch with the concerns of the part-timers, many of whom had complained to me about their low wages and had specifically mentioned the lack of incentives to work on Sundays. Indeed, there was no forum within the company for the two categories of employee to communicate their concerns, as even 'consultative' bodies like the With Circle had an implicitly limited agenda. Second, the With Circle in Nagasakiya was only consultative in a very restricted sense, as it was not intended to address basic matters of company policy and practice such as pay and high staff turnover, but only the question of how employees might perform better within the existing corporate structure.

It therefore seems to me that the With Circle might be more accurately described as concerned with self-criticism on the part of the employees rather than consultation on how corporate performance might be improved from a more general perspective. In the wider context of Japanese society, the analogy here is with the *hanseikai*, or reflection circles, that abound in Japanese organisations from schools to sports clubs, and also including companies. These are small groups that meet in order to reflect jointly on any shortcomings of the group, collectively or individually, and then suggest ways of remedying these shortcomings. For example, a football team might hold a *hanseikai* after losing a match to discuss what went wrong and how they can do better in future.

In the context of Nagasakiya, the With circle campaign might be properly considered alongside the TOUCH heart campaign described above, as both were overtly consultative, but in fact interpreted by employees as inviting self-criticism, and generally regarded as mere *tatemae* exercises. The With Circle's final report was also reminiscent of the TOUCH heart forms: a description of the current faults of employees was followed by a statement of how they planned to improve the situation, with floor and branch managers' comments appended at the bottom. Even the wording of the managers' comments was similar, exhorting the employees to 'do your best'. For example, on the report by the circle in which I participated the branch manager commented:

> Double-check your section and look out for anything unusual. Almost every day there are many things that were supposed to be done that do not get done. Together, everyone must do their best, co-operatively and individually.

Thus we return to the familiar discourse of all employees co-operating to achieve corporate goals. In this discourse, any problems at work (including matters such as staff shortages or inadequate training) appear to be the result of a failure on the part of the individual employees to try hard enough or to co-operate fully with each other. And if everyone does their best 'co-operatively and individually' the problems will be solved. Company policy itself is not called into question, and senior management is beyond criticism. Indeed, the idea of senior management as a separate entity with goals distinct from those of ordinary employees is notable by its absence, thus placing the formal discourse of the With circle campaign neatly in the realm of consensual Japanese management.

However, as we have seen, ordinary employees at Nagasakiya, whether part-timers or regular employees, did make a very clear distinction between themselves as senior management, commonly referred to as the people at the top, as distinct from 'us'. And the part-timers, who were the main target of the 'increase the efficiency of the shift' campaign, did not identify the problems of the shift as arising from lack of effort on their part. How was it, then, that the formal discourse of the With Circle campaign was left unchallenged? I think that the answer to this lies in the implicit understanding among the employees of the appropriate discourse in this context. Everyone (except the ignorant visiting anthropologist) knew what sort of statements and actions were expected of them and felt it was pointless to stray outside these limits. As Tabata has remarked regarding a range of company practices, including morning meetings, suggestion schemes, and quality control circles:

> The whole system of communication ... does not aim at communication itself; rather, it aims solely at the enhancement of efficiency and competitiveness. Only those opinions and ideas useful for increasing efficiency are gathered and adopted by management.
>
> (Tabata 1998: 210)

Also, the campaign operated within a number of significant constraints: the themes addressed were in practice defined by senior staff, few part-timers were given the opportunity to participate, and those that did were not able to participate in all stages of the circle, nor did they have a hand in the compilation of the final report. From this, most part-timers to whom I spoke surmised that the With Circle was not concerned with obtaining their views.

But perhaps most importantly, the With Circle was, like the TOUCH heart campaign, a highly public activity within the company. It was impossible to give one's views anonymously in this context, and everyone knew that his or her contribution would be assessed by senior management. Such a public forum was not seen as the correct context for criticism of company policy, which was done either privately, behind the scenes, with the outcome known only to a handful of people, or anonymously through the company union. (The company union survey, referred to in previous chapters, was one forum in which employees could be, and were, highly critical of the company.) Ironically, overtly consultative activities could not really be consultative precisely because they were overt and therefore tended to disguise tensions and problems and to obscure communication between senior and junior levels of the company.

The staff at Nagasakiya therefore adjusted what they said about the company depending on the context, with the private/public, official/unofficial distinction being particularly important for the comments that could safely be made. However, not all company-organised activities were wholly private or wholly public; many allowed for both public and private interactions between employees, thus making it possible to draw a contrast between the overt, public agenda of the senior management organising the event, and more personal, private, agendas of the participants. This contrast was particularly noticeable at social events organised by the company.

## Company-organised social events

Company social events were organised on both a branch and a regional basis, and included parties to mark the arrival or departure of regular employees, day trips, short holidays of two or three days, and all-day festivals and sports days. Aside from the parties, which were organised and financed at a branch level, social events were organised and paid for by the company union. I was told by a senior union official that the organisation of such events was one of the principal roles of the union, along with activities more familiar to a British observer: campaigning for improved wages and conditions for the union members, and providing a channel through which staff could express grievances. Union membership was limited to regular employees below the rank of branch manager and part-timers classed as *teijishain*. Participation in union events was, however, generally open to all employees, whatever their status.

Although attendance at these social events was optional for all categories of employee, in fact employee participation followed a regular and predictable pattern, with the vast majority of participants being the young unmarried regular staff, both male and female. They were also well attended by older men of the rank of manager and upwards, and by the casual workforce of the young male temporary staff. With the exception of branch-organised parties, part-timers rarely attended these events, and generally there were very few women over the age of thirty, whether part-timers or regular employees. The older women who did attend usually had a special reason for doing so: some of the reasons given by older women to whom I spoke were fondness for the particular sport being played in a company sports contest, being married to another company employee (so they could attend the event as husband and wife), or being temporarily alone owing to the husband working far away (and therefore having a lot of time on their hands).

For the younger employees, whether regular staff or temporary *arubaito*, the main reason for attending these events was simply that they enjoyed them. Most of the participants were people of a similar age, and the events were aimed at young people. Because of this, these company outings provided the perfect opportunity for unmarried male and female employees to mingle socially and to get to know each other without going so far as to formally date. These opportunities to get to know each other were important, as it is often difficult in Japan to meet people of the opposite sex except through one's work or school. Company social events attracted almost 100 per cent attendance by young male regular employees, many of whom might expect to find a bride through the company, and were also well attended by the young male *arubaito*. And for the female regular employees who were new to the company, and whose family and non-company friends were far away, few other opportunities to socialise with their own age group presented themselves. It is also relevant to note that the costs of the day's outing were met entirely by the company, so for the younger participants, whose wages were low, it was a good opportunity to get together with people of a similar age without putting extra strain on their limited budget.

As for the older male managers, their role differed depending on the kind of event concerned. For events organised at a branch level the senior staff attended mainly in a supervisory capacity, to ensure that the younger employees did not get out of hand. A typical branch-organised event consisted of a day out including a barbecue lunch at some popular leisure area, often a funfair, although the branches did also organise short trips away, perhaps to a hot-spring resort, or to go skiing. The tone was generally very informal, with no rigid timetable for the day, and the younger employees passed their time chatting and joking, commenting on each other's appearance and teasing each other. For example, one young man was nicknamed 'fox' because of the shape of his face and was teased mercilessly by the young women, although he seemed to bear the teasing with remarkable equanimity.

These branch-organised events contrasted in a number of ways with the more formal regionally based social events, at which staff from all the branches in a given geographical area gathered together. First, obviously the regional events were on a much larger scale, and in part because of this they necessitated much more formal organisation than did day trips such as the one described above. Whereas the day trips typically had few organised activities except for lunch, and the participants were left very much up to their own devices, regional events usually had a fixed timetable of events, complete with opening and closing speeches. Second, although young regular staff were still numerically preponderant and older women largely absent, senior male staff were much more in evidence at these events. This was partly because it was expected that branch managers would attend, but also because regional events provided an opportunity for male managerial staff from the level of floor manager upwards to meet friends, either from the same intake or from previous stints in other branches. These events were also attended by the managing director and the appropriate regional director, although they kept themselves at a distance from the rest of the employees.

One of the major regional social events in the Nagasakiya year was the sports day, or *undōkai*, which had been held every spring since the late 1960s. Company sports days are common in Japan and form a continuation of a practice begun in pre-school – even day-care centres in Japan have sports days. They are also sometimes organised on a neighbourhood basis as a way of creating a sense of community (Ben Ari 1991). The origin of the *undōkai* can be traced back to the *kyōto yūgikai* (Fighting and Playing Meet) first held at the Tokyo Naval Academy in 1874. In one Japanese pamphlet explaining this custom the *undōkai* is summarised in the following terms:

> the idea is to encourage participation by all, regardless of age or gender, so the emphasis is on sports that require no special skills, such as three-legged racing, tug-of-war, ball games, and relay races.
>
> Hot communication (October 1993)[9]

In 1991, Nagasakiya held its sports day for the Kanto region in the Budokan in central Tokyo, a popular concert venue, not unlike Wembley arena in London. It was attended by about twenty-five or so staff from the Koganei branch, and similar numbers came from all the other branches in the area. On the day of the sports day all Nagasakiya branches were closed.

The Koganei branch members all met at 7.45 a.m. to travel to the Budokan, arriving about half an hour before the opening ceremony at 10.00 a.m. Initially, we were ushered upstairs to our designated seating area, but after we had deposited our bags, we went back down to the floor of the arena, where we sat in a line with the store manager at the front. After all the branches had assembled in this way, coloured ribbons were distributed, with a different colour for each branch, which we were told to tie around our heads. For our branch, this was all that distinguished us from the other branches, as we were all in casual sports clothes, with the exception of the younger male staff who were members of the company baseball team and had changed into their baseball uniforms shortly after we arrived. Some of the other branches, however, wore identical brightly coloured T-shirts in addition to the obligatory ribbons.

At 10.10 a.m. the sports day formally began with a short speech by the master of ceremonies from a raised platform on the floor of the arena. Then a spotlight appeared, seeming to search the arena until it settled on a sort of royal box above the arena, lighting up the face of the managing director. A loudspeaker boomed out: 'The managing director, Mr Iwata.' The managing director then stood up, smiling, arms outstretched, to receive the applause of the audience. Two other dignitaries seated beside him in the box were also announced. Then the lights were dimmed, there was a drum roll, and slides of fireworks were projected onto a large screen, to applause and laughter. The managing director and the other dignitaries remained standing, with spotlights lighting their faces from below.

After the fireworks slideshow, three aerobics instructors mounted the stage and began to demonstrate some exercises to music, while we all followed as best we could, still lined up by branch behind the branch managers. We then returned to our seats upstairs, and the main programme began. Punctuated by a packed lunch and drinks provided by the company, which we ate in our seats upstairs, this programme consisted of a mixture of fairly ordinary sporting events, such as races, as well as more light-hearted events.

One of the more standard sporting events was a race held in separate age groups, from under thirties up to the over fifties. Each branch cheered on their own representatives enthusiastically, using cheer-leaders, rhythmic clapping, and pompons that were waved in the air. There was cheering when a branch member won, and some amusement at the efforts of the older representatives, including the Koganei branch manager, who came next to last in his group. More light-hearted events included a contest to see which branch could fit most people onto a wooden box (of the kind used for vaulting in gymnastics). This event in particular caused a great deal of hilarity.

From a non-Japanese point of view, this sports day seems at first glance to be an example *par excellence* of the corporate spirit at work. It finds a ready echo in the stereotypes, lovingly dwelt on by the media, of the serried ranks of Japanese employees doing their morning callisthenics on the factory floor. However, a closer examination throws some doubt on this interpretation. First, sports days of this kind are, as pointed out, common to all large institutions in Japan. Therefore, much the same strictures apply as were made in Chapter 4 for the company entrance ceremony: this kind of event should not be seen as part of a special type of company lifestyle but rather as continuous with general social practice in Japan. The sports day is a very familiar setting to all the participants from school and university, as is the discourse of amicable competitiveness within a general frame of corporate unity that pervades such occasions.

Second, alongside the formal events of the day, a more informal mingling of the staff was taking place. In addition to the lunch break, there were frequent breaks between events, and at any one time only a minority of the staff were participating in the races and other contests. This meant that there was ample opportunity for chatting and socialising with other employees. Most of this took place within the blocks, where we were seated separately according to branch. However, it was noticeable that many of the older male employees were circulating among the blocks, exchanging greetings with other men of a similar age, and sometimes stopping for a chat and a beer before moving on. This was a pattern I saw repeated again and again at company social events, and older male regular employees to whom I spoke commented that they looked forward to these events as they were an opportunity to meet friends they had made during their initial training or on earlier postings who now worked for a different store.

Such friendships were important not only on a personal level but also because they served as the basis for establishing one's own individual network within the company. These networks were often very important in getting things done, where the co-operation of other sections or branches of the company became necessary: it was not unusual, for example, for a branch manager to ask one of his junior managers to approach a friend in another section in order to get something done, rather than approaching the section head himself directly. It was also obvious at these events that senior figures were particularly assiduously cultivated by their male colleagues, and those who had been sidelined in the promotion stakes also tended to find themselves sidelined socially.[10]

It would therefore seem that the significance of these company-organised social events shifts somewhat depending on the perspective from which they are viewed. On a formal level, they were a celebration of the company as a corporate group, with an emphasis on symbols of corporate unity such as the Nagasakiya logo always prominently displayed. The sports day, in particular, can be read as a metaphor for the organisation and philosophy of the company as a whole, with its emphasis on the virtues of teamwork, and the competition between branches, all subsumed by a wider corporate loyalty. However, from the perspective of the company members the same events can be opportunities for strengthening personal networks or simply a free day out and a chance to socialise with others of the same age.

These events also tended to underline the way in which employees are divided by generation and gender. The networking activities of the older men, for example, were, for the most part, irrelevant to the women attending, as they were in any case excluded from the male career ladder and confined to one branch for the duration of their working lives. Thus they had neither the opportunity nor the motivation to try and establish links with employees in other branches beyond those few they had got to know during the initial training programme. Also, as remarked above (p. 110), older women in general, and part-timers in particular, only attended in very small numbers, in contrast to the situation in the stores themselves, where these employees were in the majority.

There was, however, one company-organised event at which the marginal status of the older women employees at Nagasakiya was turned to their and the company's advantage, and they were able for once to take centre stage. This was the *chōbikai,*or luxury goods sale, an event that was not strictly speaking part of the company's social calendar but which was used as a social gathering by the *oba-san* generation.

## Employee as consumer: the *chōbikai*

The *chōbikai* (literally, forever beautiful meeting) was a luxury goods sale lasting two or three days that was held three times a year at a top-class hotel in central Tokyo. Goods sold included jewellery, kimonos, and European brand-name leather goods. Everything was very expensive, with a few items carrying such a high price tag that one could only presume they were there primarily for display purposes. For example, a forty-centimetre-long gold tiger with stripes made of diamonds and emerald eyes was priced at thirty million yen – the equivalent of £120,000 at 1991 rates, enough (at that time) to buy a small house in suburban Tokyo. Customers attended by invitation only, assembling first thing in the morning at the branch by which they had been invited to be bussed to the hotel. The expressed aim of these sales, as explained to me by a senior manager, was to try to emulate the more prestigious department stores, with their tradition of supplying luxury goods and providing individual service to wealthy customers.

However, as the same manager confirmed, in fact most of those attending were not exceptionally wealthy. Rather, the unusual feature of this sale was that almost all the customers were friends or acquaintances of the sales staff in the stores. Before each sale, there was a concerted campaign within the store to get all the staff to sign up as many customers as possible to attend the sale. That is, in theory this campaign was aimed at all the staff, but in practice it was focused on the older women, in the main the part-timers but also the older female regular employees. This was for two main reasons: first these women were of the same age and gender as Nagasakiya's main target market, middle-aged women who, in Japan, control the spending of their household's income. They were therefore the employees most likely to be able to introduce suitable customers to the sale.

Second, the older women, both regular staff and part-timers, tended to have locally based networks of friends that they could call on. The part-timers were, as we have already seen, recruited locally, and thus they already possessed these networks when they joined the company. For the female regular staff, on the other hand, the picture changes over time. As women working as regular staff in Tokyo branches of the store were mainly recruited from remote rural areas,[11] the younger among them tended to lack local connections. However, unlike the male regular staff, the female regular staff spend all their working lives at the same branch, so as their length of service extends they too develop locally based networks of friends and acquaintances.

A number of the female regular staff at Koganei had married local men, generally leaving their jobs at Nagasakiya on marriage or on the birth of their first child. These women remained friendly with those of their former colleagues who were still employed by the store, and the *chōbikai* was one occasion when they had an opportunity to get together.

The *chōbikai* was therefore transformed by those who attended from a sales event to a social occasion and Nagasakiya old girls' reunion. Although some of the staff were paid to attend and to look after the customers, as a small group of thirty or so women gathered in front of the Koganei store on the first morning of the sale it became obvious that several of the customers were also part-time employees attending on their day off. As we chatted, it transpired that others were former employees of the store. Although disenchanted with Nagasakiya as an employer – one woman explained she had been forced to give up her position as a regular employee on becoming pregnant, and although she was subsequently re-employed as a part-timer had left because the part-time wages were too low – they seemed happy to return as customers and to renew their friendship with their ex-colleagues. In addition, these outings gave them the opportunity to have a day out away from their families – although almost all were married, no husbands and only a few older children attended, the younger children having been left in their father's care for the day in most cases. As it is rare for parents of young children to go out together without the children in tow, such all-female outings are one of the few opportunities married women in Japan have for a break from the daily grind of household labour, child-rearing, and, in many cases, paid employment.

When we had all assembled, we were led onto a specially hired tour coach by the deputy branch manager. After we had taken our seats, a red-jacketed tour guide gave a short speech of welcome and bowed, after which everyone clapped. This was followed by a speech by the deputy branch manager, who explained the purchasing method at the sale – it was enough simply to sign for the goods, which would then be sent to the Koganei branch to be passed on to the customer on receipt of the amount due. He also explained that free gifts would be distributed at the end of the sale, exchangeable for gift vouchers on request. As an extra spur to spend more money, he added that there would be a prize draw into which customers would automatically be entered if they spent more than ¥200,000 (about £800.00 at 1991 prices). He concluded by expressing, in very formal and deferential Japanese, his hope that we would enjoy the *chōbikai*. This, too, was greeted with applause, after which we settled back into our seats to enjoy the journey. Refreshments (canned juice, tea, and coffee) were served to us in our seats by a young male employee, and the tour guide commented on the sights as our bus swung through central Tokyo.

Once at the hotel, we were ushered to the floor where the sale was taking place and then left to our own devices. The sale was quite crowded, full of small groups of women browsing and chatting, many of them a mix of present and past employees. I was surprised to see one usually fairly dour section chief of the Koganei branch being addressed by her first name with the suffix *-chan* – a very familiar form of address in Japanese – by some other women who turned out to be her former *senpai* (seniors) who had since left the company. The section chief appeared to be thoroughly enjoying herself and was more relaxed than I had ever seen her. An hour or so after our arrival a full meal was served in the dining room of the hotel, followed by coffee, after which shopping resumed. Most people I spoke to seemed to have bought one or two items, enough to ensure that the event was highly profitable for the company and also gaining kudos for the individual employee who had invited them.[12] At about 4.00 p.m. the customers headed down to the hotel foyer to collect their free gifts and catch the coach home. In addition to this basic programme, at some *chōbikai* a guest celebrity attended to demonstrate the goods, for example a famous actress in Japanese period dramas was invited to discuss how to wear the Japanese kimono.[13]

The *chōbikai* was an event where the lines between outsider and insider were unusually blurred. Looking at the participants, it was hard to tell who were and were not current staff members, since not all the current staff were wearing uniform, and staff and customers alike were furnished with identical rosettes identifying the branch under whose auspices they were attending. The conspicuous lines of division were rather those of gender and generation. The younger regular employees, both male and female, were few in number and all attended in their working capacity. They were delegated to a service role, standing behind the displays of goods and taking orders where necessary, while the senior male managers stood on the sidelines supervising the proceedings. But the focus was on the older women, or *obasan*, both in and out of uniform, they were the customers and it was very much their day.

The usual status hierarchy of the company thus appeared to be inverted. Whether ex-employees, low-status part-timers, or older female regular employees who had 'failed' to leave at the age considered appropriate, here the middle-aged women were in a position of privilege, courted for their custom. The fact that such women often had stronger ties to their neighbourhood than to their employer was here turned to their advantage. In the context of the *chōbikai*, they became mediators between company and customer, an ambiguous mix of customer and employee. And this in turn highlighted the irony of the position of female employees at Nagasakiya – barred from significant promotion within the company, their only path to gaining status was to leave and return as the privileged outsider, the customer.

## Conclusion

Taking an overview of company-organised group events at Nagasakiya, there are two points that seem particularly noteworthy. First, group events within the company tended implicitly to highlight lines of division, often at the same time as explicitly celebrating unity. Social events tended to bring together only certain sections of the company, for example older women employees at the *chōbikai* or young regular employees on company outings. Here, the most commonly stressed divisions were those between part-time and regular staff, and differences of generation.

In addition, the horizontal divide between 'us' and 'the people at the top' was often stressed by the more junior employees, male and female, part-timer and regular employee alike. Concerning the notion of consensus, there was a general perception among these employees that their opinions were irrelevant, and that the real business of consultation and decision-making took place in the innermost of inner circles – among senior male management. Apparently consultative activities that involved these junior employees, such as the With Circle or the TOUCH heart campaign were dismissed by them as being *tatemae*, just for show.

However, it would be wrong to assume that the rank and file of the employees therefore constituted an alienated mass. For one thing, the junior employees themselves were a very diverse group. Indeed, the word group is probably misleading as the ties between different categories of junior employee, for example newly recruited male regular employees and female part-timers, were weak to non-existent. It is also evident that many aspects of corporate activities were widely enjoyed and participated in with great enthusiasm. This was the case, for example, at the company social events, which were particularly popular with the younger employees, even those who complained that the work at Nagasakiya was boring and that they had no intention of staying there long term. And even the part-timers, who rarely participated in union-organised activities, managed to create their own social event at the *chōbikai*.

This in turn highlights another important point. Group activities at Nagasakiya were not merely passively endured by employees obediently following a pattern predetermined by management. Rather, the employees acted on and frequently transformed the frame they were given. Social events that were nominally a celebration of the corporate group became opportunities for working on one's own personal network. Luxury sales became a day out away from husband and children and a chance to relax with old friends. Even the With Circle and TOUCH heart campaigns, both of which were unpopular management-imposed events, were reinterpreted by the employees as being *tatemae*, just for show, from which it followed that they could be safely ignored once a reasonable time had elapsed.

The same themes that have already been discussed in earlier chapters again arise here: notably the importance of divisions of gender and generation within the company, and the way in which the frame provided by the company may be interpreted and used differently depending on the context and on the employee concerned. The company appears not as a monolithic entity enveloping its members, but rather as a flexibly bounded arena within which official and more personal agendas and representations of company–employee relations interacted in a dynamic way.

## Changes in post-bubble Nagasakiya

By 1999, many of the features of Nagasakiya described in this and the previous chapter had changed. Numbers of staff in the branches had been reduced and working hours extended, with the store now closing at 9.00 p.m. daily. In the Koganei branch, from 153 staff in 1991, the number had been reduced to 120, only twenty-one of whom were regular staff compared with forty-nine regular staff in 1991. The number of part-timers, on the other hand, remained little changed at seventy-nine compared with eighty-two in 1991, with a similar situation for the *arubaito* – nineteen in 1999 and twenty-two in 1991. A detailed breakdown of the changes is shown in Table 6.1.

As can be seen in Table 6.1, within the context of the overall reduction in the number of regular staff, the number of male regular staff in particular has been reduced dramatically. With only six male regular staff in the store in 1999, all these were older men in senior managerial positions. There were no longer any young men in the branch, and the young women were also reduced in number. Walking around the store, it seemed that most of the employees in the sales areas were middle-aged women part-timers, or temporary student staff, with few senior regular staff in evidence. I later learned that the supervisory positions had been reduced in number, with a corresponding increase in the attached responsibilities. Instead of one manager per floor, there were two (recently increased to three) managers for the whole store who shared responsibility for all the floors between them, and instead of one section chief per section there was a new position of 'leader', which carried responsibility for several sections on one floor.

Part-timers, now in an even greater majority than previously, had somewhat better prospects for career progression in 1999 than they had had in 1991. New statuses of 'friend'[14] *shain* and 'mate' *shain* had been introduced to replace the old rank of *teijishain*, with each status subdivided into two further ranks. This gave the possibility of promotion for part-timers by moving through these ranks, but still with no prospect of an official position in the management hierarchy. In addition, a further rank of 'silver' *shain* gave long-serving part-timers the opportunity to remain with the company, at a lower hourly rate of pay, after reaching the retirement age of sixty.

*Table 6.1* Changes in staffing of the Koganei branch of Nagasakiya 1991–9

|  | 1991 | 1999 |
|---|---|---|
| *Regular staff* | | |
| Male | 21 | 6 |
| Female | 28 | 15 |
| *Part-timers* | | |
| Male | 2 | 1 |
| Female | 80 | 78 |
| *Temporary staff* (arubaito) | | |
| Male and female | 22 | 19 |

Most of the part-timers to whom I spoke seemed content with the changes and generally positive about the increased proportion of part-timers within the store. However, for the remaining regular staff things were different. There was an atmosphere of gloom at the time I visited, as they had just heard that no summer bonus would be paid to staff that year – generally the twice yearly bonus is an important element in the salaries of regular employees in Japan, and its cancellation can create real hardship. Senior staff told me that their workload and working hours had increased, and there was now simply no time for many of the company events that had previously been held for regular staff; they could not give the staff the time off. Nagasakiya no longer fielded a team for the local dance festival in the summer, there were few sporting events organised now, and the annual company trip had been dispensed with. Nowadays, I was told, the most that the company organised was an occasional day trip.

Workplace meetings had been scaled back – even the morning meeting, or *chōrei*, was now an occasional rather than a daily event, as there were fewer regular staff now available to cover such meetings. In its place was a simple daily roll call. Some also commented that the atmosphere in the workplace had become more subdued now that there were fewer young employees. Reflective, or consultative, activities remained; the campaign at the time of my visit was 'Nice Change', ostensibly a campaign to make Nagasakiya more responsive to customer needs, but no-one to whom I spoke seemed to have much enthusiasm for the campaign. Some senior managers expressed the view that the agenda of the campaign was scarcely new – responding to customers is in any case one of the fundamentals of retail. In general, it seemed that those regular employees who remained in 1999 looked back on 1991 with nostalgia – one manager referred to it as a *kachōfūgetsu*, play on words alluding to an expression meaning in Japanese the beauties of nature, but here *fūgetsu* is used to refer to a golden age of good company atmosphere (*fū* from *shafū*) and good salary (*getsu* from *gekkyū*).

Again, in its era of decline, the divisions between Nagasakiya employees were more noticeable than what united them. While regular staff suffered in the recession, seeing their numbers cut and their salary and career prospects dwindle, part-timers fared relatively well, as the company relied on them increasingly heavily in order to cut its wages bill. However, part-timers were still excluded from the mainstream corporate hierarchy, resulting in an ever-heavier workload for those regular staff remaining. It is noteworthy that as the company struggled to cut costs, many of the social events designed to create a corporate spirit among its regular employees were curtailed on practical grounds, as were the daily morning meetings, suggesting that such events should not be seen as part of the core of Japanese company practice, but rather an area that can be elaborated or cut back as economic circumstances allow. The *chōbikai*, on the other hand, in which the overt agenda, to make money for the company, was successfully re-worked by the older women staff to constitute their own social event, remained and was still participated in by older women employees, past and current.

Clearly, the fragmentation and low morale of the company workforce, especially in 1991, must be seen in the context of a company in decline. However, I would argue that even in the company's so-called golden age a tendency to fragmentation was inherent in the structure of the company and its heterogeneous workforce. This is an issue which will be returned to in the concluding chapter of this book. But first, the next two chapters reconsider the role of the company from the perspective of some of the individuals who have passed through it and examine further the importance of differences of gender and generation within the corporate context.

# 7 Gender issues

## Working women in Nagasakiya

### Gender and work in Japan

Many of the older accounts of Japanese companies (and some of the more recent ones) dismiss female employees as peripheral to company structure (see for example Rohlen 1974: 20; Larke 1994: 27), with the further implicit assumption that the company is also peripheral to its female employees' lives: their central focus is taken to be marriage, children, and the home. However, this view is problematic in that it depends very much on taking a company-centred and implicitly male-gendered perspective, and it thus underestimates the importance of paid work in the lives of a large proportion of women in contemporary Japan. If we change the frame of reference to the perspective of individual female employees, paid employment and the successive transformations of women's working roles over the course of their lives are highly significant in a number of ways – although this does not, usually, entail a rejection of the socially sanctioned roles of wife and mother.

For women as for men, paid work outside the home takes up large amounts of time and energy, and may provide an essential source of income. It is also very common in Japan for women to combine paid work with domestic roles, so that the widespread image of the Japanese woman as a professional housewife is somewhat misleading. Taken as a whole, around half of Japanese women of all ages are in employment, with the proportion rising to over two-thirds of those aged between twenty-five and fifty-four. From a comparative perspective, these figures put Japan roughly in line with the UK, France, and Germany in terms of overall participation rates (though with slightly lower figures for the twenty-five to fifty-four age group in Japan) and some way ahead of Italy, although still behind North America (Japan Institute of Labour 1998a: 15).

Labour force participation patterns for Japanese women compared with their major Western European and North American competitors are distinctive in the fall in participation rates between the ages of twenty-five and thirty-four, women's main child-bearing years, followed by a gradual rise again from the ages of thirty-five to fifty – the well-known 'M curve'.[1] This indicates the normative pattern for a large proportion of Japanese women, who join the labour force after graduation from high school or university, leave on marriage or on the birth of the first child, and rejoin when their youngest child is old enough to enter kindergarten or primary school.

Most women who rejoin the labour force after having children are given the status of *pāto*, or 'part-timer', as described in detail in Chapter 2. This employment status is, indeed, so heavily dominated by married women returning to the workforce that the term *pāto* in Japanese evokes the image of a middle-aged married woman. As pointed out in Chapter 2, this adoption of part-time status involves the acceptance of much lower rates of pay than those enjoyed by full company members, even though there may only be a small reduction in working hours.

Commonly, the life-course for a Japanese woman in a middle- to lower-income household residing in an urban area can therefore be divided into several distinct phases: dependence on parents, childhood and adolescence up to leaving full-time education; full-time employment and financial independence; marriage and care of pre-school children, dependence on husband; part-time employment combined with child-rearing and household responsibilities; retirement and the achievement of a degree of leisure. In this context, what significance attaches to the intervals in a woman's life when she is employed outside the home? And how do these intervals articulate with wider concepts of femininity and work in Japan? Given that both men and women participate actively in the labour force in Japan, what are the differences between the ways in which male and female work are viewed, and how do these in turn vary depending on generation and marital status?

This chapter will consider constructions of femininity in Japan, and the extent to which these constructions are applicable to the Nagasakiya case. More specifically, the aim is to show how individual employees are affected by notions of gendered life-course in their relationships with the company, and in the ways in which the older employees articulate the demands of company and household, through a selection of brief life histories.

## Constructions of femininity in Japan

Smith (1987) argues that in Japan men and women are seen as inhabiting socially distinct spheres. The female sphere is seen as primarily domestic and revolves around the twin roles of household manager and mother. This construction of femininity is traced back by Smith to the Meiji era, when 'The proper role for the adult woman came to be defined as the dual one of good wife and wise mother' (Smith 1987:7). Smith (1987) locates the origins of the slogan 'good wife and wise mother' (*ryōsai kenbo*) not in Confucian traditions of female subordination, but in Victorian ideals of feminine domesticity borrowed from Europe in the 1880s and 1890s (Smith 1987: 7).

As both Sievers (1983) and Kondo (1990) have pointed out, this ideal of women's role in society was not entirely a restrictive move. Indeed, in the context of the time, it in some ways represented an upgrading of women's status, in so far as this was a reversal of the Tokugawa view that women were incompetent in weighty matters such as the proper upbringing of children, a responsibility that more properly belonged to the adult males of the household (Kondo 1990: 267). The slogan of good wife, wise mother was therefore also seized upon by various early women's movements, in whose hands it became part of an attempt to improve the status of women (Sievers 1983: 110).

In Smith's (1987) account, no conflict occurs between the promotion of a domestic role for women by the Meiji oligarchs and the demands for female labour in Meiji Japan, notably in the textile industry. This is because Smith sees the paid employment stage of a woman's life-course as occurring in the period of young adulthood, the interval between completing education and marriage. In the early days of industrialisation, it was a patriotic gesture for samurai families to send their daughters to work for a time in the textile industry, but this role was later taken over by young women from poor rural families. Thereafter, and until the 1920s, women from poor families dominated the female workforce. But by the late 1920s financial necessity impelled daughters of middle-class urban families, too, to seek paid employment.[2]

Financial necessity was, however, only part of the story. Also around this time non-factory work became available to women, and this work, largely white collar office work but also as shop assistants in the developing department stores, and some professional jobs such as that of teacher, was seen as suitable for young women of good family. To help attract such women to these jobs, some companies stressed the temporary nature of the work they were offering, and suggested that this period of outside work could form part of a woman's preparation for marriage. In some cases, employers even arranged classes in skills considered suitable for marriage preparation for their female employees, such as the tea ceremony or flower arranging (Nagy 1991: 212).

For unmarried women in the workforce as much as for their married counterparts, then, work was early subordinated to the feminine roles of wife and mother. For women of all classes, the ideal representation was of a docile employee helping towards her family expenses and diligently preparing for marriage. This representation has persisted, and it is endorsed by the management and training policies of large companies in Japan today, where preparation for marriage is a recurrent theme as far as female employees are concerned.[3]

In Nagasakiya, young working women largely shared this view of their employment as being temporary, with marriage and motherhood as their ultimate goals. The alternative of becoming a 'career woman'[4] was not regarded as attractive; rather, this was seen as a choice incompatible with marriage, and those who took this path were viewed on the whole as pitiable – failures in the quest for a husband.[5] Here it is important to emphasise that marriage and child-bearing are seen as essential for the achievement of mature adulthood in Japan – the status of *ichininmae* – and women who do not marry or bear children tend to be seen as in some sense incomplete.[6] A striking example of this attitude, widely reported in the Japanese press in 1991, was the criticism of the former (female) leader of the Japan Socialist Party, Takako Doi, by a government minister who cast doubt on her fitness to be a national leader on the grounds that she had never married or had children. In this regard, he contrasted her unfavourably with Margaret Thatcher, who, he suggested, was equipped to become Prime Minister not only because of her own talent as a politician but also because she had fulfilled the feminine roles of wife and mother. Thatcher was a complete person and therefore worthy of trust in a way that Doi was not.

The point here is not that work and marriage are seen as mutually exclusive; as already noted (p. 121), a high percentage of married women are in employment in Japan, and certainly for those with family businesses, or households engaged in agriculture, it has long been standard practice for the wife of the household to participate actively in the household's economic activities. However, the dominant discourse of femininity in Japan as it developed over the course of the twentieth century places the primary emphasis on the woman's role as wife and mother, with her outside economic activities firmly subordinated to her domestic responsibilities. Both Kondo (1990) and Nolte and Hastings (1991) have argued for a class dimension here, with the role of 'professional housewife' *(sengyō shufu)* being very much a middle-class aspiration. For women from less affluent families, returning to work after an interval of child-bearing and child-rearing is the norm, and it is not regarded as reprehensible, but rather may be seen as an index of her commitment to her household (Kondo 1990: 285). Nonetheless, such outside work is almost always undertaken on a 'part-time' basis, notionally to give the woman thus employed enough time for her domestic responsibilities. These, it should be noted, have tended to remain hers alone, although there is some evidence that in recent years husbands have begun to participate more in domestic tasks. But there is also a symbolic dimension here; as already noted (p. 20), 'part-timers' often work relatively long hours in Japan, but they are not seen as full company members. There is thus a division within the company between the full company members who owe their primary allegiance to the company and the part-timers whose central focus lies elsewhere.

At the same time that the notion of femininity as defined by the roles of good wife and wise mother has taken hold in Japan, the gap between completing full-time education and getting married has become established as a distinct stage in the female life-course, and one not wholly circumscribed by the notion of preparing for marriage. The existence of a period of young adulthood between the completion of formal education and marriage in Japanese women's lives can be traced back at least to the early twentieth century, as the average age of marriage for women rose fairly rapidly from around sixteen in the Meiji era to about twenty-three in the early twentieth century (Hendry 1981a: 25). It has continued to edge up since then, hovering around the age of twenty-six during the 1990s (Japan Institute of Labour

1998a: 12). At the same time, however, the age on leaving formal education has also risen, so that the interval between education and marriage was actually at its highest point in 1930, at nearly ten years compared with a gap of eight years for the average high-school graduate in the late 1990s, and four years for a four-year university graduate.

In addition to pursuing paid employment during this interval, many women move away from their parental home, often to live in company dormitories. The development of this relatively independent stage in the female life-course has been accompanied by the appearance of a popular representation of femininity in which the young independent working woman forms a distinct category, alongside more familiar representations of women as daughters, wives, housewives, and mothers.

The earliest of these popular representations of young working women seems to have arisen in the 1920s, when the term *modan gāru* (modern girl), or *moga* for short, gained wide currency. The modern girl was portrayed in newspapers and magazines dressed in Western clothes, with short hair and long legs, given to promiscuity and cruising in the fashionable Tokyo downtown area, the Ginza. But the most striking aspect of this media image of the modern girl was her independence, specifically from ties of household or family. However, this independence did not, in most versions of the modern girl, extend beyond claiming control of her own life and leisure in a way that some feminists of the time found frivolous (Silverberg 1991: 248–9). And although the modern girl was widely perceived as a threat to the established order, this was more because of her independent behaviour in the public domain than because such women represented any organised force for change.

Furthermore, although the modern girl was represented as antithetical to the 'good wife and wise mother' ideal of femininity, there is no evidence that the real women on whom this representation was based in fact chose never to marry, and still less that they sought to establish working careers along the lines of male careers. In the popular image of the modern girl she is forever young, her passage into middle age is not recorded, and it is her appearance and her social life, rather than her working life, that are the focus of interest.

The modern girl as a popular construct declined and then disappeared in the 1930s, with the rise of Japanese nationalism and a renewed movement to emphasise women's roles as wives and mothers and to remove visible signs of Westernisation, as epitomised by the dress and comportment of the modern girl of the 1920s. By the early 1940s, the state had adopted a policy of encouraging population growth by reducing the average age of marriage and increasing the number of children per family.[7] In so far as these policies were successful, they had the effect of drastically limiting the independent phase of the female life cycle.

In the post-war era, the image of an independent young working woman has been revived and forms part of the representation of young adulthood discussed in Chapter 4. However, as with the modern girl of the 1920s, the focus of attention in these popular representations of young womanhood is not the work element in women's lives, but their patterns of consumption and leisure,[8] and their independence as manifested in their ability to support themselves financially, and their residence in rented apartments or company dormitories, separate from their families.

Many examples of such women are found in popular culture. For example, the favourite television programme and a principal topic of conversation among the young women employees in Nagasakiya in the spring of 1994 was *'kono yo no hate'*, or *The End of this World*, a drama serial featuring two of Japan's most popular young actors. The female lead played a young woman employee at a post office, whose boyfriend was a *furii arubaito*, without stable employment or even his own apartment. For some time he lived with her in the small apartment that she rented, but he was also having an affair with another woman. At the time that I left Japan, the series took a dramatic turn with the boyfriend leaving her just as she (unbeknownst to him) had become pregnant. However, she did not follow the approved Japanese norm in these circumstances and have an abortion but decided instead to keep and rear the baby independently, still without informing its father. In this, and other similar series, the world of work features quite peripherally in women's lives, and a great deal of attention is paid to their relationship with men. Marriage and children are still seen as desirable (if not always attainable). However, women are, importantly, depicted as capable of independence, taking responsibility and making their own decisions, sometimes more effectively than the male characters. Their employment does not exact from them a long-term commitment, or involve them on a career level, but it does empower them as *shakaijin*, full members of society, and provides them with the salary that makes their independence possible.[9]

In the discussion that follows of the women employees at Nagasakiya, the way in which this relatively independent stage of the female life-course is constructed by the young women working at the store is explored further, as are the transformations in women's lives as they grow older and find their own solutions to the conundrum of balancing the demands of work, marriage, and motherhood.

## Women employees at Nagasakiya

The women in Nagasakiya, both married and unmarried, come largely from lower-income families. The unmarried women are mainly from rural families, and most of the married women are from the neighbourhood surrounding the branch in which they work. Although, in keeping with the general lack of class consciousness in Japan,[10] these women do not consider themselves as belonging to a lower or working class (the term working class is not used in Japanese in any case),[11] for most part-timers the main motivation for working is the need to supplement household income to meet daily living expenses.[12] Moreover, chain store work is badly paid and low in prestige, so it tends to attract women with a relatively low level of education and no specific skills (such as word-processing or a driver's licence). As far as the Koganei branch was concerned, these women therefore stood in clear contrast to the more well-to-do local housewives, who, if they sought paid employment at all, would be likely to do something more prestigious, such as giving private lessons (for example in playing the piano or in a decorative art) or office work.

Most of the women at Nagasakiya appeared to fit fairly neatly with normative patterns of female employment and life-course. A majority of regular employees were single women under thirty, whereas part-timers tended to be aged between their mid-thirties and early fifties and were usually married, with children.[13] For most women in both groups, paid work featured in their lives mainly as a means to an end, but a somewhat different end depending to a great extent on generation. For younger women, employment in Nagasakiya provided a means of pursuing other interests, notably those related to leisure and consumption, and also, in some cases, the financial wherewithal to train for a more attractive job. Although marriage figured largely in their images of their future, for most of the eighteen-year-olds this still seemed a distant prospect, with an exciting interval of independence to be enjoyed beforehand. Few of these women considered the idea of pursuing a long-term career within Nagasakiya to be an attractive, or even possible, alternative. Turnover among this group was high, and neither the company nor their colleagues expected most of the young female recruits entering the company to remain for long. In practice, some remained for seven or eight years before leaving, having made a wide circle of friends within the company, and often maintaining contact with other past or present Nagasakiya employees for years afterwards. These were perhaps those who were seen as the most successful of Nagasakiya's female employees, particularly if they left to get married – they fulfilled social expectations in serving as diligent employees until their mid-twenties then moving on to the next approved stage in the female life-course. However, there were others who left within a year or two, without making much impression on the long-term employees or maintaining any links with the company afterwards. This was the case for the female intake to the Koganei branch in 1991. In 1999 they were long gone, with their names scarcely remembered, and their lives on leaving Nagasakiya a subject of apparent indifference to those who remained.

The older women, on the other hand, formed a more complex and varied group. Among these were a small number of regular employees, few of whom had originally intended to remain with the company long term. For these women, remaining with the company and gaining promotion was not seen as a source of unambiguous pride. Commonly, the fact of remaining for a long time (ten years or more) was evaluated negatively and explicitly associated both by the women concerned and by the younger women employees either with lacking the courage to move on or with a perceived omission in other areas of life – generally not having married or not having had children.[14] Given the value attached to marrying and having children for both sexes in

Japan, these women were not seen as enviable role models, but rather tended to become increasingly anomalous and isolated within the company. Nor did they tend to rise far, as women regular employees are not placed on the career track in Nagasakiya.[15]

The large majority of older women, however, were part-timers. Lacking in job security, barred from promotion at work, and with responsibilities for the home, children, and sometimes elderly or sick relatives, this would seem at first glance to be the most peripheral category of employee. Most of these women worked from financial necessity, and turnover was high, with many, especially the younger ones, leaving to work for better wages elsewhere, either in light industry or in one of Nagasakiya's competitors. As with the regular employees, women in this category who remained for a long time commonly remarked apologetically that they had never intended to stay so long but felt unable to go elsewhere, either because they lacked the courage to move to an unfamiliar working environment or because they lacked the skills, or simply felt they were too old to find anything else.

However, within this category there was also a smaller number of women, referred to in Chapter 2, who described themselves as 'veterans' and took considerable pride in their expertise in the workplace, gained over many years. In some cases these women achieved a higher status within the part-timer category, with company union membership. They also became well known within the local branch in which they worked, and for some of these women at least their eventual departure was marked with a company-organised farewell party and remembered subsequently. Another theme for the veterans was the notion that it was good to work and keep active as long as they were physically able to do so. Work was seen as good for the health and also as intrinsically good as opposed to leisure, which was perceived as idleness.[16] Here there was a clear generational divide in the relative evaluation of work and leisure, with the younger employees placing much greater emphasis on leisure pursuits.

There were thus broad divides between and within various categories of female employee that make any general statements on women working in Nagasakiya highly problematic. And even within each of the broad groupings outlined above there was substantial variation in the ways in which individual women viewed their work at Nagasakiya and the role of work in their lives. The next section of this chapter gives a range of brief life histories, or vignettes, for women working in Nagasakiya, both regular employees and part-timers (some of whom have already been introduced in Chapters 5 and 6), in order to give an idea of the aspirations of the younger employees and their perceptions of their relationship with the company; and, for the older women, to show some of the variety of pathways working women may follow.

## Female regular employees: changing perspectives

### Kojima-san

Kojima-san was nineteen years old when I met her in 1991. She had joined the Koganei branch of Nagasakiya the previous year, quickly becoming a popular member of staff, particularly with the other young regular employees, and often representing the branch in company-wide sporting events – she was particularly good at volleyball. The youngest of four children, she was brought up in the Ogasawara islands, technically under Tokyo's administrative jurisdiction, but in fact over a twelve-hour boat ride away. Kojima-san said she joined Nagasakiya because it had good fringe benefits – she particularly mentioned the fact that company dormitories have single rooms, whereas a lot of other chain store dormitories have several people to a room. She did not consider joining a department store because her school results were not good enough. As for why she chose the retail sector, she was quite vague – she thought it looked interesting and could not really think what else she might want to do.

She did not enjoy her work, when asked what she liked about the job she replied 'nothing really', and she complained from time to time to me about how boring it was. Although animated and cheerful on company outings, she tended to be glum and monosyllabic at work, where she was isolated as the only young regular employee in a section otherwise comprising only part-time *oba-san* – middle-aged women. Kojima-san often said she wished she could do more interesting things, but she did not appear to have any specific ideas about what else she could do. When asked if she would like to become a section chief in the future, she laughed and said 'Oh no, I'm not going to stay that long'. As to how long she did plan to continue, she was also quite vague, just saying she did not want to stop immediately.

In fact, Kojima-san did stop, quite soon after I had completed my fieldwork, after only about two years with Nagasakiya, and I suspect she may have been job-hunting for some time before that. She found a job as an insurance saleswoman based in the Koganei area and moved out of the company dormitory into her own apartment. She still came to visit her old colleagues at the Koganei branch from time to time, and they said that she was enjoying her new job and the higher salary it offered. Most people at Nagasakiya seemed unworried by her move – her former colleagues simply said it was her business what she decided to do with her life. The part-timer who continued to head the section where Kojima-san had worked did, however, complain that the remaining section members had been very overstretched after Kojima-san's departure, and that she had been obliged to start all over again training another new recruit to work in the section.

### Sato-san

I met Sato-san on the company training course described in Chapter 3. A somewhat withdrawn, nervous, young woman, she was the oldest of three children, with a younger sister in the first year of high school and a brother in elementary school. Her family lived in Nagaoka city, Niigata prefecture, a large provincial city in north-eastern Japan. She described her father as 'just an ordinary salaryman'.

She had decided to join Nagasakiya because she wanted to work in retail, and it was the only large store advertising jobs at her high school that offered places in Tokyo. She said she wanted to go to Tokyo because she thought it would be boring to spend all her life in one place. Another attraction of Nagasakiya was the single-room dormitories. She said she found the work better than she had thought it would be, having initially been very put off by her experience of the training course, when she had thought she might just give up and go home. She was, nonetheless, already thinking of leaving less than a year after entering the company, saying that the main thing that made her stay was that the (new) dormitories were so nice, and it would be hard to move out and find anywhere else as good.

Sato-san invited me to lunch at the dormitory on one occasion, and it did indeed seem very comfortable. 'Dormitory' in fact seemed a misnomer – it was to all appearances a modern block of self-contained studio flats, in which Sato-san had a pleasant, if small apartment. In the single room that served as living and sleeping space, she had arranged her futon to act as a sofa in the daytime, and next to this was a small table, and beyond that a large television and video recorder. She also had a compact disc player for music.

Although Sato-san's ambition was to marry and have children, she said she hated cooking and housework, so when I visited we feasted on a selection of pastries from the local French-style patisserie. She told me that she never cooked for herself, and claimed she would not know how and was happy to live on take-away food, much of it European style. Her main leisure interests were watching television and shopping with friends – all of whom were fellow employees living in the same dormitory, and we followed our lunch with a leisurely stroll around a department store located near the dormitory, admiring the fashions, and deciding what we would we buy if we could afford it.

Sato-san was an enthusiastic fan of television dramas, we shared some favourites as we both liked murder mysteries, as well as a series that might be most succinctly described as a Japanese version of *The Twilight Zone*. She was also a dedicated follower of the drama serial of young adult life in Japan, *The End of this World* (see p. 126) and in the realm of popular literature enjoyed the work of the unusually named Yoshimoto Banana, a woman writer who became popular in Japan while still in her early twenties. As with *The End of this World*, Yoshimoto's writing concerns the world of young adults and is more concerned with the relationships they form with each other than with the domain of work.[17]

I lost touch with Sato-san when I left Japan in 1994. By 1999 she had left, and no-one remaining seemed to remember her very clearly or to have much idea of when she had left or what had become of her, though one of the senior managers thought she might have gone back to her family in the countryside. As with many young female regular employees, she passed through the company leaving little trace behind.

### Arakawa-san

A cheerful, energetic woman, Arakawa-san was a full company member and section chief on the floor where I was employed at the Koganei branch, and she also worked as a trainer on the on-the-job training programmes for both regular employees and part-timers. She was born in Saga, a rural district on the island of Kyushu in western Japan. The second of two children in a farming household, her parents initially wanted her to succeed to the family farm, as her elder brother, who should have succeeded according to the preferred pattern of eldest-son inheritance,[18] had successfully completed university and entered a company. However, Arakawa-san was adamant that she did not want to be a farmer, and so the older brother was obliged to give up his job and return to the farm in Saga.

Having failed to persuade their daughter to take on the family farm, her parents then tried to convince her to carry on with her education, as her brother had done. However, Arakawa-san disliked studying and wanted to go to work in a city, preferably in Fukuoka, the main city on the island of Kyushu. Her parents eventually agreed to let her go to work after graduating from high school, but argued that Fukuoka was too close, only a day's journey from their farm, and that as long as she was leaving home, it would be better to go further away. Arakawa-san explained that they took this line because in Japan it is thought good for the development of character that children should live independently from their parents for a time – ideally about three years. Her parents thought that she would be less likely to give up and return home if she went to work far away – home would not then be within such easy reach. Since it had taken quite a long time to reach a family consensus about what she should do, by the time Arakawa-san came to apply for a job there were few places left open, and she had little choice as to which job to take.[19] She therefore applied to Nagasakiya by default, not because she had any positive reason for choosing to work there.

She joined Nagasakiya in 1977, and by the time I conducted my fieldwork had been there for fourteen years. She met her husband at the Koganei branch, which he joined two years after she did. They married five years later, in the same year that Arakawa-san was promoted to section chief. She achieved her promotion after her husband, a full two years after passing the necessary exam. This was because at the time the position of section chief was introduced the men eligible for the post were all promoted before the women as a matter of policy. Her husband was subsequently promoted again, and in 1991 he worked at head office in downtown Tokyo, where he still remained in 1999.

Arakawa-san, however, denied any ambition to be promoted further herself. She explained that her only reason for continuing to work was that in seven years of marriage she and her husband had been unable to have children, and as long as she had no children she felt that she would be bored staying at home. She was not interested in studying (many reasonably well-off Japanese housewives fill their time by studying or taking up a hobby – anything from

English lessons to flower arrangement) and since all her life since graduation had been bound up with Nagasakiya, she did not know what else to do.

Her husband had no objection to her continuing to work as long as they had no children, but he did expect her to do all the housework, laundry, cooking, and shopping for their home. She laughed as she told me that he just sat down when he got home and issued orders for beer, food, and so on – behaviour that is depicted in Japan as 'typical' of husbands and part of Japanese images of masculinity. As is common in Japan, he never told her when he would be working late or going out to dinner, so there were occasions when she cooked a meal and he did not turn up to eat it. I asked her if this annoyed her, and she laughed again and said, 'Of course, but I don't say a word. When he comes in I just pick up all the plates and scrape the food off into the rubbish, right in front of him.'

For married couples such as the Arakawas, Nagasakiya makes an effort to keep husband and wife in the same area of Japan, so that if the husband is transferred the wife may also be transferred to the same branch. Given this situation, I asked Arakawa-san why she chose to remain on a 'home' contract and not shift to a national one that would make her eligible for promotion.[20] She again reiterated that she had no interest in promotion, and said that she did not want to risk being transferred to another branch, even within the same area, as she would not then be able to cycle to work, as she could at present. She said that her main ambitions for the future, as far as work was concerned, were that the people she was training would do well.

Reminiscing about her early experience at Nagasakiya, Arakawa-san recalled with nostalgia the conditions in the company dormitory when she first joined. She told me that it was dirty and crowded, with three people to a room, but said that she was happy there. She said that the *senpai* (seniors) were friendly and seemed more like older sisters, and she also commented that the recruits in those days had a *gaman* (endurance) mentality. In her view, that changed from around the early 1980s, and since that time the *gaman* mentality had largely been lost with the influx of a new generation brought up in a more affluent era than that of Arakawa-san and her contemporaries. Of the new recruits in 1991 she said, 'They will do what you tell them *kichinto* (punctiliously), but nothing more.'

A postscript to this narrative was added in the spring of 1994, when Arakawa-san resigned from Nagasakiya. Although she had not had a child, and still wished to continue working, she and her husband had bought a house in a distant suburb, and she felt that she could not commute and continue to do all the domestic work in their household. The choice of location of their house was in part determined by the high price of property at that time in Tokyo, which meant that they had to move far out of the centre to find anything they could afford. However, Arakawa-san reportedly favoured this location anyway because it was popular with former Nagasakiya staff, and her long-time friend and fellow section chief, Nishiguchi-san, who had resigned earlier in the year in order to marry, had also bought a house in the same area.

Arakawa-san told me she planned to get a new job as a part-timer in a different company, probably another store, close to her home, as she would get bored if she gave up work altogether. Asked if she had any regrets on leaving Nagasakiya, Arakawa-san's eyes wandered around the store, where we were talking, 'Well ... everyone's so young now, you see. Did you know the average age of women regular staff has dropped to twenty-one?'

At thirty-four, Arakawa-san found herself isolated. All her female contemporaries had already resigned, and she was increasingly an anomaly: a middle-aged woman in Japanese terms but still a regular employee and childless. She must also have been expensive for the company to continue to employ, given her accumulated seniority,[21] and a young male regular employee had long been waiting in the wings in her section, explicitly groomed for the position of section chief. This would have been an important consideration for the company while it struggled with a situation of economic decline, and for her the resignation bonus on offer after sixteen years of service would have been a considerable help in financing their new home. Whether or not she was actually encouraged to leave I was not able to discover, but it seems likely that a number of factors combined to make Arakawa-san eventually give up her position at Nagasakiya.

By 1999, when I asked about Arakawa-san, I was told that her husband still worked at head office, and that his wife, was 'just a housewife'. Arakawa-san's old friend, Nishiguchi-san, had divorced, and, so rumour had it, had returned to her natal home in the countryside.

### Watanabe-san

Like Kojima-san, Watanabe-san was the youngest of four, in her case all girls. Although their home was in Kagoshima, on the island of Kyushu, only one sister had remained there. The two oldest had gone first to Tokyo and then on to the US, where they now lived. Watanabe-san had been inspired by their example to find a job in Tokyo, and this was her main reason for choosing Nagasakiya, although she also mentioned the fact that one of her seniors from school worked in a branch of Nagasakiya near the Koganei branch, and that she had been impressed by the Nagasakiya pamphlet.

Twenty-seven years old at the time I conducted my fieldwork, Watanabe-san had already clocked up nine years as a regular employee at Nagasakiya, and had recently been promoted to section chief. However, she said that she did not aspire to any further promotion and laughed at the idea of being a 'career woman', '*Nagasakiya de kyaria ūman wa chotto iya desu ne*' (Being a career woman at Nagasakiya is sort of a yucky idea isn't it?). She said she felt rather stuck in a rut and wanted to do something 'by myself', although, like Kojima-san, she was quite vague about what that something might be. She also said she found the human relations at Nagasakiya 'a bit difficult'.

Watanabe-san was old enough to have experienced the former dormitories at Nagasakiya and recalled how awful they were – an old wooden building with three people to an eight tatami-mat room[22] infested with insects. Like some other employees of the same generation, she was indignant about this, commenting that the company had lied about the dormitories in the recruitment material. She said she had moved to a privately rented apartment as soon as she could afford to do so – in her case, four years after joining. She did say, however, that there was a good side to the old dormitories in that they enabled one to establish close, friendly relations with *senpai* (senior employees), a situation she contrasted with the current state of affairs, where she felt employees were more isolated from each other, just individuals (*kojin, kojin*).

Watanabe-san appeared to have many friends within Nagasakiya as well as friends from her hometown who had also moved to Tokyo. As far as outside work interests were concerned, her greatest enthusiasm seemed to be directed towards travel: she aspired to go to the US as had her sisters, and she was interested in all things American, although she worried about her inability to speak English.

Somewhat to my surprise, in 1999 Watanabe-san was one of only two female regular employees I had known in 1991 who remained at Nagasakiya. Now married, but as yet with no children, she had the new position of 'leader'. With the restructuring of employment at Nagasakiya, many of the former junior managerial positions had disappeared; now two or three managers per store were each in charge of several floors, and one or two leaders on each floor were each responsible for several sections. This replaced the former system of one manager per floor, and one section chief per section. Watanabe-san's new position thus left her in the same relative position in the management hierarchy, but with a greater workload than before. She seemed to have reservations about her new remit, in part because she felt torn by the demands of her intermediate position between management and ordinary employees (a position that had probably become more demanding as the number of people in this intermediate role decreased), and in part because she felt that however hard she tried at work, other staff were not following her lead in making a similar effort themselves. In this respect, she commented on the high turnover of part-time staff, and the lack of training provided for part-timers.

> Part-timers don't always have the fighting spirit to do the job straight away, like regular employees do … there are those who come in with no experience at all, and you have to teach them everything from scratch … There isn't any training, so they just have to watch what the people around them are doing … It varies. There are people who really want to get stuck in, and develop their skills. But there are also people who give up after a day. It really goes between two extremes … there aren't many part-timers who stay for a long time.

She also commented that now there were very few young regular employees in the company, so she felt that the atmosphere had become rather gloomy and subdued.

Watanabe-san still seemed to have little enthusiasm for further promotion within Nagasakiya, although she no longer had any immediate plans to leave. She said that if she had children she would leave, but as long as she had no children she preferred being out at work to staying at home, as it gave her a chance to meet and talk to all sorts of people. Now aged thirty-five, and with Japan in recession, her options had narrowed considerably since we had last met. As she had no skills other than sales, she doubted that she could find a job in another field, and thought that of the chain stores Nagasakiya had particularly good human relations – a comment which contrasted with her evaluation of the situation in 1991. As far as becoming a manager was concerned, she still seemed to find the existing managers less than exciting role models, commenting,

> I don't really think I want to be a manager. If I'm honest ... well, if I became a manager I'd earn more ... I wonder ... but if I look at the managers we've got now, well, I don't want to be rude, but ...

Being married, Watanabe-san found, combined well with working – in fact she said that life had become much easier since she had married. She and her husband share all the housework and cooking, on the basis of whoever is home first cooks (often her husband, as Nagasakiya regular employees in 1999 worked until 9 p.m., a result of the liberalisation of Japan's Large Store Law). Her interest in travel continues, and by the time of my return visit she had succeeded in her long-held dream of visiting the US on holiday, with her husband.

### Ushijima-san

Besides Watanabe-san, the sole female regular employee in the Koganei branch remaining in 1999 from those I had known in 1991 was a truly exceptional woman who had risen to be one of only three women floor managers in the whole of Nagasakiya. Ushijima-san was transferred to the Koganei branch only about a month before I completed my fieldwork, but she had also worked there some years previously and seemed well liked by those who had worked with her. Aged forty-three, unmarried and likely to remain so, and one of the most successful women in the company, of the women I knew Ushijima-san approximated most closely to the popular image of the 'career woman'.

Ushijima-san was born in a small town in Yamanashi prefecture, near Tokyo. She was the younger of two sisters and her father was a salaryman. Ushijima-san went to a commercial high school, originally intending to seek office work rather than a position in sales, but in the event her choice was constrained by the fact that she wished to leave home, and therefore she had to look for a company with a dormitory. She took, and passed, a number of company entrance examinations, including that for Takashimaya, one of Japan's most prestigious department stores, but she chose Nagasakiya because they had space available in their dormitory and Takashimaya did not. This was in 1966, just before Nagasakiya's major period of expansion, and Ushijima-san remembered it as being a good time to join from a career point of view, although perhaps not so good from an individual point of view as employees were very much subject to transfer (she noted that this was less so for female employees). Ushijima -san herself has been transferred four times, but always within the same area of western Tokyo, and she is now classified as a zone employee, that is, one subject to transfer within a limited zone; she noted that this system of dividing employees up into home, zone, and national employees has only been in existence since about 1987 or so.

Ushijima-san's first promotion came in 1970, when she attained the rank of section chief, and in 1985 she became the first woman floor manager in the Nagasakiya group. Commenting on the dearth of women in senior positions in the company, she said that at the time she joined women's work was conceived of as *koshikake* – a stopgap between school and marriage. In the 1960s, most women regular employees only stayed for three years, almost no-one had stayed as long as ten years, and few for five years. There were also few part-timers – almost all female employees were regular employees in their late teens and early twenties. She said that Nagasakiya was in no way unusual in this – a similar situation obtained in all Japanese companies at the time. Career advancement did not really seem to be a possibility for Ushijima-san's generation, nor was it Ushijima-san's original intention to make a career within the company. But when she reached the age of about twenty-eight with no marriage prospects on the horizon, she realised that she was probably going to stay single, and, with hindsight, she thinks that this probably facilitated her rise to manager, as she had no conflicting demands on her time. 'Being single, my time is my own'.

Aside from her unmarried status, she attributed her promotion to her own liking for the work, and to the support of those around her, both superiors and subordinates. But she said it was not easy being a woman in a responsible position, as such women are still rare, and the general assumption, both of customers and within the company as a whole, is that only men hold such positions. For this reason, a customer with a problem will often insist on speaking to a male employee, even if he is a new recruit, in preference to speaking to Ushijima-san. Speaking in 1991, Ushijima-san could see no possibility of further promotion but added that it had once seemed impossible for her to get as far as she has. 'I'll take it as it comes.'

Ushijima-san had less to say than did other female employees about her life outside work, simply saying that she liked to play golf in her free time, which she does mainly with friends from outside the company. On the subject of work, however, she had a lot to say, and was full of enthusiasm about new schemes she hoped to introduce at the Koganei branch, such as a rotation scheme to familiarise employees with the work of sections other than their own. 'I've only just got here, *kore kara charenji suru* (from now on I shall 'challenge'[23]).'

In 1991 Ushijima-san was one of six floor managers in the Koganei branch of Nagasakiya. She had been transferred there when a neighbouring branch closed and doubled up with another floor manager, with whom she shared responsibility for a single floor. By 1999, the male floor managers alongside whom Ushijima-san had worked had mostly either left the company or had been moved to one of Nagasakiya's subsidiaries. Not one had achieved promotion. Within the Koganei branch, the number of floor managers had been reduced to a total of two, sharing responsibility for the whole store. Ushijima-san was one of these and had the reputation of being the more dynamic of the two. Procedures that had lapsed in other parts of the store, such as morning meetings of staff, were not allowed to lapse in the areas under Ushijima's control. She was widely respected and liked by the older female staff, if perhaps less so by some of her younger subordinates. One of the veteran part-timers expressed the opinion that she might yet become Nagasakiya's first woman branch manager. Unfortunately, when asked by the senior male staff if she would be willing for me to interview her again, she was the only Koganei staff member to decline – saying she was simply too busy.

## Regular female employees: an overview

Varied though the above accounts are, there are some common themes that can be identified. For most of the women joining Nagasakiya as regular employees, their initial motivation is a highly practical one, in which considerations such as the availability and quality of dormitory accommodation play a large role. In their early years as Nagasakiya employees they do not tend to see their work as a long-term career, and when work does become long term this is generally expressed as something unplanned and fortuitous, a reaction to events in their personal life, such as not getting married or not having children, rather than a career choice. In this it would seem that Nagasakiya women are not particularly unusual – Creighton (1996: 209) notes similar views among regular female staff in department stores.

Moving on from Nagasakiya is not, however, a simple matter of resigning on marriage or childbirth. Women leave for reasons other than to get married; for example, in Kojima-san's case, to pursue another line of work or, in the case of Watanabe-san's sisters, to travel. At the same time, women do get married and continue working, although usually not indefinitely, as Arakawa's case shows. But with the passage of time, these individual variations are lost, and inquiries about half-remembered female employees a few years later are more likely than not to elicit responses along the lines of 'I'm not sure, but I think she probably got married', or 'she went back to the countryside' (with the implication that she returned to her natal home to get married), or 'she's just a housewife now'. In the normative generalised account, work for regular women employees thus always tends to be counterposed to their (supposed or imagined) domestic role, with the assumption that there is a progression from one to the other.

Marriage remained an ultimate goal for the young women employees of Nagasakiya, the unquestioned final destination of the path of young adulthood. But this goal remained hazy and distant for many, with no connection apparently made between the daily toil of a housewife and their own inability and disinclination to cook or keep house. In the meantime, they enjoyed their new-found independence, working conscientiously but reserving their enthusiasm for leisure pursuits, whether individual or company organised, and orientating themselves very much with the world of young urban adults and consumers.

For those who, for varying reasons, remained after most of their generation had left, a change in attitudes can be seen. Work, and the skills they had developed, rather than a stop-gap or a means to an end, became increasingly an index of identity, separating and distinguishing them from other less experienced employees. Thus, Arakawa-san complains of younger regular employees not putting more than they have to into their work and bewails their lack of mental toughness, and eight years on Watanabe-san complains of the lack of expertise of the part-timers who now form the majority of the work-force. These women may not seek promotion, but they take pride in their own competence at their work. At the same time, the acquisition of increased status and responsibility, combined with increased age, tends to isolate them from their fellow women, in particular the younger regular employees, to whom they often seem to represent a feared, rather than a desired, possible future. This is all the more evident in the case of Ushijima-san, who has succeeded in becoming a well-respected and very hard-working manager, deeply committed to and enthusiastic about her work, but who is more likely to be cited by younger colleagues as an example of a future they do *not* want than of a role model to be aspired to.[24] However, in all this it needs to be remembered that the contrast between younger and older women is not absolute: the one turns into the other, often with a corresponding change in outlook. This is demonstrated by the case of Watanabe-san, who in 1991 looked with disfavour on women who made a career in Nagasakiya, but eight years later had become one of the longest-serving employees in the branch.

At the same time, the above accounts are suggestive of changes over time in Nagasakiya as a company and the position of women within Nagasakiya. When Ushijima-san joined the company in the 1960s most women working there were regular employees who stopped a few years later. Marriage was seen as incompatible with continuing employment as a regular employee, and Ushijima-san herself attributes her ability to make a career for herself within the company to the fact that she remained single. For Arakawa-san, joining the company a decade later, marriage no longer implied immediate resignation. However, Arakawa-san had little support from her husband in dealing with domestic chores and felt increasingly isolated in the company. Ultimately, moving house provided the spur to leaving. In contrast, Watanabe-san, some six years Arakawa-san's junior, found that marriage made it easier to work rather than harder, as she and her husband shared domestic chores, and he would often cook for them both in the evenings. Combining marriage and work did not seem to be an issue for her, although, like Arakawa-san, she had no children, and said that she would have stopped work if she had.

Although it would be rash to draw too firm conclusions from a few accounts, the varying experiences of these women do indicate that within a cultural frame that broadly views women as properly focusing on the domestic sphere, particularly after marriage, there is room for both individual variation and generational shift. The ways in which the demands of outside work and looking after home and family are balanced is also an important issue for the part-time employees, as discussed in the next section.

## Part-time work, long-term commitment?

Part-time working by women, in Japan as elsewhere, is widely depicted as a way of reconciling work and family. The assumption is that family comes first, and that part-time work can be fitted around this, enabling the part-time woman worker to fulfil multiple roles, both at home and in the workplace. It is also assumed that the workplace comes a clear second to the home for the woman concerned. However, looking at individual cases in Nagasakiya the picture appears more complex, with some part-timers showing considerable involvement in and long-term commitment to the company. Conversely, it seems that the company itself is relying ever more heavily on these women, and increasingly it puts considerable pressure on them to remain with the company at the same time as other categories of employee are being encouraged to leave. This in turn creates a situation in which it becomes problematic to continue to view part-time workers as peripheral and dispensable: a section of the part-time workforce, at least in retail, is emerging as an indispensable core, on which the company relies for its everyday operations.[25] This is an issue that will be discussed further in the concluding section of this chapter. Here we begin by examining the involvement of these long-term core part-timers through a description of three of the so-called 'veteran' part-timers of Nagasakiya, and one of the rare women to cross the part-time/regular employee boundary.

### Matsumoto-san

Of these narratives, Matsumoto-san is exceptional on two counts: first she is not an employee of the Koganei branch, but works in a branch in the Osaka area. I met her while participating in the company training course, where she was acting as trainer. Second, and more importantly, she is the only woman I met at Nagasakiya who has been able to make the transition from part-timer to regular employee status. This is very unusual and was not considered to be a possibility by any of the other part-timers I interviewed.

In 1991 Matsumoto-san was in her forties and had been with the company for ten years. On graduating from high school she joined a department store, Daimaru, near her home in Osaka, where she worked until she got married four years later. She then had a ten-year break, during which time she had three children. Also during this time two other important changes took place in her life: her mother became ill and came to live with her and her husband, and Matsumoto-san began to suffer from depression. She saw a doctor who advised her to get out of the house more, and when she said she found this difficult he suggested that she get a job outside the home.

She was able to find a job as a part-time sales assistant at the Osaka branch of Nagasakiya (she decided to work at a large store because of her previous work experience) working from 9.45 a.m. to 4.00 p.m. These were unusual hours – generally part-timers at Nagasakiya work until 4.45 p.m., but she wanted to be home when her children returned from school, and also she did not want her husband to find out that she had taken a job, as it was not uncommon at that time for Japanese men of Matsumoto-san's generation in middle-income households to forbid their wives to work. She managed to juggle work responsibilities and housework and childcare for some years, with the help of her mother, who by that time was sufficiently recovered to take on the lion's share of the housework.

Gradually, she became more involved with the company, taking on more responsibility and staying later in the evening. Then her section chief left, and, as she had pretty much taken on a section chief's responsibilities by then anyway, the store asked her to become a regular employee and section chief. Matsumoto-san found it hard to say no directly to this offer – company requests in Japan are generally interpreted as orders, with the only option other than acceptance being to leave the company. She therefore replied in evasive terms hoping that they would give up the idea, as she could not possibly accept the job without telling her husband, who still did not know she was working. (Section chiefs work weekends, when most husbands are home.) However, the store did not give up, and she eventually found she was boxed into a corner and had to talk to her husband about it. To her surprise, he was very supportive, so she took the job and has subsequently added the task of training new recruits to her other responsibilities.

Matsumoto-san's life was very busy. She finished work at about 8.00 p.m. every day and returned home by 8.30 p.m. She then started preparing dinner, to be ready by 10.00 p.m. Her sons helped her with the cooking – her eldest son was then nineteen. By 1991 her mother could no longer help as much as she used to – she was seventy-six and tired easily. However, Matsumoto-san was content with being a section chief and was satisfied with her work at Nagasakiya, particularly because it enabled her to make friends, though she also enjoyed the work itself. She did not aspire to becoming a floor manager, as that would involve accepting transfers, and she did not want to be moved away from her family.

### Miura-san

In 1991 Miura-san was a *junshain* (a sub-category of part-timer), who worked in the delivery section of the Koganei branch. Born in 1940 in the Tokyo area, but evacuated to Yamanashi prefecture during the war, Miura-san returned to live in Tokyo at the age of eight. The younger of two sisters, she was trained from the age of twelve in flower arranging, and from the age of fourteen in the tea ceremony. Miura-san's aunt was a teacher of the tea ceremony who had no children of her own, and Miura-san was originally intended to succeed her, but gave up this idea when she married at the age of twenty-five. Miura-san's sister has now succeeded their aunt as teacher at her tea ceremony school. Miura-san's husband is an ordinary company employee, and they have one daughter.

Unlike most part-timers, Miura-san did not claim to work from financial necessity, but traced her involvement with Nagasakiya back to her long-standing friendship with the general office manager at the Koganei branch, 'the Chief', who is described in more detail in Chapter 8. He originally persuaded her to join Nagasakiya when she was thirty, telling her, 'It's not yet time to take it easy (*mada asobu jikan janai*), you should come and work with us'. She duly joined a branch a few stations down the line from the Koganei branch, where the Chief was currently office manager, and she worked there until it closed down ten years later. She then took a six-year break during which she concentrated on being a housewife and mother, before again being persuaded by the Chief, who was by that time office manager at the Koganei branch, to go and work there.

Again unusually for a part-time female employee, Miura-san does not live near the Koganei branch – it takes her about one hour by train to get to work. Her sole reason for choosing this inconvenient location was her friendship with the Chief. She commented particularly that he let her take responsibility for running the delivery section, a job that is usually entrusted to a man, and she was also authorised to act for him when he was absent. She had a great admiration for the Chief and told me that he had all the qualifications for becoming a branch manager but simply did not seem to want to. Like most part-timers, however, Miura-san denied that she enjoyed her work, saying,

> I don't exactly *like* it, but I'm still physically strong, so it seems the natural thing to do. Anyway, having my own work cheers me up. Though I never thought I would do this kind of work – I was brought up to do tea and flower arranging. But the people are friendly here.

On another occasion, when we were discussing the large number of housewife part-timers working at Nagasakiya, she commented,

> I think it's a good thing [for women to go out to work]. If you stay at home, you can do housework, or study, but if you go out to work I think it makes you develop in yourself,[26] you're not just staying at home. Well, I

suppose you could do that staying at home, but ... Well, I've done that once, stop work to be a housewife, but when the children get bigger, you feel you want to do something, don't you? I didn't really know exactly what, just do something, get out of the house.

Regarding her life outside the company, when we spoke in 1991 Miura-san said that she had little free time since her father was ill. Saturday and Sunday were days off for her, and one day she rested while on the other she tried to study the English alphabet so that one day she could teach it to her grandchildren. She had once planned to use her Nagasakiya wages to pay for her studies, but found that it went mainly on clothes and treats for her family. The housework was left entirely to her – her husband thought that it was women's work. When asked about her plans for the future, Miura-san said she hoped she could help her grandchildren to learn English, and also that she would like to take up the tea ceremony and flower arranging again as a hobby.

When I revisited Nagasakiya in 1999 Miura-san was still there, and she had taken up one of the new statuses of part-timer that had been introduced in the reorganisation of Nagasakiya, thus gaining both a somewhat better salary and also a membership of the company union. She was due to reach retirement age shortly, but hoped she would be able to continue work after retirement as a 'silver' employee – another new status introduced for part-timers who had passed retirement age. She was awaiting the results of a medical test and the approval of her immediate superior and of the store manager. However, the Chief, who had encouraged her to work for so many years, was no longer there to support her application – he had taken voluntary early retirement that spring after a transfer to a loss-making subsidiary of Nagasakiya some years previously. Miura-san was unsure whether the current management of the Koganei branch would approve her application.

Miura-san had once again taken up the tea ceremony and flower arranging, and she talked with enthusiasm about the various exhibitions and events organised by the flower-arranging school to which she belonged. However, she was emphatic that this was 'just a hobby'. In 1998, her aunt, who had also been her teacher of flower arranging and the tea ceremony, had died at the age of ninety-four, and Miura-san's sister had succeeded her. Miura-san said with approval,

She carried on to the end, until she was 94, she was doing flower arranging and the tea ceremony. Until she was 94 she carried on working without slacking. Right until the end, until she drew her last breath. If you keep working, it makes you strong in mind and spirit too *(seishintekini shikkari suru)*.

### Noguchi-san

Noguchi-san was in some respects closer to the norm for Nagasakiya's part-time employees than was Miura-san. She chose Nagasakiya because it was convenient, just fifteen minutes' walk from her house, and had no particular senior figure to whom she was attached. Although she was originally introduced to the company by another friend who was working there part-time and had heard that they needed more staff, this friend had long since ceased working for the store. Her complaints about the company, although more articulate than those of many part-timers, also echoed the general grumbles I frequently heard from other part-timers I worked with.

In her late forties, both Noguchi-san and her husband were born in central Tokyo. They moved to the Koganei district twenty-seven years ago, as this was the home area of Noguchi-san's mother, and they were given some land by her mother on which to build a house. Given that land prices in Koganei have sky-rocketed since then, this makes Noguchi-san nominally fairly well off, but this wealth remains tied up in the Noguchis' property. She described her husband as 'just an ordinary salaryman'.

Noguchi-san started work immediately after graduating from high school, and until she got married she worked as a hairdresser. She gave up work when she got married and rejoined the workforce as a Nagasakiya part-time employee in 1983 when the younger of her two children reached the age of ten. In 1991 she told me that she planned to continue as long as her health was good, and said she liked the work – she felt it suited her, she got on well with her work mates and felt the store had a friendly atmosphere. She made a clear distinction, however, between those employees who were ordinary shop assistants, whether full- or part-time, and the senior managerial staff, from floor manager upwards. She felt the latter had 'no connection' with her (*kankei nai*), a sentiment echoed by most part-timers with whom I spoke.

Her main complaints about working at Nagasakiya centred around the high turnover of staff, particularly female regular employees, and the difference in the treatment accorded regular employees and part-timers. On staff turnover, she said that she wished the management would be more careful in their recruitment of staff and screen out those who were likely to stop soon. Otherwise the long-serving part-timers ended up teaching new staff the job from scratch again and again. She also complained that new regular employees earned more than part-timers who, like herself, had many years' experience. She thought that this was unfair and happened because the part-timers are women, and management think that women only need to earn pocket money as their husbands support them. Noguchi-san disagreed strongly with this way of thinking, saying that the husband's salary is irrelevant.

It was Noguchi-san who told me of the abortive attempt by part-timers to set up their own union within the company as a way of making their voices heard. But she thought there was no chance of doing this, owing to management opposition and the fear that most part-timers had of losing their jobs if they made an issue of it. She said that although most part-timers she knew would like to have a union, probably no-one would talk to me about it because of their fear of the consequences of being known to have pro-union sympathies. This, again, was in sharp contrast to the regular employees, who have their own union fully approved of and supported by the company.

As was generally the case for the married women to whom I spoke, Noguchi-san took sole responsibility for the work of running her own household, doing the cleaning, laundry, and cooking in the evening – she worked at Nagasakiya from 9.45 a.m. to 4.45 p.m. five days a week – and on her days off. When she gets too tired she takes time off work, and sometimes goes on short trips with friends. She also takes one long (by Japanese standards) holiday a year, about five to seven days, in the summer. She has made many friends at Nagasakiya, all part-timers like herself, and she sometimes sees them in her free time. They get together usually just to chat or go shopping. But she also has friends from her neighbourhood and still sees old school friends too. Here, again, Noguchi-san was probably fairly typical of the part-time female workforce, who, unlike most of the female regular employees, have usually lived for a long time in the Tokyo area, and are part of an extensive social network, in which Nagasakiya plays a role, but not necessarily the predominant one.

In 1999, Noguchi-san was still working in Nagasakiya, having now accumulated sixteen years' service with the company. However, unfortunately my brief visit to the company coincided with her holiday, so I was unable to see her again on this occasion.

### Kimura-san

The part-timer I came to know best at Nagasakiya was Kimura-san, who unofficially headed the section in which I worked. She had joined Nagasakiya in 1972, when her children were aged twelve and thirteen, and chose this job because it fitted in with taking care of the children and because she had previously worked in a shop before having children. After nine years with the company she was able to obtain the then newly introduced rank of *teijishain*, a status of part-timer that entitled her to membership of the company union. However, as a part-timer she was never able to obtain any official position of responsibility, despite acting as an unofficial section chief for many years and training several new regular employees who in due course became section chiefs themselves (including Arakawa-san, whose story is given above). Like Noguchi-san, Kimura-san complained of the high turnover of regular female staff, and she was also critical of some of her fellow part-timers who seemed to lack commitment to their work. She placed herself and other long-serving part-timers in a separate category of 'veteran' and took pride in her expertise and knowledge of her work. Although senior male managers in interviews with me frequently referred to retail work as 'basically unskilled', from Kimura-san's point of view her job required both skill and experience. She was often frustrated that her experience and knowledge of the product range she sold was not used by senior management, and felt her views were not listened to.

At the time that I worked in Nagasakiya, Kimura-san was continually anxious over whether she would be able to continue working there, and for how long. She felt that as a part-timer her job was not secure and worried about the sales figures for our section, as she feared that if the section did badly its sales area might be reduced, with a consequent loss of jobs. At fifty-five, she was approaching retirement age, and hoped to be able to continue working for the company until she retired.

When I returned in 1999, I found that Kimura-san had left four years previously, after twenty-three years at the Koganei branch of Nagasakiya, one year short of the retirement age, which had been recently increased from fifty-eight to sixty for part-timers. This departure had, however, been compelled not by the company or its financial problems but by Kimura-san's husband's ill health; already unwell in 1991, his health had subsequently deteriorated, and she had given up work to care for him. She was remembered by all the staff I spoke to, including the senior male managers, and as she continued to live locally I was able to arrange to meet her.

We met at Nagasakiya, in the section where we had previously worked, where I found Kimura-san chatting with the current staff. Adjourning to a local coffee shop, I found Kimura-san relaxed and cheerful, eager to talk about her grandchildren and her new pet bird, and to show me their photographs. She told me that her work at Nagasakiya had become too much for her when her husband was hospitalised, and she found it increasingly difficult to manage her daily shopping and visiting him in hospital (a forty-minute train ride away) after work. She had therefore decided to take early retirement and received a company pension from Nagasakiya. This was smaller than it would have been had she stayed until retirement age, but it still left her better off than many former part-timers who had not paid into this scheme, which was optional for part-time employees. She took evident pride in telling me that the management of the store had tried to persuade her to stay on and had held a big leaving party for her, at which she was given a ring as a leaving present and a large bunch of flowers. She also told me (again with some pride) that by the time she left she had become Nagasakiya's highest-paid part-timer. She added that the sales figures for the section at which we had worked had fallen since her departure, and she had been asked to return, as a 'silver' employee – a position recently created for retired former part-timers (at a lower wage than ordinary part-timers).

Kimura-san's achievements within Nagasakiya were clearly important to her, as was the recognition she felt she had received from the management of the store at the time of her departure, and subsequently in their efforts to encourage her to come back. I asked her how she felt that formal promotion had never been open to her, and she paused and thought, 'At the time I just thought that was normal, although I don't think so now.'

Although Kimura-san's husband recovered, and she no longer needs to care for him, she expressed no desire to return to work. She enjoys her retirement, despite the limited income she and her husband have, and she feels that as long as they have their health that is the most important thing. She now finds time for hobbies – going for walks, caring for her pet bird, making clothes, and making handicraft items out of Japanese paper. She feels that Nagasakiya has gone downhill in recent years, the greetings of staff to customers are no longer as bright and cheerful, and the quality of goods sold has deteriorated. She also feels awkward, as a 'veteran', going shopping there, and thinks seeing her there may make current employees feel uncomfortable and self-conscious. Although she still shops at the (separately managed) basement food section, on the whole for clothes (which occupy most of the rest of the store) she prefers to either make her own or shop elsewhere. However, she still maintains links with a number of the employees there and sometimes meets them socially. She socialises with the women there of a similar generation, both the older part-timers and Ushijima-san, the woman manager mentioned earlier (pp. 135–7), for whom Kimura-san has great respect, saying that she is the top woman in Nagasakiya and could become Nagasakiya's first woman branch manager.

Kimura-san was less complimentary about the younger women employees and commented that the young in Japan now were losing their sense of duty (*gimu*), and thought only of their own rights (*kenri*). According to Kimura-san, even in the changed economic climate of post-bubble Japan, few of the young women employees entering Nagasakiya stayed for long.

## Narratives of maturity: employment and the married woman

A number of common themes run through the above narratives. One is the notion of work as important to well-being, both physical and mental. There is a strong bias against perceived idleness here – even if finances permit. If a woman cannot find a socially approved outside activity to engage her in the time when she is not occupied with household tasks, it is thought proper and healthy for her to go out to work. Thus Arakawa-san explained that she wished to continue to work because she had no interest in studying (an approved alternative for relatively well-off women) and no small children to occupy her. Matsumoto-san invokes medical advice as her reason for re-entering the workforce, and Miura-san repeats the argument put to her by the Chief, 'It's not yet time to take it easy'. Even after retirement age, there is a noticeable emphasis on staying active, perhaps through work (as in the case of Miura-san's aunt) or possibly through some sort of hobby (as for Kimura-san). Other older women at Nagasakiya spoke about the possibility of engaging in some kind of volunteer work after retirement.

It is important to note, though, that these alternatives to paid work are contingent on the woman's financial situation. Kimura-san was at pains to explain that she was able not to work because of the pension scheme she had paid into over the many years at Nagasakiya. However, she also pointed out that many part-time employees are not in as fortunate a position as she is, particularly as many switch jobs frequently and may not pay into any pension scheme. For these women, depending on their husband's work situation – also possibly precarious given the current state of the Japanese economy – and overall family income, there may be little alternative to seeking work after retirement. This is a situation that retail companies such as Nagasakiya have been able to capitalise on by instituting new post-retirement positions at lower pay, subject to satisfactory health checks and management approval.

The view of women's outside work as an appropriate, even laudable, alternative to being a full-time housewife, exists in counterpoint to the widely perceived opposition of husbands to their own wives working. This opposition may derive from social norms concerning the husband's role as 'pillar of the household' and main financial provider, as examined in further detail in Chapter 8, where notions of masculinity require at least a token opposition to one's wife participating in the labour force. That such opposition may be more token than real is suggested by Matsumoto-san's experience, an experience echoed by many of my female acquaintances, who commented, 'of course they (husbands) say they're against our working, but when it comes down to it and they see the extra money coming in, they're glad we're doing it'.

The unspoken bargain here, as in many societies where women work outside the home, is that the husband will tolerate the situation as long as the wife continues to fulfil her role within the home, taking responsibility for all household chores and caring for children. By this bargain the masculinity of the husband and the femininity of the wife are preserved. Successful performance of this dual role is the badge of the mature woman, and it is something that the women I met took pride in rather than complaining about.

Indeed, performing this undoubtedly exhausting balancing act serves as one public marker for women of the possession of a quality much prized in Japan and thought to be an essential part of mature adulthood for both sexes – the ability to endure and persevere – *gaman*. Whereas for men *gaman* may be displayed solely in the workplace, through putting in long hours and taking few holidays, for women *gaman* is displayed in the equally long working days they put in caring for their families and engaging in outside activities. And just as the man is subject to the judgement of his fellows if he fails to leave the company late every night, so are women's daily routines scrutinised and judged by their neighbours.

Early rising, engaging in activities outside the home during the daytime, and returning home to perform shopping and cooking tasks, and awaiting the husband's return in the evening constitute the normative daily routine. Early rising can be gauged by the time at which the bedding is hung outside to air and the laundry to dry. Both these should be done first thing in the morning before going to work. Presence or absence from home in the day time can be assessed by almost any passer-by glancing in the windows, and Kondo records the irritation of her landlady at the disparaging comments of her mother-in-law's friends, who would peer through the window in the daytime and find her 'idle' – engaged perhaps in reading a book (Kondo 1990: 278–9).

To engage in outside work or study for the mature woman thus provides a visible sign of industriousness that raises her status in the eyes of the neighbourhood – provided always that her bedding is still aired at the correct time of day, and that she is otherwise seen to be fulfilling her domestic role.[27] Within this context, women seem almost to vie with one another for endurance points, recounting tales of studying by waking at 4.00 a.m. every morning to study while the rest of the family sleeps, or perhaps 5.00 a.m. to prepare lunch boxes for children and husband before preparing for work herself. Food is bought fresh daily, and ready-made dinners are shunned – as in the example of Matsumoto-san, who still takes pride in preparing a 'proper' dinner for her family, despite the increasingly heavy demands of work, which in 1991 continued until 8.00 p.m. every night.

This quality of *gaman* in the mature adult, whether female or male, is often contrasted with the perceived absence of this ability in young people, and an exposure to *kurō*, suffering, is often said to be a necessary part of the process of maturation. Arakawa-san recounts leaving her Kyushu home for Tokyo and the cramped conditions in the company dormitory as a part of this *kurō*, which she now believes to have disappeared, with correspondingly deleterious effects on the new recruits. Older employees often blame a lack of *gaman* or an inadequate sense of duty (*gimu*) for the high turnover rates among young female employees, a common source of complaint, voiced by both Noguchi-san and Kimura-san in the narratives above. However, it is also noticeable that complaints about the change in the younger generation are a constant across the time period surveyed, as is the nostalgic recall of an earlier era when things were different.

The performance of this balancing act between home and workplace, which wins a woman approbation in the eyes of her neighbourhood and at least acceptance of the situation by her husband and family, also marginalises her from the point of view of the workplace. The domestic demands on female employees tend to be seen as incompatible with taking on a responsible senior position in the company, with the result that the stereotype of the career woman is a single woman living alone. It is significant that Ushijima-san attributed her success at least in part to her single status and that consequently 'my time is my own'. And the reason given by Matsumoto-san for not seeking promotion beyond the rank of section chief was that this would involve accepting transfers, with correspondingly disruptive effects on her domestic life. But perhaps the most telling example here is that of Arakawa-san, who, despite an expressed desire to work, in the end resigned citing as a reason the inability to fulfil her domestic duties and commute to work at Nagasakiya.

Whether or not Arakawa-san actually resigned because other pressures had been brought to bear is, in a sense, irrelevant. The point is that it was an explanation that was instantly accepted, with no apparent surprise among her fellow employees that a woman who had accumulated sixteen years of experience within the company, and was an efficient and well-liked section chief, should give up her job to become a low-paid part-timer in another store. From their point of view, Arakawa-san was following the approved norm in putting her domestic life first, and her planned move to part-time status in another company was appropriate to her age and marital status.[28] By making this move she fulfilled the expectations of Japan's idealised female life-course.

However, it is also evident from these narratives that not everyone follows this idealised life-course, and that much greater commitment may be made to a company by its female employees than the marginalisation of women in the official company discourse suggests. Ushijima-san's case illustrates that it is possible for women to stay single and to develop a career, although the link she makes between her single status and her success in work terms is suggestive of the barriers faced by married women of her generation in Japan.

The case of Watanabe-san, on the other hand, suggests that the idea of women taking responsibility for all domestic duties may be changing in recent years. However, it is noteworthy that Watanabe-san said she would give up work if she had children, so although it may be the case that marriage is no longer a compelling reason to give up the position of regular company employee, for women having children is still seen as incompatible with pursuing employment on the career track in Japanese companies.

Of the other cases considered, Matsumoto-san shows that for women marriage can be combined with a high level of commitment to the company, given a supportive family, whereas the cases of Miura-san and Kimura-san show the dedication and personal loyalty that may be brought to the company even by the low-paid female part-time employees. This divergence from the gendered norms of company–employee relations may also be seen in the narratives of male employees given in Chapter 8, in which, in the mirror image of the narratives given above, dedication to and absorption by the company are often far less than that depicted as the norm for male company employees in Japan.

# 8 Company men and pillars of the household

## Sources of identity

### Introduction

As described in the preceding chapter, employment and the domestic sphere interact in Japanese women's lives in a complex fashion. Although marriage puts pressure on women employees to prioritise the domestic sphere, the Nagasakiya case supports Kondo's (1990) finding that for lower-income women in urban Japan the division between employment and domesticity is rarely clear cut. Indeed, part of the construction of mature womanhood in Japan would seem to be the ability to cope with the demands of both domesticity and activities outside the home, whether this involves paid employment, or, for more well-to-do women, studying, taking up a hobby, or doing voluntary work.

Similarly, for men constructions of masculinity are more complex than the depiction of the Japanese man as a 'salaryman' enveloped by his company would imply. As for women, generation is important, with an analogous period of young independent adulthood between entering the workforce and getting married. And for men too, marriage and ensuing domestic responsibilities constitute an important watershed: indeed, mature manhood is linked with, and dependent on, constructions of the male role within the household.

An important notion here is that of *daikokubashira*,[1] a term literally meaning big black pillar, referring to the main pillar supporting a traditional Japanese house, which at one time would have been blackened with age and smoke from the hearth. However, it also has a secondary meaning, translated into English as breadwinner, referring to the head of the household and his support for the household through his outside economic activity. Without the *daikokubashira*, the house would collapse, and this term very vividly conveys the importance of the (usually male) head of the household to the household. Although this term can be applied to women, it is more usually associated with men, and becoming the *daikokubashira* of one's own household is an index of mature manhood.[2]

The concept of *daikokubashira* also serves to link company and household now that Japan is largely urbanised and most of the male population are employees of one sort or another. It is through his work at the company that a man is able to fulfil his role of *daikokubashira*, and his obligation to fulfil this role gives the company an important hold over him that is absent in the case of a female employee. An employee of a large company is a more desirable husband and son-in-law than an employee of a small company, and certainly more desirable than a casual labourer, and hence there is a good deal of pressure on young men to find such employment at least by the time they enter their mid- to late twenties and are approaching marriageable age. The free part-time worker (*furiita*) phenomenon commented on in Chapter 3 is therefore characteristic of young unmarried men, with a shift to more secure employment evident as men approach the age of marriage. This pattern is reinforced by the peculiarities of the Japanese labour market, which favours far greater mobility among young men than their older counterparts (Tabata 1998: 209).

The apparent envelopment of mature men by their companies in Japan is therefore, ironically, a phenomenon very much contingent on notions of mature masculinity as defined by the role in the household, with salaryman and *daikokubashira* being logically paired concepts. As is the case for women, the quality of *gaman* is important, but for the man this is manifested by the ability to endure long hours of hard work outside the home. Male company employees in Japan are internationally famous for the long hours they work at the office, and Kondo (1990) recounts how the male artisans in the company where she worked would put in twenty-two-hour days during busy periods (Kondo 1990: 244). However, at the same time, one aspect of these feats of endurance is the ability to be an effective support to the household, which, according to survey data, most Japanese men prioritise above the company for which they work (Rōdōshō 1987 cited in Tabata 1998: 211).

However, this ideal normative destiny for the mature man of becoming a hard-working company employee and thereby an effective pillar of the household is cross-cut by quite a different discourse on masculinity, as manifested in Japanese popular culture. Images of the salaryman's life in Japanese comic books and films tend to be quite negative, portraying a world of servile sycophantic juniors, time-servers, and tyrannical superiors. In so far as there are heroes in this genre, their appeal tends to be in the way they subvert the formal system for their own ends. One example is the popular manga character Section Chief Shima Kosaku, an upwardly mobile and highly manipulative section chief who wins praise from his superiors for his loyalty and dedication to the company while the reader is made aware that his main interests in life are winning promotion and seducing as many women as possible. In a volume published in the early 1990s Shima himself reflects that 'I don't have any particular loyalty to the company.'[3]

As far as the domestic side of the salaryman's life is concerned, the father of the family too is often portrayed in a less than sympathetic light, often a target for the bullying of wife and children in an inversion of the supposedly normative role of the father in the household. In one such portrayal, the comedy film *Crazy Family*, directed by Ishii Sogo, the father eventually asserts himself by attempting to murder his wife and children, a drastic solution to which, the viewer is led to feel, he has been driven by their impossible demands.

The figure of salaryman and father thus is often portrayed as more victim and figure of fun than role model. Heroic masculinity tends to be cast in a different mould. Even in comic books that glorify the ideals of *gaman* and dedication to work, the protagonists are often not company employees but artisans, who perfect their skill through a long and arduous apprenticeship. Examples include carpenters, sushi makers, and even in one story, thieves. Here, Kondo's account of constructions of masculinity among the artisans with whom she worked becomes relevant:

> A full-fledged artisan is also a full-fledged *man*: able to make a living by his arm or technique, tough and able to withstand long hours and deprivation, in stereotype and sometimes in actuality a strong silent type, the embodiment of one sort of masculinity … a mature artisan is a man who, in crafting fine objects, crafts a finer self.
>
> (Kondo 1990: 241)

The artisan may thus be closer than the salaryman to an ideal of Japanese masculinity, but at the same time falls outside the elite of the Japanese workforce. The social hierarchy and cultural constructions of masculinity cross-cut and pull in opposite directions.

Nor is it only the ideal of the male as a company employee that is undermined in Japanese popular culture: the notions of the male as a harmonious member of the group and a pillar of the household are also called into question. In stark contrast to company discourse on harmonious group relations, the male heroes of Japanese comics, popular literature, and film are often loners, rejecting both group affiliation and domesticity, true only to some higher goal (such as retribution for wrongdoing, a popular theme in period dramas) and perhaps one or two select male friends. This type of male hero has been identified as an archetype of masculinity in manga (Schodt 1983) and in film (Barrett 1989) and *anime* (Standish 1998), as well as in more general discussions of popular culture (see, for example, Buruma 1984).

In period dramas, one example of this type of male hero may be found in the popular saga set in the Tokugawa era of the assassin Baian, who features both in short stories and in a television drama. Baian is publicly an acupuncturist and a doctor, but he also works as an assassin in secret. His only close friend is a man, also a hired assassin, and he treats women with a contempt that, we are told, stems from his hatred of his mother, who left home when he was a small child, taking his sister with her but leaving Baian behind. In one of the early Baian stories he ends up murdering his long-lost sister, only later discovering her identity. Baian, however, feels no remorse, and the reader is made to feel that, promiscuous and treacherous like her mother, the sister richly deserved her fate (Ikenami 1991). The Baian story is particularly interesting in that it counterposes a pure and honourable masculinity with a corrupt and polluted femininity. This tension finds its expression in a male violence that is, in a number of Baian stories, directed against women.[4]

A more recent example of the unattached male as hero is the popularity of the *furiita* (free temporary worker) as a character in television dramas in the early 1990s. The favourite television drama of the young Nagasakiya employees, *'kono yo no hate'*, referred to in Chapter 7, featured one such man as its main character. This particular archetype runs in direct opposition to the role of salaryman: the *furiita* rejects the notion of attachment to a single company as an infringement of his freedom and independence. The *furiita* is also the inverse of the ideal represented by the *daikokubashira*; in television dramas at least, he rarely has his own apartment and appears unable and unwilling to support a family. The *furiita* is thus depicted as turning his back on domestic ties, remaining a romantic loner, heir to a long tradition of similar male characters in Japanese popular culture.

It has been argued that these apparent challenges contained in Japanese popular culture to the *status quo* of Japanese society are mere safety valves in an oppressive culture (Buruma 1984). It can also be argued that one should be wary of giving these alternative discourses of masculinity too much weight since those who produce these images – comic book illustrators and writers, film producers, writers of popular novels – are themselves outsiders to the elite company system, artisans of a kind who might be expected to glorify alternatives to the salaryman. However, it seems that in narratives of life-course produced by mature Japanese men there is a recurring sense of inner conflict between these competing discourses of masculinity: material and social success as represented by the elite track of becoming a large company employee; the responsibilities to home and family encapsulated by the notion of *daikokubashira*; and the personal, idiosyncratic, pure masculinity represented by the loner who refuses normative social values. Often it seems that this conflict is expressed in life histories full of what ifs and might have beens, where the compromise of self is enforced by the transition at marriage, at which point romantic ideals of masculinity are abandoned and the unglamorous roles of company employee and father become inescapable. The very centrality of the company in the masculine life-course becomes for many a matter of apprehension or regret, with more or less secret dreams of escape and independence far from uncommon.[5]

In the changed economic climate of the late 1990s, these themes of inner conflict and regret have become even more marked among the older male employees, as they face seismic changes in company organisation and, often, the premature curtailment of their career. At the same time, the role of *furiita* has become more entrenched as more companies in Japan cut back on hiring and more young men take up this kind of casual work.[6] Although the percentage of young men opting for this type of employment still appears relatively small – only just over 11 per cent of men were non-regular employees in 1996 compared with over 30 per cent of women (Japan Institute of Labour

1998a: 27) – the role of *furiita* had, by the turn of the century, become well established. The business sections of bookshops abounded with advice manuals for *furiita* and part-time workers, with titles such as 'What no-one ever taught you: manual for tasty *furiita* and part-time work' (Nakamura 1998). And in popular culture, *furiita* continued to provide heroes for film and television drama. For example, one of the most popular Japanese television dramas of 1999, *Gift*, has as its main character a man who has lost his memory and now works as a messenger, a job that has become the archetypal trendy occupation for the young *furiita*. In many ways, this character is an extreme example of the archetypal loner. Without memory, he is rootless and lacking in family ties, and his job involves minimal interaction with others. At the same time, the quality that makes him a good messenger is his persistence, his ability to deliver the most unwelcome of packages to the most unwilling of recipients. In this way, he personifies the admired quality of *ganbaru* (trying one's best), but in a transformed social context.

The following narratives give some concrete examples of the workings of these themes in individual lives. Although most of the material presented here was gathered during the prosperous era of the early 1990s, the seeds of later trends such as the increasing importance of the *furiita* as an alternative pattern of employment for young men are already visible here. As far as possible, the subsequent fate of these employees in the recession is also indicated, and the effect of the recession on male employees within Nagasakiya is discussed in more detail in the concluding section of the chapter.

## Work and the young man

### *Chida-san: the furiita*

Chida-san, in terms of job status one of Nagasakiya's floating pool of temporary staff, joined the Koganei branch shortly before my fieldwork ended, in 1991. Cheerful, and energetic he worked long hours (usually around forty-eight hours a week) and seemed at ease in the workplace, rapidly taking on a range of tasks from which (at that time)[7] temporary staff were usually excluded, such as helping out behind the cash register. Talking to him, I discovered that he had been employed by another nearby branch of Nagasakiya that had recently closed. He had worked in the other branch for one and a half years, that is since shortly after graduating from high school, and he had no immediate plans to leave the company, thus prompting me to ask him why he had opted for non-regular employee status. He replied that:

> I didn't want to become a regular employee, so I didn't join in the recruitment drive at high school. I don't like being tied down, and if you're a regular employee there are so many rules you have to follow. I like the freedom of being a temp *(arubaito)* – when I want to take time off I take it – and it doesn't make much difference to the salary.

There used to be lots of people like me at my old branch, but there aren't many here. What happened to the rest of them? Well, some of them moved to other branches, some stopped working for Nagasakiya. We had a choice – either transfer to another branch or one month's severance pay.

I worked with my father for a while after I graduated – he has a sales business. I'm the eldest son, and I live alone with my father. My parents are separated – my mother took the other children and I stayed with my father. But I like working with electrical goods. I like sales too, but I prefer electrical goods. In my last branch I worked in the electrical goods section, that's why I took the job there. I hope I can move to that section in this branch. Now I'm working in haberdashery, which has nothing to do with electrical goods, but never mind. If I can't change sections here, I may try my ex-floor manager – he's moved to the Fusa branch, and he may be able to find me a place there.

You know in Akihabara, (Tokyo's main electrical goods shopping area) everyone is an *arubaito* like me, there aren't any salarymen. You have to be really good there – the competition is tough, and the strong eat the weak. But that's all part of capitalism, isn't it? I would have liked to work there, but it's too far to travel.

For Chida-san, there was no real incentive to become a full company member. He did not lose out financially, as his monthly earnings, although calculated on an hourly rate, were generally on a par with the wage received by new male entrants. Of course, he did not receive the benefits on offer to regular employees, most notably the subsidised dormitory accommodation, and he was not eligible either for promotion or for regular pay increases. However, as an eldest son living with his father, the former was unnecessary and the latter irrelevant, as he stood to inherit his father's business in due course. For this reason, too, the job security offered by regular employee status was not important to him. Working as a temporary employee represented an ideal stop-gap solution.

Chida-san's remarks exuded a mild contempt for those who chose the salaryman route, stressing instead the virtues of being an *arubaito*, both for the freedom this conferred and for the fact that in the absence of guaranteed job security one's job depended on how good one was. He therefore showed a pride in '*arubaito* culture' not, perhaps, far removed from the feelings of those who, like his father, opted out of the salaryman scenario and started their own businesses. Although Chida-san's family circumstances made *arubaito* status a particularly attractive option, a number of other young male *arubaito* in the company took a similar view, and several older male regular employees who had also worked as *arubaito* for a time seemed to look back on this period of their lives with nostalgia. For many of them, as will be explored further in the narratives which follow, their time as *arubaito* was a period of relative freedom to follow their own aspirations before marriage forced a transition to the more constricted world of the regular employee. Predictably, by 1999 Chida-san had left Nagasakiya, as had all the temporary staff who had been there in 1991. He was not remembered by any of the current staff, and no-one could tell me what had become of him.

### Kobayashi-san: the regular employee

Kobayashi-san was very unlike Chida-san in a number of respects. A twenty-five-year-old English literature university graduate, he was generally very quiet and withdrawn, except when drunk, when he revealed an unsuspected sense of humour and a generally well-concealed ability to speak English. Although as a male university graduate he was being groomed for managerial rank, he showed no obvious aptitude or enthusiasm for the practice managerial tasks allotted to him, and he was a source of concern and irritation to his floor manager, as described in Chapter 5.

Kobayashi-san was a native of Tokyo but lived in the company dormitory in preference to his family home. He explained that he was the youngest of three brothers, the other two of whom were married, and that his mother was dead. His eldest brother together with his wife and four children lived with Kobayashi-san's father (a salaryman), and the other brother lived separately. Kobayashi-san said that he had had to leave home to make room for his elder brother's family. It is not common in Japan for siblings of the household heir to remain long in the same house after adulthood, and I imagine there may well also have been some tension in the household arising from the fact that the mistress of the house, responsible for the feeding and general care of its members, was no longer Kobayashi-san's mother but his brother's wife.[8]

Kobayashi-san said that he had chosen Nagasakiya because it was located near his family home and had a good dormitory, and because he had thought it would not be too demanding (*hima sō datta kara*).[9] He aimed to become manager in due course if he stayed with Nagasakiya, but he was considering leaving as he was concerned about the store's economic difficulties. He speculated optimistically about the prospects of the chain being taken over by a competitor who might offer better working conditions and a brighter future.

About the job itself, Kobayashi-san commented that it was not particularly interesting, but it was easy, and he had no problems in getting on with the other staff. His social life remained firmly centred outside the store, with most of his friends coming from the nearby area in which he had grown up.

Despite his lack of enthusiasm for the company, in 1999 Kobayashi-san was still a Nagasakiya employee, although now transferred to head office and working in the company's health insurance section. As far as I was able to discover, all the young male regular employees who had worked in the Koganei branch of the store in the early 1990s remained with the company at the end of the decade but had been transferred either to managerial positions in other branches or to head office. For these employees, many of whom were now married with children, Nagasakiya had fulfilled the implicit promise of long-term job security made to its core male employees. The experience of their older colleagues, however, was somewhat different, as explored in the next section.

## Company men? Middle-aged middle managers at Nagasakiya

### The Chief

One of the most forthcoming of the managers at the Koganei branch was the general office manager, a genial and very popular man who was aged forty-eight at the time I began my fieldwork. Referred to and addressed by all the employees simply as 'Chief', he had apparently limitless energy and good humour, amusing himself by running the wrong way up the down escalators before the store opened in the morning and complaining about the discomfort of having to wear a tie in hot weather, arguing that this was a most inappropriate European cultural import given the high humidity of a Tokyo summer. He would boom out greetings to me every time we met, varying the language used between English, French, and Japanese, and he often engaged me in conversation on the subject of Mrs Thatcher, for whom he had a deep admiration. He gained promotion and a transfer to head office shortly after I left, and the affection in which he was held by the other employees was evidenced by a very well-attended leaving party held at the store and various other drinking venues thereafter.

The chief was born in 1943, in Tokyo, and was evacuated to Okayama prefecture to escape from the war-time bombing. In 1950 he returned to live in the family home in Tokyo, which had fortunately escaped being destroyed by the fire bombing. The second son and last of four children, he described his childhood as 'ordinary'. His father worked as a salaryman, and the family must have been reasonably well-off, for the Chief attended a private high school and then went on to take two degrees at Waseda, one of Japan's most prestigious private universities. He initially studied mechanical engineering, and although he did not enjoy it persisted until graduation then re-entered to take a degree in economics.

By the time he completed his second degree he had decided he wanted to be a journalist, but he failed in his attempt to get a job on a newspaper and joined a petroleum company instead. However, he lasted just two years there before having an argument with a senior and walking out, unfortunately for him shortly before he was due to marry. His parents-in-law refused to let the marriage go ahead unless he found another job, so he took the first thing he could find, which happened to be Nagasakiya. At that point he said he felt he did not care where he worked, '*doko demo ii*', anywhere would do. In fact, he said he thought this move had turned out well, as he liked the 'sticky' (friendly, close)[10] atmosphere of Nagasakiya and felt that it suited his personality.

Asked about the future, when I interviewed him in 1991, he said that he would still like to be a journalist and felt this would suit his independent, self-centred (*wagamama*) personality. He expressed uneasiness about the future of Nagasakiya; he hoped its current position would improve, and said he would be sad if it were to be taken over, but he thought this was a possibility as Daiei had recently acquired a large number of Nagasakiya shares. If there were to be a takeover, lay-offs would be inevitable in the Chief's view, so he hoped that Nagasakiya could at least hold out for a merger. But he hastened to add that these matters were well outside his control, and he did not really know much about the company's strategy in this respect – such questions are left to top management.

The Chief had very firm views on Japanese companies and Japanese culture, and at this point veered off into more general concerns, effectively taking over the interview until it was curtailed by an unexpected power cut that plunged the whole store into darkness. He traced the distinctive nature of Japanese company relations to the feudal era via the wartime kamikaze, and suggested that the same loyalty once addressed by a Japanese man to his lord, or to the emperor during the war, was now directed at the company by some people. As far as the different roles of men and women were concerned he made a distinction between the generations, grouping the over forties together as *kaisha ningen* – company people – and saying that for his generation the norm was for the man to go out to work while the wife stays at home and looks after the children. For the under thirties, in his view, such clear gender distinctions no longer applied.

He expressed contempt for what he described as imported American ideas – freedom and independence – saying that these notions were not really understood by the Japanese and were only paid lip-service to as a result of American influence and pressure. He said he thought it would take the Japanese another hundred years to really assimilate these notions. In any case, he saw the practical implications of freedom as being largely negative; pointing at the US, he said that freedom just resulted in a society where people have to carry guns to protect themselves, and where poverty is endemic. He thought that instead of being so preoccupied with freedom the US would do better to tackle the poverty in their country by using taxation to redistribute income and raise the level of the poor.

It seemed to me that the Chief's statements were riven with contradictions, particularly where his personal conduct and motives for joining Nagasakiya were juxtaposed with his idealised image of the kamikaze salaryman. Again, on personality, his description of himself as independent and self-centred contrasted sharply with his condemnation of the idea of independence as an alien US import and his stated preference for a company with a 'sticky' atmosphere. On gender differences too, it was striking to me that the same man who had persuaded Miura-san (one of the women described in Chapter 7) to work for the company on the grounds that it was not yet time to take it easy should state so unequivocally that for women of his generation their proper place was in the home looking after their children. Perhaps something of my feelings showed on my face, because the Chief ended the interview with a brief lecture on the relative merits of different cultures' ways of thought.

You know, WASP thinking is not the only way of looking at the world. Here in Japan, the influence of Buddhism is very strong, the idea that everyone can become a Buddha after death. You Europeans have a very black and white way of thinking, but things are not so clear cut to us, because of the influence of Buddhism. So you should try to understand the other person, don't always think you are 100 per cent right. I would like foreigners to understand Japan, but I am not sure Nagasakiya is a good example ...

Eight years later, on my return visit to Nagasakiya, I learned that in the course of the company's restructuring the Chief had been transferred to a subsidiary of Nagasakiya a few years previously, where he was the number two. He had then taken early retirement, leaving the company a few months before my visit, at the age of fifty-six. At the time of my visit, he had enrolled in a gardening school near his home in Omiya, a suburb of Tokyo. We were able to arrange to meet one evening after his school had finished and went out for a meal.

He seemed quite unchanged, still as energetic and talkative as ever, full of ideas and plans for the future. In general, he was reluctant to talk much about Nagasakiya and his experience of restructuring. He grimaced when asked about the subsidiary he had been transferred to, and said it was already in the red when he joined, and that his time there had been difficult *(taihen)*. His comments nearly a decade previously about being a company man notwithstanding, he seemed to have few regrets at having retired early. He explained, 'You go to the company every day like this (miming holding onto a strap in the train), then you do overtime, then you come home again ... it's not much fun *(tsumaranai ne)*.' And on adjusting to his new life outside the company, 'I always tried to keep those two things separate, the company and me, save a part for me *(jibun)*.' Like all those employees who took early retirement from Nagasakiya, the Chief received a generous retirement package and did not seem to be suffering unduly financially, although he commented that to retire at this age did cause some problems, as there were no jobs for men of his age in Japan. Also, he still had loans to pay off, and a child in the second year of high school who he had to finish putting through education. Regarding lifetime employment he was now dismissive, simply saying that it no longer existed in Japan, and that looking at what happened to men of his generation younger employees could no longer believe in it.

However, he was emphatic that he did not see his situation, or that of his contemporaries also facing an early end to their careers, as being especially deserving of sympathy.

Yes, you can say we have problems, but it's nothing if you compare it to what some people have to endure. What about disabled people? What about if I were blind? Then I couldn't see the face of the person I love. Even if I wanted to go to Tokyo Tower, get on the bus, I wouldn't know which bus to get on, I'd have to ask someone. It would be terrible. I'm OK.

So far, the Chief seemed to be enjoying his retirement. He had already travelled around northern Japan since stopping work, and, when he had completed his gardening course, he planned a trip around western Japan to visit famous sites associated with the war 'against the Americans'. After that, he was vague about what he wanted to do, but said that once he had met his financial obligations he wanted to give something back to society, although he did not yet know how. He thought he might like to do something to help people in Vietnam, who, he felt, had suffered terribly 'mainly because of the Americans'. If he could, he would like to do something directly, but if not he would give money:

Even 10,000¥, it's not much for us, but it's a lot over there. If I give 10,000¥ a month, over a year it's 120,000¥, then if I do that every year it will mount up to quite a lot.

For much of our conversation, the Chief talked animatedly of international politics, cultural and religious differences between Japan and 'the West', the deleterious influence of America on Japan in the post-war era, and his (mostly negative) perception of the changes in post-war Japan. He returned frequently to the topic of the kamikaze pilots, and asked rhetorically if they had given their lives for the Japan we see today. He concluded our meeting by presenting me with a book on the kamikaze pilots as a parting gift. He opened it to show me some photos of young men in uniform. 'They all died. I don't know if you can read this or not, but if you can …'

### Yamaguchi-san

In terms of personality, Yamaguchi-san, a floor manager at the Koganei branch, and also a mid-career recruit, could not have been more different from the Chief. A gentle, soft-spoken man in his early forties in 1991, he was always smiling and had a great fondness for children, taking charge of my small daughter on company trips, carrying her around and soothing her to sleep while his male colleagues drank beer.

Although he was the eldest son in his family, Yamaguchi-san lived with his mother-in-law (his father-in-law was dead), his wife, and their sixteen-year-old daughter. His own mother was dead, and his father lived with his older sister – living with a daughter rather than with the eldest son is unconventional in terms of the norm of eldest son succession to the household in post-Meiji Japan but has become an increasingly common pattern in recent years. Yamaguchi-san went to a fairly high-ranking private university, where he studied politics, economics, and the media. On graduating in 1972, he joined a company, Hoya garasu, making spectacles and for a time thought of setting up his own company as an oculist. It was at this time that many discount spectacle shops were starting up, however, and the competition for small businesses in this field was intense. A friend of his tried to start up his own business but went bankrupt, so Yamaguchi-san decided instead to join a small spectacle shop in Yokohama as an employee.

During his four years at Hoya garasu, Yamaguchi-san married a young woman he had known from his high-school days, and their daughter was born in 1975. He remembers the period as an employee at the small shop in Yokohama, from 1976 to 1980, as a happy time, since his daughter was a small child, and he was able to find plenty of time to play with her and take her out. He attributes the good relationship he has with her now to the time they spent together when she was small. However, after four years at the Yokohama shop, Yamaguchi-san decided that he had better join a more stable company where his future prospects would be secure (by this time he was thirty, an age after which changing companies becomes increasingly difficult in Japan). Not many large companies at that time were accepting mid-career recruits, so, like the Chief, he did not so much choose Nagasakiya as end up there through lack of other options. However, he did express a preference for working in retail both because he enjoys the customer contact and because for retail employees time off is taken during the week, not on Saturday and Sunday. Yamaguchi-san explained that all public places in Japan are impossibly crowded during the weekend, and having time off during the week enabled him to take his daughter out without having to fight the crowds.

Evidently, for Yamaguchi-san family considerations have been important throughout his life in constraining his choices relating to work. Like the Chief, his entry to Nagasakiya was largely constrained by family pressures – one factor that encouraged him to seek more secure employment was that both of his parents-in-law and his wife had become ill. Medical treatment can be expensive in Japan, and the kind of backup that large company welfare schemes can give in this situation was probably an incentive for him to move, though he did not give this as a reason. He did explain to me, however, that family considerations were the reason that, unusually for a male employee, he opted to take the status of zone employee, thus opting out of transfers outside a specified geographical area, and putting himself on a promotion ladder that stops at the rank of floor manager. Yamaguchi-san simply said that his family could not be moved, and he did not wish to leave his family.

Yamaguchi-san enjoyed his work at Nagasakiya, he liked sales and in 1991 his main hope for the future was stability, rather than promotion. He was willing to accept moves within the company, as long as he could remain in the same area of western Tokyo. He found Nagasakiya an exceptionally friendly company, and he also enjoyed the contact with customers. His leisure time was divided between Nagasakiya-linked socialising or *tsukiai*,[11] non-Nagasakiya friends and family. He practised the Japanese martial arts of judo and aikido once a week on one of his two days off, and his fellow practitioners formed one circle of friends, with the other being old high-school friends, a group that includes his wife. His daughter was, at that time, a focal point in his life, and he would often engage me in conversations about child-rearing and education.

In the restructuring of Nagasakiya in the mid-1990s, Yamaguchi-san was transferred to one of Nagasakiya's subsidiary retail outlets in a branch in another part of western Tokyo. As of 1999, he remained an employee within the Nagasakiya group, broadly defined, but in the periphery rather than the core of the group's operations. However, with Nagasakiya having been placed in the hands of the receivers in February 2000, there must be a question mark over the fate of those like Yamaguchi-san employed by subsidiary companies – prime candidates for any sell off aimed at rationalising what remains of the Nagasakiya group.

### Kohama-san

Kohama-san, the branch manager at Koganei at the time I joined, had, until the restructuring of Nagasakiya in the mid-1990s, a career more in keeping with ideal norms for Japanese male company employees than either the Chief or Yamaguchi-san. Originally from north-eastern Japan, he joined Nagasakiya immediately after graduating, and the only unusual feature here was that he was a graduate of a junior college, not a four-year university, as is usual with male recruits.

Kohama-san was also able to offer positive reasons for his choice of Nagasakiya. Although most of his college friends went to banks or other companies in the financial sector, such work did not appeal to Kohama-san, who said he preferred sales to office work as he wanted to do something where one could see immediate results from one's efforts. In Nagasakiya, such results could be obtained in two senses: sales targets give the employee a ready measure of his achievements, and at the time he joined the company (around 1970), it was a relatively high-ranking company within the chain store sector, and prospects for the company to expand and for the individual to achieve promotion within it looked good.

For Kohama-san, employment at Nagasakiya initially seemed to fulfil this early promise. He achieved promotion rapidly, attaining the rank of floor manager in just five years, and that of deputy branch manager three years after that, while still in his twenties. A mere thirteen years after joining the company he reached the rank of branch manager, the first of his intake to reach this level (most of them had still not achieved the rank of branch manager seven years later). Barely into his forties, Kohama-san was both younger and had a lower level of education than most of his male subordinates at managerial level.

Kohama-san was eager to make himself appear friendly and accessible, and to de-emphasise differentials of rank, saying that Japan's strength was the ability of employees to co-operate, and that even a young female employee at the bottom of the store hierarchy could speak freely to him.[12] He also stressed the importance of socialising after hours, and said that in post-war Japan differentials of rank could be forgotten in this non-work context. In this sense, he felt that Japanese society had changed from the more status conscious pre-war period. He characterised Nagasakiya as the most 'democratic' and 'free' of the large chain stores.

Kohama-san did not talk much about his family, which consisted of his wife and two children. He had been transferred many times in the course of his career at Nagasakiya, and until his posting to the Koganei branch his family had followed him wherever he went. On this occasion, however, it had not been convenient for them to do so, and Kohama-san therefore lived alone in a company-owned apartment a short walk from the store. As his wife and children lived in another suburb of Tokyo he was able to visit them on days off. When asked how he felt about his frequent moves, he did not mention family considerations as a problem, but said that the most difficult thing about moving was dealing with the different dialects and customs that exist in different parts of Japan.

In the event, Kohama-san's and my period of employment at the Koganei branch coincided closely, with Kohama-san joining and leaving a few months earlier than I did. As I had been his protégée at the branch, he came to say goodbye to me personally in the section where I worked, and to offer to introduce me to the branch manager who would be taking over from him when he left. I asked him if he would be sorry to go, and he said that he would, as he felt he had only just started to settle down at the Koganei branch, and one year was really too short. He also said that the transfer had come as a surprise to him, and in fact there was no job for him to go to. His current post had been given to the branch manager of a neighbouring branch that had to close, and he had been named as branch manager of a projected future branch that would open in around a year's time. But for the moment, there was no work for him to do. I suggested that this was a perfect opportunity for him to take some leisure time with his family, but he demurred, looking less than happy about the situation.

Although Kohama-san was given a well-staged leaving party, arranged to do double duty as a farewell to him and a welcome to the new branch manager, attending the Chief's party subsequently made me realise that Kohama-san's party had been rather lacking in warmth. And at a subsequent company social event where I ran into him, I found him for the most part standing alone with his drink, being deliberately avoided by his former subordinates at the Nagasakiya branch, who instead clustered around the new branch manager. On this occasion, Kohama-san complained to me that his current position as branch manager without a branch, and without named employees, left him utterly bereft of a social network.

Kohama-san's position was made more difficult by the fact that he had spent most of his working life up to his transfer to Koganei in western Japan, and therefore he had few personal contacts among staff in the Tokyo area. And, having graduated from a junior college, unlike most male employees, who tended to be university graduates, he was excluded from the various old-boy networks within the company. In retrospect, I realised that even when he had been branch manager at Koganei, it had often been difficult for him to personally order that something be done when co-operation from employees at head office or at other branches was involved, instead having to ask his subordinates to use their connections on his behalf. In a sense, then, Kohama-san provides an example of the vulnerability of even a male employee of a large company who apparently does everything by the book, works hard, and achieves promotion. Without a personal network that is highly contingent on, for example, the university attended and having a long enough posting somewhere to establish social bonds as well as formal ties of superior–subordinate, a male Japanese company employee may find himself in a very isolated position.

Kohama-san did not survive the restructuring of Nagasakiya and took early retirement from the company at the beginning of 1999. In contrast to the Chief, who remained in touch with managers at Koganei, and was easy to contact through the company, those I spoke to were vague about what had become of Kohama-san, and my attempts to contact him came to nothing.

## Overview: male employment in times of change

What do these narratives tell us about the employment experiences of men at a large company in Japan? The first point to make is the variation in attitudes to work and the company depending on age. These narratives suggest that for younger men, both in the 1970s, when the older generation of managers joined the workforce, and in the early 1990s, employment was not necessarily viewed as a lifetime commitment, the then current ideologies notwithstanding. For men in their twenties, especially in times of economic prosperity, a degree of employment mobility has long been noted in Japan (see, for example, Clark 1979: 150–4). In the narratives above, we can see an approach to employment characterised by both flexibility and a high degree of pragmatism: Kobayashi-san feared for the future of the company in 1991, and he hoped either to leave of his own accord or for the company to be taken over in order to secure his own future. Chida-san, in an account that appears in opposition to most popular images of the male employee in Japan, chose to work as a temporary employee, using the company as a source of income and experience, before his projected move into his father's small independent business. This narrative finds an echo in other stories from senior managers at Nagasakiya (including some not quoted here) whose careers led them in the opposite direction, from temporary employees, or employees in small businesses elsewhere to regular employees at Nagasakiya.

The accounts of the Chief and Yamaguchi-san also point to the importance marriage and family considerations play in the life-courses of many men, with employment at a large company often seen as a necessary sacrifice that has to be made in order to get married or to ensure the security of one's household. These were themes echoed by many of the older male employees, both mid-career recruits and those who joined straight from university. For many of Nagasakiya's male employees, working for Nagasakiya was seen as something to be made the best of, often less a career choice than a compromise, making do with what was available.

This leads to what should, perhaps, be a fairly obvious point, but one which has been neglected in analyses of Japanese companies: the importance of business fluctuations in company life and the relationship between company and employee. On the one hand, when Nagasakiya was growing, it provided a haven for mid-career recruits who wished for the apparent security of income and employment offered by a large company. At that time, many male mid-career recruits joining the company were guided by the lack of other comparable opportunities in Japan's relatively inflexible labour market rather than any particularly positive feelings for the company itself. And for new graduates joining during this period, an important factor was that as a company that was expanding, Nagasakiya appeared to offer relatively good prospects for rapid promotion.

As Nagasakiya went into decline, however, a more complex mix of motivations became evident for joining, or remaining with, the company. For new recruits, such as Kobayashi-san, choosing to join Nagasakiya seems often to have been influenced by the same sort of pragmatic factors that were important for new female recruits, attractive dormitory accommodation again features as an important reason, whereas other male recruits of Kobayashi-san's generation cited factors such as not being able to get in to their first choice of company or  the more attractive working conditions and less stringent sales targets in Nagasakiya in comparison with its competitors.

A survey conducted by the company union in 1991 found that only a little over a third of the male employees of Nagasakiya felt glad that they had joined the company, whereas just over a quarter professed an active dislike for the company – a figure that rose to nearly 45 per cent of the twenty-five to twenty-nine age group. By the late 1990s, after the restructuring of the company, many of the male managers to whom I spoke had become still more negative in their evaluation of Nagasakiya. In August of 1999, an atmosphere of gloom prevailed after the announcement that summer bonuses had been cancelled owing to the company's financial difficulties, and one manager remarked tersely, 'It's hard for those who have left, but it's also hard for those of us who remain.'

One store manager recalled his own changing feelings about work at Nagasakiya. In 1969, when he graduated from university, he had decided that he wanted to work in a chain store – principally because one of his teachers at university advised him that this was a growth area in retail. At that time, the leading chain stores were Nagasakiya and Daiei. Of the two, Nagasakiya appealed to him more as Daiei's business focused on food, an aspect of retail in which he was not particularly interested. Talking to me in 1999, he reflected on the results of this decision, made in the teeth of parental opposition – his father had wanted him to enter the civil service, a career which he saw as offering greater stability.

> Up to about ten years ago I would have said it had all worked out really well for me. Then, over the last ten years we've had all this restructuring, lots of things have happened, and it's been really hard, at work, and in my life, and for my family too it's been extremely hard. But I think this difficult period will last maybe another year or two, and then things will improve. Basically, I chose this job myself, of my own free will, so I will stick with it. Those are my principles.
>
> For the future? I would like to continue with work that suits me, like now, as branch manager, I'll take it one day at a time, one month at a time, one year at a time, and just do my best. I've been with this company for thirty years, I'm fifty-five now. So I've got five more years until I reach retirement age – all I can do is take it one day at a time.

For an employee such as this store manager, now in his fifties, there are few options, as other companies are unlikely to hire a man of this age. The 1991 company union survey showed a marked difference in the future career plans of male employees depending on age, with over a third of employees under thirty expressing the wish to leave the company for another job or to start their own business, in the future, as against only a quarter of those aged thirty to thirty-four, 12 per cent of those aged thirty-five to forty-two, and less than 10 per cent of those aged forty-three or over. As pointed out above, mobility is easier for younger men in Japan, owing to the relative lack of mid-career employment opportunities, and it is more common for the young to express the desire to move than it is for their elders, who may feel they have little choice; nearly a quarter of all male employees at Nagasakiya questioned in 1991 about their future job plans answered that they had no choice but to continue working for the company, and it seems likely that this percentage was higher in the older age group.

For the older men already in 1991, and even more so in 1999, the main question was whether or not they would be able to retain their existing jobs. Kohama-san appears above as an early casualty of economic pressures on the company – and also illustrates the importance of strong personal networks in safeguarding one's position within the company. Another manager, who had already experienced redundancy from a chain store that was taken over twenty years previously said in 1991 that his ambition was simply to continue as he was. He added, 'now most people will say this, but before they would have been hoping for promotion.' Sadly, this manager was another casualty of the restructuring programme.

As the economic situation in Japan as a whole worsened in the 1990s, and Nagasakiya went into deeper crisis, the young men with whom I worked in 1991 also found that their options had narrowed. Most companies at this time cut back on recruitment, and opportunities for mobility for mid-term recruits were curtailed. Men who in their twenties had thought of leaving found themselves in their thirties still with the company and now with young families to support. All the young men I had known at the Koganei branch in 1991 remained with the company in 1999. It seems likely that for this age group Japan's economic crisis had decreased their potential mobility, although it should also be borne in mind that their own increasing age would also have this effect, as job mobility has long been lower for men in their thirties than for men in their twenties.

At the same time, Nagasakiya, increasingly desperate to cut costs, sought to divest itself of its most expensive employees, the older male managers. By the time I returned in 1999, most of the older male managers I had known had either left the company entirely or had been transferred to a subsidiary company. From the older men's point of view, the lifetime employment system they had assumed would offer them security until retirement was, at the least, under threat, and some, such as the Chief, cited above, stated that in their view the system no longer existed.

Among the older men who remained in the company, there was some disappointment at the way in which things had turned out for them personally, combined with a feeling that the changes taking place were unavoidable, caused by events beyond Nagasakiya's control. A senior manager at head office commented:

> In my personal opinion, lifetime employment is about loyalty to the company, a feeling of unity within the company, I think it's a really good system. Now that system of support within the company is at a crossroads. This isn't just for us, it's the whole Japanese economy ... There's a feeling that we would like to keep this system, it's the basis of the Japanese company, but if business conditions are not favourable we can't put it into practice ... I think it will revive when the situation stabilises.
>
> The situation at the moment is extremely hard. For my generation in Japan, we gave the best years of our youth working for the company for low wages. In return, as we got older we expected we wouldn't have to work so hard, but our wages would increase. I am fifty-three now, I worked hard for low wages when I was young, and now just as I thought I could start taking it easy a bit, lifetime employment disappears.
>
> But for young people now, maybe it's good lifetime employment has gone. They can get a salary in proportion to the effort they put in.

Discussing the changes in Nagasakiya during the 1990s, the older managers all seemed to agree that being a company man was a thing of the past, something that differentiated their generation from those that followed.

Changes in Nagasakiya were related to broader changes, both in the Japanese economy and in general mores and attitudes to work. But there was also perhaps a tendency to romanticise the past and to exaggerate their own generation's degree of identification with the company. As illustrated by the narratives of the Chief and Yamaguchi-san, the role of work and the company, even in the lives of the older generation of Japanese men, is a complex one, and personal inclinations, ambitions and family situation all affected the choices men made in their working lives for their generation as for the present one, within the ever-changing context of wider economic constraints and opportunities.

Already in 1999, senior managers looked back on 1991 with nostalgia, as a golden age of the company. It is beyond doubt that the problems of Nagasakiya had worsened considerably in the interim, with dramatic effects on the lives of older male employees in particular. However, as the material presented above shows, in 1991 there was already widespread discontent and anxiety about the future among male employees. The picture of the utterly dedicated company man in the Nagasakiya case appears here primarily as an image evoked by the older generation as a source of identity and a protest against changes in the company system.

## Conclusion: gender, maturity, and work – the Nagasakiya case

Taking as a whole the narratives in this chapter and in Chapter 5, it would seem that there is a great deal of overlap in the ways in which employee–company relations are constructed for both men and women in the early period of adulthood that precedes marriage. For both, Nagasakiya offered adult status, a way to leave home and live independently, and a salary that empowered them as a new generation of urbanised consumers.

Within this frame, long-term commitment is expected of men, but not of women, leading some men who do not wish to make such a commitment or to accept the constraints imposed by company membership to opt instead for the role of temporary employee, or *arubaito*, while working full-time at the company. For women, who are not considered as committed to the company in any event, and who would not be able to leave home without the dormitory accommodation offered by the company, *arubaito* status has few attractions, and I did not meet any female *arubaito* except for the floating student population while I was working at Nagasakiya.

For both men and women, marriage appears to be a watershed, marking the transition to a second stage of adulthood in which obligations to others, both in the domestic sphere and in the workplace, become more emphasised. From this juncture, for women life becomes notionally centred on the household, and for men on the workplace. However, neither is as completely enveloped by their gendered spheres as the common opposition in publications on Japan of salaryman to full-time housewife[13] would suggest. Just as married working women cannot be entirely defined with reference to the household, the company cannot be assumed to be the all-enveloping focus of the Japanese male employee's life. Official company discourse notwithstanding, to a large extent the man's work outside the home serves to validate him as *daikokubashira* and mature male, and it is this, rather than loyalty to or love of the company, that serves to bind him to his employer. And although discourse on company life directed at outsiders may stress company loyalty and harmony (as in the Chief's explanation of 'the Japanese company'), other forms of discourse such as personal histories, or responses to an internal company survey not intended for outside eyes, reveal other, more personal, agendas and frustrations, for men as well as for women.

# 9   Rethinking the Japanese company

Returning to the issues raised at the beginning of this book: what are the broader implications of the Nagasakiya case for the study of Japanese companies as a whole? The first point to be made here is that the idea of 'the Japanese company' itself needs to be problematised. Although there is a general idealised notion of a distinctive Japanese employment system to which companies in Japan, and particularly large companies, have aspired, this is only one of a number of discourses available to companies as they seek to present a distinctive image of themselves. Companies have also been influenced by prevailing trends in youth culture, and more broadly by the tension between a work-and-save ethic widely seen as conservative, and more recent pressures in Japan to emphasise consumption and leisure.

This tension may be particularly evident in retail companies, where work and consumption are inextricably linked. In encouraging young employees to be active consumers and to value their 'private time', the company may also hope to garner valuable information about current consumer trends. So, in Nagasakiya, at the same time as young employees were encouraged to look for their own 'sense of style', and window shopping in other stores constituted a prime leisure activity for the new recruits to the regular workforce, the knowledge and expertise thus gained could be redirected to the benefit of Nagasakiya. Shopping and 'private time' can thus also become an extension of work and commitment to the company, as was highlighted in the recruitment brochures of 1999. At the same time, this revaluing of leisure and consumption could be, and often was, invoked as a critique of the 'company men' or *kaisha ningen* of an earlier generation.

Agency is also important here. Companies have themselves, in Japan as elsewhere, become products that are repackaged and marketed to their customers, business partners, and potential recruits with the help of specialist corporate identity consultants. The decision to promote a certain kind of company image in a particular way is thus one taken in consultation with specialists from outside the company who may seek to create a new corporate image to appeal to certain target audiences. Hence the responsiveness of corporate recruitment brochures to youth culture, but hence, also, the disjunction with the more conservative discourse generated in other contexts, such as the company entrance ceremony, by senior company managers. In the late twentieth and early twenty-first century, the creation of corporate identity has become a complex process in which a number of competing voices can be heard.

Another important factor to consider is that of the changing Japanese economy. As recession becomes prolonged, and more companies succumb to bankruptcy or takeovers by other (sometimes non-Japanese) firms, aspects of the Japanese employment system such as lifetime employment and seniority-based pay come increasingly under scrutiny. Features once vaunted as lying at the base of Japan's economic success are now open to criticism as expensive and inefficient – although the evidence suggests that retaining, or restoring, long-term employment for a section of the workforce remains an ideal for many companies. These broader economic trends may further undermine the idea of the 'company man' in favour of promoting a more varied and flexible workforce. In this regard it is worth quoting a recent report by the Ministry of Labour which suggests that young people in Japan are beginning to attach more importance to selecting an occupation rather than selecting a particular company, 'the mindset of young workers is shifting away from "joining a company" to "taking a job" (Ministry of Labour 1998b: 53). At the same time, as has already been noted, the number of young people taking part-time and temporary work is rising, and some kinds of temporary work, such as that of messenger, have become fashionable.

On the other hand, owing to the recession there is now an imbalance between those seeking long-term employment with a large company and the shrinking number of jobs available. This in turn means that companies are in a position to ask more of their new recruits than they were a decade previously, thus possibly encouraging a revival of more conservative discourses of company–employee relations, as can be seen in the changes in the Nagasakiya recruitment brochures at the beginning and end of the 1990s.

Against this background, at the moment it is hard to predict which of the various competing discourses of company–employee relations will become dominant in the years to come. The Nagasakiya case is at least suggestive of the range available, and the complex ways in which different kinds of images of the company may be evoked in different situations.

What, then, of the idea of the company as community? One way to assess the relevance of this concept is to look more closely at the boundaries demarcating companies. In the retail sector, the most visible boundary is that between the employees who work as sales assistants and their customers. This boundary is marked by dress, with female sales assistants in large stores wearing uniforms (male sales assistants wear suits and ties); language, in the formal greetings and polite language that must be used to customers; and demeanour, in the correct bows, smiles, and bodily postures taught to all employees. It also has its own symbols, e.g. the corporate logo and badge worn by employees, the notebook, containing the company song and a note pad, which is distributed to all employees; the company song, motto, and mission statement are all known by employees, but not by customers. In addition, it is marked by a variable set of events with a strong ritual aspect, such as the morning meetings and other meetings organised by the company.

It is, however, a permeable boundary. The same individuals move back and forth between the roles of employee and customer, marking the transition with appropriate shifts of dress and language. This ambiguity in the roles of employee–customer was used by Nagaskiya to expand the knowledge base of the company and in events such as the special luxury goods sales or *chōbikai*, where employees past and present switched to the role of customer for a day, and also, hopefully, brought along their friends. Links across the customer–employee boundary in this context and in the daily life of the store were intrinsic to the company business – as in all retail or service sector companies.

Another sort of boundary is that between Nagasakiya and its rivals within the chain store sector. Nakane (1970) famously argued that in Japan the vertical structure of companies means that people doing similar jobs for different companies have no ties with one another, whereas people doing different jobs in the same company are closely linked. In the Nagasakiya case, however, as is common for retailers in Japan, many of the part-time employees had previous experience working for one of Nagasakiya's competitors, and indeed this experience was one reason why they continued to seek jobs in retail. Conversely, it was common to leave Nagasakiya for a job in another large store that offered better conditions. There are thus a number of factors linking part-time shop assistants regardless of the company for which they work, and again the boundary between Nagasakiya and its rivals appears very permeable. However, this boundary is more likely to be crossed by certain kinds of employees, that is the part-timers (or regular female employees who resign from regular status and seek re-employment as a part-timer in another store). As far as male regular employees were concerned, although I did come across instances of managers who had changed companies (as outlined in Chapter 8) only one of these had previously worked in another retailer, and even in this case it was not one of the large chain stores that were Nagasakiya's principal competitors.

From an outside point of view, however, there was an appearance of corporate unity at Nagasakiya that masked the divisions apparent to anyone who worked there. The common uniform (for women), or shared dress code (for men), language, and the other symbols of employee status tended to obscure differences among the different statuses of employee – except in the case of the *arubaito*, who were marked out as different by the aprons they wore over their regular clothes. The main available means for differentiating among staff for the customer were therefore generation and gender, but other more subtle distinctions remained invisible.

In a manner reminiscent of Cohen's comments, cited in Chapter 1, that the same community will appear very different from different sides of the community boundary (Cohen 1985: 75), there were many more complex divisions and tensions within Nagasakiya when looked at from an employee's perspective than when looking at the company from a customer's perspective. Employment status, length of service, gender, and generation all played a role, with different criteria of ranking often cross-cutting each other, especially within the female workforce. Within this complex picture, different boundaries within the company marked off different categories of employee. One of the most important of these internal boundaries was that between regular staff on the one hand and part-time and temporary staff on the other. As described in Chapter 6, this boundary was marked in the organisation of many of the company meetings and events, with different meetings organised for different categories of employee. At the same time, there were further divisions within each category: divisions of gender within the category of regular employee, divisions between part-timers and *arubaito* within the category of non-regular employee, and the more nebulous and largely unformalised division between veteran part-timers and those part-timers who were just passing through. Within what may appear as a single corporate community from the outside, then, united by a shared symbolic code, there were numerous smaller groupings.

Among these groupings, a hierarchy can be seen in which the apex is occupied by the male regular staff. These employees were destined for future managerial roles, and might, until recent events, look forward to continuing with the company from graduation until retirement age. In this, Nagasakiya seemed to conform closely to the ideal norms for large Japanese companies in general. I also found that male employees tended to provide the official voice of the company. For any general queries about the company, even long-serving, very experienced female staff would tend to suggest that I asked a male manager, who would be assumed to have the requisite knowledge and expertise to answer my questions. Senior male staff were thus constituted as experts and guardians of the officialised company discourse.[1] It is no surprise then that this discourse tended to reflect a somewhat conservative and male-gendered perspective, which conflicted in some interesting ways with the viewpoints of female employees, as well as with those of younger regular staff both male and female.

One notable instance of such a conflict was in the view of the role of the company during a woman's life-course. The official account given by male managers was that women regular staff would work until they got married or had children and would then stop work to become housewives. Part-time female staff constituted a floating element of the workforce. For them, work was a secondary consideration to family responsibilities, and the income derived from such work was assumed to be supplementary to the main family income. All female staff were seen as doing work that required little skill and were hence replaceable. A high turnover of female staff and a short length of service was not seen as a particular problem; indeed, in some ways it was desirable for regular female staff not to stay too long as they received wage increases related to length of service. New, younger, female staff, or alternatively part-time staff, were seen as just as effective in the workplace, and they had the advantage of being considerably cheaper. As far as the notion of corporate community was concerned, it appeared, from this perspective, to be limited to the male regular staff; these were the staff members who, in the words of one of the male managers, 'ate from the same rice pot',[2] and whose future prospects depended on the company.

Listening to the women employees, however, a different picture emerged. For the younger women, Nagasakiya was frequently seen as a springboard to other things, not necessarily marriage, but also possibly a different job, travel, pursuit of leisure interests, or more training. Entering the company was a gateway to adulthood, but in the sense of an interlude of young, single, independent adulthood, before undertaking the responsibilities and restrictions of marriage. Some indication of this may be gleaned from the narratives in Chapter 7 and also from the company union survey. This showed that although around 28 per cent of female employees intended to stop work if they got married or when they had children, another 17 per cent said they did not intend to get married immediately but wanted to leave the company anyway. Presumably many of these planned to go on to other things. A further 19 per cent of regular women employees stated that they wanted to continue working for Nagasakiya long term. A majority of these, however, were over the age of thirty-five, whereas only around 3 per cent of the under twenty-fives chose this option. This may be indicative of the ways in which women employees' agendas change over time, as is suggested by the cases of Watanabe-san and Ushijima-san described in Chapter 7.

Turning to the part-timers, the depiction of these women as a floating element of the workforce is misleading. A significant proportion of the part-timers at Nagasakiya were long-serving employees – the 'veterans'. In 1991 the company union survey showed that of the part-timers affiliated to the union as *teijishain*, nearly half had over ten years' service with the company. These long-serving part-time staff took a different view from that of the male managers in their evaluation of the skills necessary to be an effective sales assistant and in their view of the importance of retaining female staff. They were critical of the high turnover of female regular staff in part because this created a burden in terms of training. From their point of view, the departure of such a staff member meant the loss of valuable knowledge and skills. This stands in contrast with the view of senior male managers that a minimal level of knowledge and skill was necessary in order to do a sales assistant's job.

This difference in perspective is understandable in the context of the different career paths of male and female employees. For male staff, a career in Nagasakiya meant frequent rotations and experience of a range of work, including liasing with buyers, departments that produced own-brand goods, and other centralised work done from head office. Typically, an initial period as sales assistant in one of the branches would lead on to one of the more centralised jobs or a managerial role in a branch. In this context, being a sales assistant was seen as relatively low-level work.

For women, on the other hand, whether part-time or regular staff, unless appointed to a position in one of the branch offices or at head office, their entire career at Nagasakiya would be that of sales assistant. The long-serving women developed an in-depth knowledge of their product range and of the mechanics of running their section in which they took pride. From their point of view, this was a skilled and demanding job, and training other women to do it represented a considerable investment of time and energy.

A number of the long-serving women, including part-time staff, developed considerable dedication to their job, and they expected similar dedication from other women with whom they worked. Given the practice of assessing work performance by section, there was always pressure from co-workers to do one's best to achieve sales targets and to complete allotted tasks, even if this might mean difficulties in juggling work and family commitments. Taking family holidays at inconvenient times from the store's point of view, although condoned by male managers who did not expect female employees to prioritise work over family, might well be resented by female co-workers, as can be seen in the tensions between Kimura-san and Morinaga-san described in Chapter 5. The income from working at Nagasakiya was also vital to the household budgets of many of the female part-timers, who were unhappy at the widespread view of part-timers as working for pocket-money (and also complained of their low wages).

Viewed in this way, it is problematic to depict female employees, and more especially female part-timers, as peripheral and temporary employees, and male staff as permanent core employees, constituting the real corporate community. From the perspective of head office, men stand at the centre of the corporate group; from the perspective of everyday work in the branches the majority of work is organised and carried out by women, some of whom have worked in that branch for far longer than their male superiors. And, as described in Chapter 8, for men as well as for women, career paths and the role of the company in their lives were often more complicated than the idealised images of gender roles in Japanese companies suggest.

Moreover, since the recession, the position of senior male managers has been precarious in Nagasakiya, with many of them forced out to subsidiary companies or into early retirement. In contrast, the numbers of low-paid female part-timers have increased, and the age until which they can continue working has been raised. Increasingly, the female part-timers have become an indispensable part of the workforce, and one in which long-term commitment is no longer exceptional. Core and periphery in Nagasakiya at least, and probably more widely in the retail sector, have become shifting and relative concepts, which do not correspond neatly to gender divisions.

How far this may presage wider changes in the Japanese corporate sphere, it is at present hard to pass judgement. The retail sector is a special case in that it has long had a high proportion of female employees and of part-timers. The ways in which restructuring has affected employment patterns in this sector are not necessarily, therefore, a good predictor of what will happen in other parts of the economy. But the case of Nagasakiya does suggest that it is worth reassessing some of the widely made assumptions about the divisions between regular and part-time, male and female employees in Japan, and their relations with each other and with the company for which they work.

The view of the company as community is also in need of reassessment. The Nagasakiya case suggests that the view of the Japanese company as a bounded entity, with a clear distinction between outside and inside, is at best limited, and largely irrelevant to the retail sector. Rather, in the retail sector boundaries are contingent, permeable, and constantly shifting. Also, in the Nagasakiya case, the company did not mean the same thing for all its members, and for those who did not plan to stay for long the idea of company as community may have limited significance.

However, the ideal of the corporate community remained important, at least in some contexts, albeit vague in terms of precisely whom it encompassed. The importance of teamwork and co-operation among employees was frequently emphasised by Nagasakiya management, and older employees in particular often evoked nostalgic images of community in their accounts of a past Nagasakiya. It was striking that these accounts tended to be located in the past and contrasted with current attitudes, particularly among young employees. This seemed to be a constant theme from 1991 to 1999; by 1999 the early 1990s, when I had worked in Nagasakiya, had become embellished by a patina of nostalgia and was regarded as a golden age when young employees were still plentiful and lifetime employment was not yet under threat. Although Nagasakiya's bleak prospects in 1999 justify this view to some degree, my recollection is that 1991 did not appear to be a golden age at the time, and there was just as much nostalgia then for earlier times, although then on the basis that in a less comfortable era employees had really been close and learned to co-operate with each other.

Nostalgia aside, though, it seemed that in the Nagasakiya case, the ideal of corporate community did have some practical benefits for the employees, at least temporarily, as Nagasakiya's problems worsened and restructuring accelerated. According to the managers to whom I spoke in 1999, although the company had begun to close and sell off unprofitable branches, it had pursued this policy in consultation with the company union and in such a way as to minimise job losses. The majority of stores closed had been in areas where another branch of Nagasakiya was nearby, and staff could be offered jobs at the neighbouring branch. This was particularly important for female regular staff, who were recruited on a branch basis, and might not be prepared to relocate to a distant area. As for the male regular staff, the majority of whom were on national contracts, they could simply be reassigned anywhere in Japan if necessary. In this reallocation of staff, part-timers too were offered alternative employment at neighbouring branches where possible. This seems indicative of the extension of the company-as-community boundaries to include at least some of the part-time workforce, although it may also have reflected a more general move to increase the number of part-time employees in the company while cutting back on recruitment of regular employees, especially women.

The overall effect of these policies was that surviving branches were sometimes temporarily very overstaffed (although this tended to sort itself out through natural wastage over time) – as I witnessed during my fieldwork when the branch for which I worked absorbed a large number of employees from a neighbouring branch. In addition, the company's reluctance to close branches where there were no other branches nearby to which employees could be transferred meant that the rationalisation of unprofitable branches was slow. In February 2000, as the press speculated over the apparent impending collapse of the Nagasakiya group, executives of potential buyers of Nagasakiya's core chain store business commented that many of the branches were unprofitable and hence would not make an attractive purchase. In addition, it seems from comments made to me by senior managers that the company's huge debts had been exacerbated by the generous early retirement packages with which it pensioned off a large number of its ageing male managers.

To a great extent then, the decisions of Nagasakiya's executives during the period of restructuring seem to have been guided by a sense of responsibility to care for the company employees, reflecting the ideal of company as community, even where the policies adopted did not appear to be in the company's best interests financially in the short term. The calculation was presumably that in the long term the company would recover and rebuild; large Japanese companies have historically tended to maintain some degree of overstaffing during lean periods, which has helped to provide a base for renewed growth when times improve. Sadly, however, at the time of writing, it appears this calculation has failed, and the future of all Nagasakiya employees must now be in doubt. It is too soon to tell how the ideal of company as community will fare in the wider context, but the Nagasakiya case perhaps indicates the resiliency of the ideal as well as some of the ambiguities and tensions that may exist in practice within the workforce of an apparently unified corporate community.

# Notes

## 1 The changing face of the Japanese company

1 'Corporatism' in Japanese is *kaishashugi*, from *kaisha*, meaning company, and *shugi*, meaning -ism. This is a rather neat play on words, as it is also an inversion of the Japanese word for socialism, *shakaishugi*.
2 The influence of Foucault (1972, 1980) is also acknowledged in Kondo's discussion of 'discursive strategies' and the 'play of power' in the deployment and contestation of idioms such as the company as family (Kondo 1990: 161; 212).
3 That is, *honne* is supposed to be about how things 'really' are, but in practice the interaction between *honne* and *tatemae* is a subtle one, and, as in any culture, how things 'really are' is a relative concept.
4 See Bourdieu (1977) on officialised discourse.
5 In government statistics the term large company is generally applied to companies with more than 1,000 employees.
6 See Japan Institute of Labour (1998a: 26).

## 2 Nagasakiya and the retail sector in Japan

1 The department stores derive a large proportion of their income (up to one-third, according to Creighton 1991) from the twice-yearly gift giving in Japan that takes place in summer and at the new year, *ochūgen* and *oseibo*. Gifts given at these seasons are to people to whom one is socially indebted – for example teachers, corporate superiors, or, for small businesses, their connections in larger corporations who have brought them work over the previous year. Many of these gifts are therefore corporate purchases or destined for people with whom the giver has some sort of business connection. The items given are fairly standard and usually of practical value – gift boxes of beer are one of the most popular items for men, and women often receive boxes of brand-name soap. But as, if not more, important than the item given is the wrapping in which it is presented (see Hendry 1993) with the most desirable wrapping being the instantly recognisable paper of one of the department stores.
2 See Ueno 1998 for a more detailed examination of the Seibu group.
3 See Chapter 4 for a detailed account of the training given to new full-time staff at Nagasakiya.
4 This is not unique to Japanese retail – large numbers of part-timers are also employed by the UK's leading retailers. However, there are certain special features in the way in which the workforce is divided into different employment statuses (not always closely linked to working hours) in Japanese retail, as explored in greater detail (pp. 20–2).

5 According to the owner of one large store to whom I spoke, the consent of small retailers was sometimes eventually obtained through bribery, but he assured me this had not been the case for his store!

6 This contrasts with the situation in the UK, where small retailers often welcome the opening of a large store in their area on the grounds that it will attract custom to the area. Part of the explanation for this lies in the different structure of retail in the UK, where chains of small speciality shops (e.g. chemists, clothing, shoes) grouped together in a high street or shopping centre tend to dominate. As these are chains, they can offer low prices that department stores cannot usually undercut. Such independently owned stores as do exist in the UK are usually small niche businesses that are not in direct competition with either the UK chain stores or the department stores. In contrast, in Japan the large retail units can, and do, compete successfully for the same custom as many of the small independent shop owners. That said, opposition to the opening of a new large store in Japan is to some extent selective, with the fiercest opposition coming from those independent businesses that are most directly threatened.

7 See for example Larke (1994).

8 The provision of parking facilities has become important with increasingly widespread car ownership and with the congested conditions and very limited parking spaces available both in city centres and in most suburbs.

9 Defined in this survey as 'those whose scheduled working hours per day are shorter or whose ordinary working days per week are less than those of regular workers' (Japan Institute of Labour 1998a: 26).

10 The percentage of the part-time workforce employed in wholesale and retail has remained at around the 40–45 per cent range since 1975, with 1994 and 1996 showing a slight increase.

11 Figures calculated from statistics in Japan Chain Stores Association 1998: 34–5.

12 This pattern is also described by Clark in his account of a medium-sized manufacturing company. Clark tells us that the shift to recruiting new graduates was partly in order to cut the wage bill by employing more young men who could be paid low wages, but more importantly,

> School recruiting was a customary practice among companies of Marumaru's size, and in adopting it Marumaru was declaring its newly gained position in Japanese industry. Moreover, now that Marumaru was substantial enough to have its own company way of life' (*shafū*), it was best to recruit young people without experience elsewhere which might prejudice their receptiveness to what they were told at Marumaru.
>
> (Clark 1979: 156)

13 Lam (1992) cites a 1981 Ministry of Labour survey showing that nearly three-quarters of firms hiring university graduates only recruited male university graduates, and another 1983 survey showing that very few women university graduates work in large enterprises – 18.7 per cent compared with 60.5 per cent of male university graduates (Kawashima, 1983, cited in Lam 1992: 52).

14 The way in which life-course expectations for women in Japan are constructed is explored further in Chapter 7.

15 A (Japanese) management perspective on this issue is given by Takeuchi (1982).

16 Despite its name, it has no connection with the city of Nagasaki in Kyushu – the name of the store was taken from the name of the futon shop owned by the founder's parents.

17 Until 1989 food sales were handled by a subsidiary company.

18 Company figures show 5,518 full-time employees for 1982, but only 3,329 for 1987.

19  Anonymous surveys were carried out by the Nagasakiya company union every five years about its membership, with the aim of assessing work and company consciousness. As these were restricted to union members, most part-time staff were excluded from the survey, although one sub-category of part-timer was admitted to the union shortly before I began my fieldwork, and therefore featured in the results for the 1991 survey. The discontent reflected in the 1986 survey therefore reflects the views of the regular staff at Nagasakiya at that time.

20  See Appendix 1.

21  This is probably an underestimation as it does not include the temporary staff, who work on short-term contracts.

22  1999 figures from Japan Chain Store Association, 1991 figures from Nagasakiya.

23  This situation is fairly typical of male employees of large companies in Japan.

24  An example of one man who chose this option is discussed in Chapter 8.

25  From 1948 to 1963 both male and female recruits with only a middle-school or high-school education were accepted. In 1964, graduation from university (for men) and from high school (for women) became a minimum requirement.

26  It was at this time that the chain began to sell food. This is a type of business for which less highly educated male staff are targeted than for other sections of the store.

27  Female enrolment in four-year universities increased markedly during the 1990s in Japan but still lags behind that of men. In 1997 43.4 per cent of men went on to a four-year university compared with 26 per cent of women (Asahi Shinbun 1998: 248).

28  Nursery provision is not universal in Japan, and nursery places must be applied for in advance. Compared with Western European countries, nursery provision in Japan is more extensive than some, such as the UK, but does not reach the level of near universal provision that exists in, for example, France.

29  In several cases I came across, it was common knowledge among a group of friends that one of their number intended to quit as soon as possible, with in one case a new recruit planning from the outset to spend only one year at Nagasakiya. However, this kind of information was usually withheld from the management of the company, as it was known that such plans would be disapproved of, or might even lead to the new recruit's job offer being withdrawn. In addition, when young women did leave they often gave false reasons for doing so.

30  Quoted in Wakisaka (1997: 147).

31  Pachinko is a popular slot machine game resembling pinball.

32  Fire risks were always a sensitive subject with Nagasakiya after a serious fire in one of their branches resulted in several fatalities.

## 3  Recruitment

1  See Naganawa (1999) for a detailed explanation of this system.

2  By 1990, only 35.2 per cent of high-school graduates were entering the labour market compared with 60.4 per cent in 1965, and 44.6 per cent in 1975 (Japan Institute of Labour 1998a: 19).

3  These jobs were increasingly filled by illegal foreign workers (Oka 1994).

4  For example, the ratio in Hokkaido was 0.59 in 1989, and for Kyushu (despite the urbanisation of the northern part– Kita Kyushu city and Fukuoka) 0.80, with Tohoku not faring much better at 1.08. In contrast, the ratio in North Kanto for the same year was 2.10, and for South Kanto 1.49 (JETRO 1991: 119).

5  The importance accorded this strategy by employers is evidenced by 1991 figures for housing starts, showing an overall slump of 20 per cent in June over the same

month in 1990, but for the same period an increase of almost 50 per cent in the construction of company housing for employees.

6 'Key money' refers to a non-returnable payment by the tenant on first renting the flat. It is usually equivalent to one or two months' rent.

7 Some landlords insist on this, and prohibit the use of the cheaper oil-fired heaters on the grounds of fire risk.

8 For example, Seibu, a department store that is particularly good at playing the image game, was rated top among the large stores in a recent league table of good companies to join produced by the *Nikkei Shinbun*, Japan's economic journal. (*Nikkei Business* 1989: 20) However, the same store did not even make the top ten in terms of sales in 1990 (Ryūtsū Keizai no Tebiki 1991: 390–1).

9 One example was the popular series, *kono yo no hate*, described in more detail in Chapter 7.

10 There are echoes here of a wider preoccupation in Japan with 'internationalisation'. *Kokusaika*, the Japanese word meaning internationalisation, is a buzz word that crops up in most current writing on Japanese society, replacing the once fashionable *kindaika* (modernisation) (Goodman 1990).

11 The data presented here are taken from briefing materials used by a firm of corporate identity consultants.

12 Foreign loan words are widely used by the younger generation in Japan.

13 This is an approximate translation, which preserves the feel of the original. However, a number of the words used are interesting because of their range of meaning and could be translated in different ways, for example *kosei* is translated here as personality, but could also be translated as individuality. The original Japanese is: *Hitori hitori kosei ga chigau. Dakara, jibunrashisa tte taisetsu nanda to omou. Fasshon ni jibunrashisa o ikasu yōnu shigoto mo jibunrashiku shitai yo ne.*

14 It is noteworthy here that the term used was *shain*, i.e. regular employees, given the tensions existing between young regular employees and the part-timer staff.

15 In the brochure the term *puraibēto taimu*, from the English private time, was used.

16 Here the Nagasakiya brochure echoes the film director imagery used by a rival chain store group, Seiyu, in the same year. In Seiyu's case, the imagery was used as a reference to the group's activities in producing films, a feature that helped Seiyu to be more successful than many of its rivals in the retail sector at attracting new recruits in the early 1990s. A recruitment officer in Seiyu commented to me that many of these recruits joined Seiyu primarily in the hope of joining the film department, although a majority of these ended up in sales, and many, disappointed, subsequently left.

17 The food section of Nagasakiya dates only from 1989.

18 The English term is used in the original.

19 I would surmise that this was aimed at male recruits, as I saw no evidence during my return visit in 1999 to suggest that promotion beyond a very junior level was any more of a possibility for the average female recruit in 1999 than it had been in 1991.

20 Interestingly, the word '*yume*', dream, is not used in the interviews with male employees, who instead talk about what they want to do in the future, giving a much more concrete, planned, feel to their statements.

21 The word used here was *amae*, indicating a passive dependency, expecting indulgence from others. *Amae* has been much discussed in the literature on Japan – see, for example, Doi (1973).

22 The word *amae* is again used here: *Amae o furikita.*

23 There is an extensive literature on notions of the self in Japan, see, for example, Moeran (1984b), Rosenberger (1992), Hendry (1992), Lebra (1992a).

24  School cliques: this refers to the practice of some companies of recruiting via an old-boy network linking current employees with prospective recruits attending the same university. For reasons discussed above, Nagasakiya had difficulty attracting university recruits of a consistent calibre as the labour shortage began to bite, and they may have made a virtue of necessity in vaunting the absence of *gakubatsu* in Nagasakiya in the company's recruitment seminars.

## 4  Member of Nagasakiya, member of society: company entrance and narratives of adulthood

1  This is the line taken by official Japanese government publications, e.g. Nakamura (1988) as well as by most independent commentators, e.g. Dore and Sako (1989).

2  Rohlen does note in his account of training at the bank in western Japan that a considerable part of the training programme was devoted to the transmission of technical skills. His contention is not that such transmission is unimportant, but rather that induction training also has a significance that goes beyond the question of skill acquisition.

3  Some extra training programmes, usually lasting not more than one hour, were offered to part-time staff at the store. However, such courses took place very irregularly, and most staff began work with little formal instruction beyond a short introductory video.

4  Drinking is illegal until the age of twenty in Japan, although everybody, company superiors included, tends to turn a blind eye as far as eighteen- to twenty-year-olds are concerned, as long as they do not get too out of control.

5  As well as the written text of rules on appearance, the textbooks show pictures of what a Nagasakiya employee should look like, with detailed annotations. These pictures were prominently displayed in all the classrooms of the training centre.

6  *Yada* is an all-purpose word for something one dislikes/does not want to do, used a lot by children and adolescent girls.

7  Although the importance attached to senior–junior relations in Japan is well documented, the link between classmates at school, that is pupils in the same year, is also stressed and even given its own special term, *dōkyūsei*.

8  Formal gift-wrapping in Japan is described in detail by Hendry (1993).

9  In Japan, blood type is thought to be related to personality, and asking about blood type is a popular ice-breaker when trying to get to know someone, much as asking about one's star sign might be in Britain.

10  This may be an oblique reference to a Japanese proverb: *ishi no ue ni mo sannen*, literally on a stone three years, meaning that if you put up with something for long enough, you can derive benefit from it.

11  The seating plan was decided by the company. Segregation by gender is not unusual in Japan, nor is the practice of 'men first'. In my daughter's kindergarten in Japan, whenever the children were all gathered together in the main hall they lined up beforehand in their classrooms with all the boys going in first, ahead of the girls in their class.

12  1991 in the Western calendar.

13  The following section of the speech is a reconstruction of the founder's words made with the help of my own notes and those of another new recruit. It was not possible to take a verbatim account, as I was not able to use a tape recorder during the ceremony.

14  The term chain store is used in Japanese as a foreign loan word, so by no means all people know the meaning of chain. The president therefore translated chain into Japanese *(kusari)* for the benefit of his audience.

15 Originally, masterless samurai. Now used to denote someone who has failed university entrance and is studying to re-sit it.

16 As for the president's speech, the following is a reconstruction of the speech from my own notes and those of another new recruit.

17 The word used was a compound of Nagasakiya and *jin*, the word for person, people.

18 Here, he is referring to the notebooks that were distributed to us on arrival. Pages 4–7 of the notebook were left blank, with instructions to use them to take notes on the managing director's speech, and page 3 was reserved for notes about the president's speech.

19 The notion of *gimu* has been widely stressed as central to the Japanese value system in literature about Japan, notably by Benedict (1946). It is, however, an unpopular word with younger Japanese people, who see it as old fashioned.

20 The words used in Japanese were *kokoro no junbi*; literally, preparation of the heart, although, as discussed in Chapter 4, *kokoro* is also commonly used to mean mind and spirit.

21 In Japanese, *jibun o shitsukeru no wa jibun de aru*. The use of the term *shitsukeru* is interesting here, as it is a key word in the discourse of child-rearing in Japan. It cannot be readily translated by any single word in English, as it expresses the notion of moulding the child's character to make it into a social being but without the negative connotations of the English term 'discipline'. For a detailed discussion of this notion, see Hendry (1986: 11–14).

22 Salaries on entry vary according to the recruit's educational level – university or high-school graduate.

23 Reading manga is a common pastime in Japan among both children and adults, and one can often observe businessmen on their way to work absorbed in a comic book. For the managing director of a large company in Japan to talk about his favourite manga, or comic book, is therefore less incongruous than it would be in England, but it is nevertheless an astute touch in so far as manga are firmly part of popular, youth culture, and claiming to be a manga reader de-emphasises the distance between the middle-aged managing director, who is also a graduate of the university of Tokyo, and his audience, composed in the main of eighteen-year-old high-school graduates.

24 This word was used in English in his speech.

25 This case will be explored in more detail in Chapter 7.

26 See, for example, Hendry (1986: 140) for a description of an entrance ceremony to a Japanese pre-school.

27 This was not the case for all recruits: Nagasakiya has an extensive network spreading throughout Japan, and some recruits applied to join branches to which they could commute from their parental home.

28 The importance for young Japanese people of acquiring certain types of consumer goods and of acquiring up-to-date information on what is, and is not, fashionable among their contemporaries is explored by White (1993).

## 5 Harmony and consensus? Employee relations in the workplace

1 As with so much else in the store, the organisation of daily work in Nagasakiya changed considerably with the restructuring of the 1990s, and the consequent reduction in staff levels. This chapter is mainly concerned with the situation in 1991. A consideration of the changes over the 1990s is given at the end of Chapter 6.

2 I never saw female regular employees below the rank of section chief take a

morning meeting, but their male counterparts did so regularly as part of their grooming for higher management positions.

3  The only misdemeanours really taken seriously are stealing from the company, or, in the case of older married men, having an affair with a member of staff. Both of these are causes for dismissal, but they are rare, or at any rate rarely discovered.

4  'Attribute' in Nakane's (1970) model refers to personal qualities both inborn (such as gender, or caste in India) and acquired (for example position within company).

5  'If we postulate a social group embracing members with various different attributes, the method of tying together the constituent members will be based on the vertical relation' (Nakane 1970: 24).

6  From this perspective, the different career paths of men and women owed more to differences in the level of education than to any notion of intrinsic differences between the two, an idea that reflects the official company line on this question. However, the principle of sorting employees according to educational level tends in practice to follow gender lines, as explained in Chapter 2.

7  The rate for a new part-timer working a twenty-five-hour week worked out at about 60 per cent of the starting salary for a female high-school graduate regular employee working a thirty-five-hour week. That is, they received 60 per cent of the salary for doing 70 per cent of the hours. Although this discrepancy does not seem huge, it should be borne in mind that part-timers paid at this rate did not receive the twice-yearly bonuses received by regular employees, nor were they eligible for paid holidays or sick leave. Furthermore, regular employees received substantially higher increases in pay than did the part-timers as their length of service increased, so for the longer-serving employees the gap between the two widened considerably.

8  During my fieldwork, I only encountered one exception to this rule limiting eligibility for the post of section chief to regular employees, the case of Matsumoto-san in the Osaka branch, who was asked to become section chief while she was still a part-timer. Her acceptance of this position did, however, involve changing to the status of regular employee. It seems, though, that this instance was very unusual. A detailed account of Matsumoto-san's career is given in Chapter 7.

9  Fellow part-timers could also, on occasion, be the target, as the cases of Morinaga-san and Kimura-san illustrate (p. 91).

10  An example of this is given in Chapter 7. Analogous pressures are noted by Ogasawara (1998: 59).

11  The importance of relationships among wives of businessmen in the upper echelons of the business world has been commented on by Hamabata (1990).

## 6  Unity and fragmentation: group events within the company

1  Quality control circles (described in more detail on pp. 103–9) are a kind of small group activity that have become associated with close employee involvement with the company and a 'Japanese' style of management.

2  A special category of part-timer, benefiting from company union membership. See Chapter 2 for a detailed explanation.

3  The arrival and departure of ordinary part-timers was announced only at the daily morning meeting on their floor.

4  TOUCH heart was also the motto of the company (see Appendix 1). The motto was in English, a not uncommon practice in Japan, conveying an international, modern image, and also giving it an enigmatic quality that lent itself to elaborate exegesis.

5  A 1972 survey found that nearly a third of the companies responding to the survey did not pay their employees for time spent in quality control circles (Asian Productivity Organization 1972: 14).

6  Uy Onglacto (1988) cites a survey conducted by the Japanese Union of Scientists and Engineers in 1983, which shows that such topics accounted for 85.6 per cent of circle themes.

7  This word was used in English.

8  The word used in Japanese was *sunao*.

9  This is taken from one of a series of pamphlets distributed to subscribers (together with the monthly telephone bill) by an international telephone company in Japan.

10  This was the fate of a former branch manager of the Koganei branch as described in Chapter 8.

11  See Chapter 4.

12  Sales were all recorded by name and credited to the employee who had introduced the customer. Those whose customers spent the most could expect a small cash prize.

13  The kimono is not now generally worn in everyday life by most Japanese women, and the correct manner of putting it on and wearing it are skills that are no longer automatically acquired.

14  For both 'friend' and 'mate' *shain*, the English words were used.

## 7  Gender issues: working women in Nagasakiya

1  A similar pattern can be seen in South Korea (Women's data book 1991: 91).

2  In 1931 one commentator wrote of the effect of the recession on the middle classes:

> It is a situation in which women, who, until now, moved on after girls' schools to flower arranging and sewing and who did not know the taste of poverty, are suddenly facing the storms of life.
>
> (Kawasaki Natsu, *Shokugyō o kokorozasu hito no tame ni*; Genninsha
> 1931: 21, cited in Nagy 1991: 205)

3  Rohlen writes of the training undergone by women entrants to the bank where he conducted his fieldwork:

> A special theme in the women's training is the interpretation of work as a preparation for becoming good wives and mothers .... It is said, for example, that learning proper etiquette and polite language ... will make them more cultivated, charming, and graceful, and therefore more attractive to their husbands and better examples for their children. Learning how to keep records and handle money will aid them in their responsibilities as keepers of the family purse strings.
>
> (Rohlen 1974: 198)

4  This term is used as an English loan word in Japanese.

5  This sort of attitude is noted by Buruma in his examination of the portrayal of career women in television dramas:

> Okura Junko, heroine of 'The Dazzling Desert' ... is single, pretty, in her thirties and a successful designer ... But is Junko happy? No ... she is miserable. Her life, as the title of the series implies, may be dazzling, but it

is also a desert. At one point she laments that 'when a woman becomes like me, it's the end of everything'.

(Buruma 1984: 39)

6  To some extent the same holds true for men, but in the case of men there are alternative discourses of masculinity available that are notably absent for women; for example, the notion of a 'pure' masculinity untainted by female contact described by Buruma (1984) and discussed in more detail in Chapter 8.

7  Various methods were used to this end, such as financial incentives to have large families and the banning of contraception and abortion (Miyake 1991: 278–9).

8  The older members of this category of young single women, from around their mid-twenties until marriage, are important targets for advertising because of their relatively high disposable income.

9  There are important contrasts here with the situation experienced by young unskilled female employees in the UK, where low wages and the absence of subsidised accommodation for single people combine to make marriage and/or childbirth the path to achieving a home of one's own and the independence associated with adulthood. For a more detailed discussion of this point see Westwood (1984).

10  Government surveys repeatedly show that the vast majority of Japanese consider themselves 'middle class'.

11  There is no notion in Japan of a class defined by work. Most people refer to themselves as *'futsū'* – ordinary – and the class inflection is provided by references to people seen as different. In the Nagasakiya case, the employees' self-reference as *futsū* was opposed to *ojō-san* (young lady), thus placing the Nagasakiya employees at the lower end of the social scale.

12  In the 1991 Nagasakiya company survey, 68.6 per cent of the part-timers surveyed gave financial necessity as their main reason for seeking part-time employment outside the home. (This survey only covered the *teijishain*, a special sub-category of part-timer (see Chapter 2), but from my observations at the Koganei branch I would guess that this is a fairly close reflection of the general pattern for part-timers.)

13  In 1991 roughly two-thirds of female regular employees at Nagasakiya were under thirty, with an average age of 24.2; for the part-timers surveyed the average age was 40.6, and 84.5 per cent were over thirty (Nagasakiya company union survey 1991).

14  See McLendon (1983) on the pressure on regular female employees not to remain with their company past the age of around thirty, and Ogasawara (1998: 60) on the peer pressure to marry, preferably at around the same time as one's *dōkisei*.

15  Although the career track is theoretically open to women in Nagasakiya, I did not come across any instances of women being placed on this track during the decade of my interest in this company.

16  This is also a view highlighted by Kondo (1990: 278–9) in her work on middle-aged part-time women workers in a small confectionery factory in downtown Tokyo.

17  Yoshimoto's work is also interesting in its explorations of notions of gender, with one of the main characters in one of her stories switching gender from male to female.

18  Eldest son succession to the headship of the household, or *ie*, was enshrined in Japanese law during the Meiji era, but before that time it seems that there was considerable regional variation in inheritance and succession patterns. Post-war occupation reforms established the equal rights of all children to inherit household assets, but in practice, in rural areas at least, all children save one tend to renounce

these rights, with eldest son succession being the ideal (see also Hendry 1981: 28–9 for more detail on variations in post-war inheritance practices).

19 See Chapter 3 for a detailed explanation of the rigidities of the Japanese recruitment system.

20 The home and national systems are explained in detail in Chapter 2.

21 The financial implications for large Japanese companies of retaining women employees long term, when they are limited to low-ranking, relatively unskilled positions, but nonetheless receive pay based on their length of service, have been explored by Roberts (1994). She argues persuasively that the company she studied did not want women employees to remain long term because of the high costs involved, and the perceived irrationality of paying high wages for low-skill work. However, as regular employees, their job security was guaranteed, and because of their gender it was not thought appropriate to resolve the situation by allowing them to rise to more senior ranks. The solution the company opted for was therefore to bring indirect pressures to bear on the older women employees to resign.

22 Rooms in Japan are commonly measured in tatami mats. One tatami mat = approximately 1.6 2 m (1.8 m × 0.9 m) according to the Japan Institute for social and Economic Affairs (1990: 87), although tatami mats may vary somewhat in size depending on the area of Japan.

23 An English loan word used with the meaning of 'do one's best, take initiatives'.

24 Again, similar attitudes towards senior female staff are noted for the department store sector (Creighton 1996: 212).

25 This point is also made by Wakisaka (1997: 147–8).

26 *Jibun o migaku* – literally, polish yourself, with the implication of becoming a more mature person.

27 The delegation of such tasks to hired help is both frowned on and extremely rare, and children of either sex are not now routinely called upon to help as parents tend to fear that this will interfere with their studies. This is in contrast to the situation in pre-war Japan, when it was common for children to be involved in domestic tasks from an early age.

28 This was despite the fact that, since she had no children, she did not actually need the main benefit that part-time work offers: shorter hours to fit in better with the school day, and the flexibility to take time off as necessary for the exigencies of childcare.

## 8 Company men and pillars of the household: sources of identity

1 Daikoku, or Daikokuten, is also the name given to the god of prosperity. Although associated with Buddhism, and the deity known as Mah k la in Sanskrit, in Japanese Daikokuten can also be read as Ohkuninushinomikoto, a Shinto deity. The two have become widely confused, and in popular religious practice Daikokuten has come to be regarded as one of the seven deities of good fortune.

2 For the eldest son and successor of a household this role also extends to providing for his mother and unmarried siblings after his father's death, even if they are not in fact co-resident.

3 Kinsella (1996: 108) points out, however, that the long-running Section Chief Shima Kosaku series of manga have become more conservative over time; the examples cited here are taken from the earlier volumes of the series.

4 Notions of masculinity as pure, opposed to femininity, which is polluted, are of ancient origin in Japan, going back to the Shinto creation myths as described for example by Ohnuki-Tierney (1984: 36). The link between violence against women

in popular culture and notions of purity and masculinity has been commented on by Moeran (1986).

5  This pattern is not confined to the salaryman working for a large company but is also expressed by many small independent businessmen. For example, Plath (1980) cites a middle-aged realtor who regrets never having fulfilled an early dream to become a politician and sees his life in the property business as an unpleasant necessity largely forced upon him by the responsibilities of marriage, 'Sometimes I tell myself ... that if I hadn't got married I could have done what I really wanted to. Under the marital yoke it became impossible' (Plath 1980: 56).

6  For figures on male non-regular employees see Japan Institute of Labour (1998a). For a recent report on changes in the employment patterns of young people in Japan see Naganawa (1999).

7  By the time of my return visit in 1999, the numbers of regular staff had been scaled back to the point where all daily tasks, including operating the cash register, were shared among whoever happened to be in the store at the time, whatever their official job status.

8  Relations between unmarried adult siblings still resident in the household and the wife of the household heir are often tense, as she, although once a stranger, has become a permanent member of the household, whereas they, despite being born there, are expected to leave (at least on marriage if not before) and establish themselves elsewhere.

9  Literally, 'it looked leisurely', from *hima*, a word used to mean spare or leisure time.

10  The Japanese word he used was *anko*, a word literally meaning a sticky sweet red bean paste used in Japanese sweets, but it is also used metaphorically in other contexts. The use of this word provides a vivid image of a feeling of group cohesiveness.

11  *Tsukiai* is a kind of socialising that is done with people with whom one is linked by work (either clients or fellow employees), and has the ring of obligation rather than pleasure, although of course in practice it tends to be a mixture of the two.

12  This kind of statement was often made by Nagasakiya's senior male managers, and in some ways serves to emphasise the importance of gender and age in the corporate hierarchy as 'young' and 'female' are used here as symbolic indications of low status.

13  See, for example, Vogel (1963).

## 9  Rethinking the Japanese company

1  See Bourdieu (1977: 41–3). It has been noted by Bourdieu and others that men are frequently nominated by informants as official spokesmen, and that this tends to create a gender bias in officialised accounts.

2  A Japanese proverb cited to me by one of the male managers. It means to depend on a common source of support, and hence to have common interests.

# Appendix 1

## Nagasakiya Motto and Statement of Management Vision 1991

1. Management vision:    To be loved by the customer
To aim to be a diversified general merchant

2. Motto:    Expand – network of kindness
Join together – network of trust
Extend – network of competitiveness

3. Standards of action:    TOUCH heart

1. The keyword TOUCH
TIMELY: make management and store appropriate to the times
ORGANISATION: Management organisation bringing together know-how
UNITE: All employees unite their efforts
COMMUNICATION: Close consensus within the company, dialogue with customers
HUMANITY: Considerate service with a human touch

2. The keyword HEART
The hearts of the customers
The united hearts of all employees – from regular employees to management

3. These two keywords together make TOUCH heart
This means:
Make contact with (touch) the customers' hearts
Link together (touch) all the employees' hearts
– from regular employees to management

# Appendix 2

Timetable of initial training course for female high-school graduates, March 1991

| Time (h) | Day 1 | Day 2 | Day 3 |
|---|---|---|---|
| 07.00 | | | Wake up<br>Wash |
| 07.30 | | Wake up<br>Wash | Roll call<br>Exercises |
| 08.00 | | Breakfast | Breakfast |
| 08.30 | | | Cleaning |
| 09.00 | | Roll call<br>9.20 talk by<br>personnel manager | Go over test<br>distributed before<br>course |
| 10.00 | | Summary of the<br>contents of the<br>company training<br>course<br>(20-minute break)<br>10.40 Employment<br>standards | Gift wrapping |
| 11:00 | | Welfare<br>Insurance | |
| 12.00 | Reception | Lunch | Lunch |
| 13.00 | | Manners in the<br>workplace (video<br>and talk)<br>(10-minute break) | Fire awareness<br>and training<br>(10-minute break) |
| 14.00 | | 14.20 Dealing<br>with customers<br>(video and talk) | |
| 15.00 | Orientation<br>Rules of course | | Dealing with<br>customers 1: |
| 16.00 | Medical<br>examination<br>Administrative<br>formalities | (10-minute break)<br>Let's get to know<br>each other | basic expressions,<br>movement,<br>wrapping practice |
| 17.00 | | Communication<br>games and<br>educational games | |
| 18.00 | Dinner | Dinner | Dinner |
| 19.00 | | | Test |
| 20.00 | | | |

| Day 4 | Day 5 | Day 6 |
|---|---|---|
| Wake up | Wake up | Wake up |
| Wash | Wash | Wash |
| Roll call | Roll call | Roll call |
| Exercises | Exercises | Exercises |
| Breakfast | Breakfast | Breakfast |
| Cleaning | Cleaning | Cleaning |
| Dealing with customers 2 (content depending on sales assistant trainer) | Basic calculating | |
| Taking money and goods etc. | (10-minute break) | (10-minute break) |
| | Basics of colour images | Test |
| Lunch | Lunch | Lunch (change clothes) |
| The correct knowledge and use of credit card slips etc. at the cash register | Basics of colour images | Collected from centre |
| (15-minute break) | (10-minute break) | |
| | Separate training by section | |
| | Vocabulary | |
| | Special characteristics of section | |
| DO! SPORT | Flow of goods | |
| | Basic knowledge of materials | |
| Dinner | Dinner | |
| Meeting | Visit to local branch of Nagasakiya | |

# Appendix 3

Nagasakiya training course for new company members 1991: course rules

## Main points of daily schedule

| | |
|---|---|
| 07.00 | Rise |
| | Wash |
| 07.30 | Exercises |
| 08.00 | Breakfast |
| | Cleaning |
| 09.10 | Lectures begin |
| 12.00 | Lunch |
| 13.00 | Lectures |
| 18.00 | Dinner |
| 19.00 | Lectures |
| 20.00 | Bath |
| | Free time |
| 21.30 | Dormitory gates close |
| | Self-study |
| 23.30 | Lights out |
| | Go to bed |

## Living rules

### 1 Timekeeping

1　Keep to the scheduled time.
2　Assemble 5 minutes before (lectures, exercises, etc.).

### 2 Greet others first, brightly and cheerfully

1　When passing each other in the corridor:
morning: *Ohayō gozaimasu* (good morning)
midday: *Konnichiwa* (hello)
evening: *Konbanwa* (good evening).

### 3 *How to walk in the corridors*

1   Don't make a noise (only wear slippers after a bath).
2   Don't run.
3   Don't walk while having a private conversation.
4   Answer *hai* (yes) when called.

### 4 *Toilet*

1   Be careful to be economical in your use of water.
2   Don't go into the toilet with your shoes on.
3   Arrange your shoes neatly when you go in.
4   Arrange the toilet slippers neatly when you go out.

### 5 *Going out*

1   Going out is only permitted between 8.00 p.m. and 9.30 p.m. (only in order to go shopping).
2   Before going out, enter your name and room number in the going out register.
3   Be quiet when you go out, as the centre is in a residential area.
4   Always put your slippers in the shoe cupboard.
5   Going out alone is forbidden.
6   When you go out, say, *ittekimasu* (I'm going out).
    When you come back, say *kairimashita* (I'm back).

### 6 *Dress*

1   Wear tracksuits during lectures.
2   Put your name plate on the left side of your chest.
3   Keep your track suit top's fasteners neatly done up.

### 7 *Dormitory rooms*

1   Don't put photos etc. on the door or walls.
2   After getting up, fold up the bedding into four, and place your pillow on top of it.
3   Don't speak in a loud voice.
4   After lights out, go to sleep quietly.
5   When you leave the room, don't forget to turn out the lights.

### 8 *Cleaning*

1   Cleaning is done by everyone, every morning.
2   The cleaning rota is posted up on the blackboard.

3   Rubbish from the rooms is thrown out daily (material to be burned should
    be separated from material that should not be burned).
4   Take the initiative to clean the blackboard after lectures.
5   Put the desks straight 5 minutes before lectures begin.

### 9 Meals

1   Since it is crowded at mealtimes, be considerate of others and finish
    quickly (breakfast is in separate base groups).
2   Don't leave food.
3   When you have finished, return your dishes and cutlery promptly.
4   When you start eating say *itadakimasu*.
    When you finish eating say *goschisōsama.*

### 10 Bathing

1   No bathing outside the prescribed hours.
2   The last person to use the bath must report to the office afterwards.

### 11 Use of the television room

1   Keep to lights out time.
2   Don't speak in loud voices and make a disturbance.
3   Always tidy up rubbish.

### 12 Other

1   Deposit valuables at office.
2   Inform the office if you feel unwell.
3   Do not make long telephone calls.

### 13 Rules for lectures

1   Greetings for the beginning and end of lectures:
    Beginning:   *Kiritsu, rei* (stand up, bow)
                 *Onegaishimasu* (please)
    End:         *Kiritsu, rei*
                 *arigatō gozaimashita* (thank you).
2   Don't lean on your elbows, don't fold your arms across your chest, don't
    cross your legs.
3   Always take notes.

### 14 Roll call

1   Morning roll call, 7.25 a.m., either in the new hall or on the 2nd floor.

Each room leader should say: room number X, Y members, Y present, all present and correct.

2    Evening roll call, 10.00 p.m. at reception, as above.

### 15 Smoking and drinking alcohol are forbidden

Those who do not keep the above rules score zero points and will be reported to the store manager of the branch to which they have been allocated.

Always keep your dormitory rooms tidy as it is sometimes essential to enter them during lecture hours.

# Bibliography

Abegglen, J. (1958) *The Japanese Factory*, Glencoe, IL: The Free Press.

Abegglen, J. and Stalk, G. (1985) *Kaisha, the Japanese Corporation*, New York: Basic Books.

Alvesson, M. (1993) *Cultural Perspectives on Organizations*, Cambridge: Cambridge University Press.

Anderson, B. (1991) *Imagined Communities*, London: Verso.

Arai, S. (1991) *Shoshaman: a Tale of Corporate Japan*, Berkeley: University of California Press.

Asahi Shinbun (1998) *Japan Almanac 1999*, Tokyo: Asahi Shinbun.

Austin, L. (ed.) (1976) *Japan: the Paradox of Progress*, New Haven: Yale University Press.

Bachnik, J. (1992) 'Kejime: defining a shifting self in multiple organizational modes', in N. Rosenberger (ed.) *Japanese Sense of Self*, Cambridge: Cambridge University Press.

Bachnik, J. (1994) '*uchi/soto*: Challenging our conceptualizations of self, social order and language', in J. Bachnik and C. Quinn (eds) *Situated Meaning: Inside and Outside in Japanese Self, Society and Language*, Princeton: Princeton Unviersity Press.

Bachnik, J. and Quinn, C. (eds) (1994) *Situated Meaning: Inside and Outside in Japanese Self, Society, and Language*, Princeton: Princeton University Press.

Barrett, G. (1989) *Archetypes in Japanese Film*, London: Associated University Presses.

Barth, F. (1969) 'Introduction', in F. Barth (ed.) *Ethnic Groups and Boundaries: the Social Organisation of Culture Difference*, London: George Allen and Unwin, pp. 9–38.

Befu, H. (1980) 'The group model of Japanese society and an alternative', *Rice University Studies* 66(1): 169–87.

Bellah, R. (1957) *Tokugawa Religion: the Values of Pre-industrial Japan*, Glencoe, IL: The Free Press.

Ben-Ari, E. (1991) *Changing Japanese Suburbia*, London: Kegan Paul International.

Ben-Ari, E. and Eisenstadt, S. N. (eds) (1990) *Japanese Models of Conflict Resolution*, London: Kegan Paul International.

Ben-Ari, E., Moeran, B., and Valentine, J. (eds) (1990) *Unwrapping Japan: Society and Culture in Anthropological Perspective*, Manchester: Manchester University Press.

Benedict, R. (1946) *The Chrysanthemum and the Sword*, Boston: Houghton Mifflin.

Bernstein, G.L. (ed.) (1991) *Recreating Japanese Women, 1600–1945*, Berkeley: University of California Press.

Bestor, T. (1985) 'Tradition and Japanese Social Organization: Institutional Development in a Tokyo Neighbourhood', *Ethnology* 24(2): 121–35.

—— (1989) *Neighbourhood Tokyo*, Stanford: Stanford University Press.

Bourdieu, P. (1977) *Outline of a Theory of Practice*, Cambridge: Cambridge University Press.

—— (1984) *Distinction: A Social Critique of the Judgement of Taste*, London: Routledge.

Brinton, M. (1992) 'Christmas Cakes and Wedding Cakes: the social organization of Japanese women's life-course', in T. S. Lebra (ed.) *Japanese Social Organization*, Honolulu: University of Hawaii Press.

—— (1993) *Women and the Economic Miracle: Gender and Work in Postwar Japan*, Berkeley: University of California Press.

Buruma, I. (1984) *Behind the Mask: On Sexual Demons, Sacred Mothers, Transvestites, Gangsters, and other Japanese Cultural Heroes*, New York: Pantheon.

Chalmers, N. (1989) *Industrial Relations in Japan: the Peripheral Workforce*, London: Routledge.

Clark, R. (1979) *The Japanese Company*, New Haven: Yale University Press.

Clarke, P. B. (ed.) (2000) *Japanese New Religions in Global Perspective*, Richmond: Curzon.

Cohen, A. (1985) *The Symbolic Construction of Community*, London: Routledge.

Cole, R. (1971) *Japanese Blue Collar: The Changing Tradition*, Berkeley: University of California Press.

—— (1979) *Work, Mobility and Participation: A Comparative Study of American and Japanese Industry*, Berkeley: University of California Press.

Cook, A. and Hayashi, H. (1980) *Working Women in Japan: Discrimination, Resistance and Reform*, Ithaca: Cornell University Press.

Coulthard, M. (1977) *An introduction to Discourse Analysis*, London: Longman.

Crawcour, S. (1978) 'The Japanese Employment System', *Journal of Japanese Studies* 4(2): 225–45.

Creighton, M. (1988) *Sales, Service, and Sanctity: An Anthropological Analysis of Japanese Department Stores*, unpublished PhD thesis, University of Washington.

—— (1991) 'Maintaining Cultural Boundaries in Retailing: How Japanese Department Stores Domesticate Things Foreign', *Modern Asian Studies* 25(4): 675–709.

—— (1992) 'The *depāto*: merchandising the West while selling Japaneseness', in J. Tobin (ed.) *Remade in Japan: Everyday Life and Consumer Taste in a Changing Society*, New Haven: Yale University Press.

—— (1996) 'Marriage, Motherhood, and Career Management in a Japanese "Counter Culture" ', in A. Imamura (ed.) *Re-imaging Japanese Women*, Berkeley: University of California Press.

—— (1998) 'Something More: Japanese department stores' marketing of "a meaningful human life"', in K. MacPherson (ed.) *Asian Department Stores*, Richmond: Curzon.

Czarniawska-Joerges, B. (1997) *Narrating the Organization: Dramas of Institutional Identity*, Chicago: University of Chicago Press.

Doi, T. (1973) *The Anatomy of Dependence*, Tokyo: Kodansha.

—— (1985) *The Anatomy of Self*, Tokyo: Kodansha.

Dore, R. (1965) 'The legacy of Tokugawa education', in M. Jansen (ed.) *Changing Attitudes Towards Modernization*, Princeton: Princeton University Press.

—— (1973) *British Factory, Japanese Factory: the Origins of Diversity in Industrial Relations*, Berkeley: University of California Press.

—— (1986) *Flexible Rigidities*, London: Athlone Press.

—— (1987) *Taking Japan Seriously: A Confucian Perspective on Leading Economic Issues*, London: Athlone Press.

Dore, R. and Sako, M. (1989) *How the Japanese Learn to Work*, London: Routledge.

Duncan, W. (1974) *Japanese Markets Review 1974–5*. Essex: Gower Press.

Edwards, W. (1989) *Modern Japan Through its Weddings: Gender, Person, and Society in Ritual Portrayal*, Stanford: Stanford University Press.

Foucault, M. (1980) *Power/Knowledge: Selected Interviews and other Writings 1972–1977*, C. Gordon (ed.), New York: Pantheon Books.

—— (1972) *The Archaeology of Knowledge*, New York: Harper Colophon.

Frager, R. and Rohlen, T. (1976) 'The future of a tradition: Japanese spirit in the 1980s', in L. Austin (ed.) *Japan: the Paradox of Progress*, New Haven: Yale University Press.

Fujimura-Fanselow, K. and Kameda, A. (eds) (1995) *Japanese Women: New Feminist Perspectives on the Past, Present and Future*, New York: Feminist Press.

Geertz, C. (1973) *The Interpretation of Cultures*, New York: Basic Books.

—— (1983) *Local Knowledge*, New York: Basic Books.

Gennep, A. van (1960) *The Rites of Passage*, London: Routledge and Kegan Paul. Translation of *Les Rites de Passage*, Paris: Nourry, 1908.

Gluck, C. (1985) *Japan's Modern Myths: Ideology in the Late Meiji Period*, Princeton: Princeton University Press.

Goodman, R. (1990) *Japan's 'International Youth': the Emergence of a New Class of Schoolchildren*, Oxford: Clarendon Press.

Goodman, R. and Refsing, K. (eds) (1992) *Ideology and Practice in Modern Japan*, London: Routledge.

Hamabata, M. (1990) *Crested Kimono: Power and Love in the Japanese Business Family*, Ithaca: Cornell University Press.

Hazama, H. (1963) *Nihonteki keiei no keifu*, Tokyo: Nihon noritsu kyokai.

Hazama, H. and Kaminsky, J. (1979) 'Japanese Labour Management Relations', *Journal of Japanese Studies* 5(1): 71–106.

Hendry, J. (1981) *Marriage in Changing Japan: Community and Society*, London: Croom Helm.

—— (1986) *Becoming Japanese: the World of the Pre-school Child*, Manchester: Manchester University Press.

—— (1987) *Understanding Japanese Society*, London: Croom Helm.

—— (1992) 'Individualism and Individuality: entry into a social world', in R. Goodman and K. Refsing (eds) *Ideology and Practice in Modern Japan*, London: Routledge.

—— (1993) *Wrapping Culture: Politeness, Presentation, and Power in Japan and Other Societies*, Oxford: Oxford University Press.

Hickson, D. and Pugh, D, (1995) *Management Worldwide: the Impact of Societal Culture on Organizations Around the Globe*, London: Penguin.

Hirschmeier, J. and Yui, T. (1975) *The Development of Japanese Business 1600–1973*, London: Allen and Unwin.

Hobsbawm, E. and Ranger, T. (1983) *The Invention of Tradition*, Cambridge: Cambridge University Press.

Honda, K. (1993) '*Pātotaimu rōdōsha no kikan rōdōryoku to shogū seido*' [Utilisation of part-time workers and their compensation programs] *Studies of the Japan Institute of Labour No. 6*, Tokyo: Japan Institute of Labour.

Hunter, J. (ed.) (1993) *Japanese Women Working*, London: Routledge.

Ikai, S. (1988) *Shōrai no gotoshi: inō no shōnin Iwata Kōhachi* [Like the wind in the pine trees: Iwata Kohachi, maverick retailer], Tokyo: Shikai Shobo.

Ikenami, S. (1991) *Master Assassin: Tales of Murder from the Shogun's City*, Tokyo: Kodansha International.

Imamura, A. (ed.) (1996) *Re-imaging Japanese Women*, Berkeley: University of California Press.

Inagami, T. (1988) *Japanese Workplace Industrial Relations*, Tokyo: The Japan Institute of Labour.

Inohara, H. (1990) *Human Resource Development in Japanese Companies*, Tokyo: Asian Productivity Organization.

Inoue, S. (1997) 'Changing Employment in Japan', *Japan Forum* 9(2): 160–5.

Jansen, M. (ed.) (1965) *Changing Attitudes Towards Modernization*, Princeton: Princeton University Press.

Jenkins, T. (1994) 'Fieldwork and the Perception of Everyday Life', *Man* (NS) 29: 433–55.

Johnson, C. (1982) *MITI and the Japanese Miracle: The Growth of Industrial Policy 1925–1975*, Stanford: Stanford University Press.

Kamata, S. (1982) *Japan in the Passing Lane*, New York: Pantheon Books.

Kaneko, S. (1997) 'Diversification of employment types and changes in the employment system', *Japan Forum* 9(2): 154–60.

Kawashima, Y. (1983) *Wage Differentials between Men and Women in Japan*, unpublished PhD thesis, Stanford University.

—— (1995) 'Female workers: an overview of past and current trends', in K. Fujimura-Fanselow and A. Kameda (eds) *Japanese Women: New Feminist Perspectives on the Past, Present and Future*, New York: Feminist Press.

Kinsella, S. (1996) 'Change in the Social Status, Form and Content of Adult Manga, 1986–1996', *Japan Forum* 8(1): 103–13.

Koike, K. (1983) 'Internal Labor Markets: Workers in Large Firms', in Shirai, T. (ed.) *Contemporary Industrial Relations in Japan*, Wisconsin: University of Wisconsin Press.

—— (1988) *Understanding Industrial Relations in Modern Japan*, London: Macmillan Press.

Kondo, D. (1990) *Crafting Selves: Power, Gender, and Discourses of Identity in a Japanese Workplace*, Chicago: University of Chicago Press.

Krauss, E. S., Rohlen, T., and Steinhoff, P. (ed.) (1984) *Conflict in Japan*, Honolulu: University of Hawaii Press.

Kumazawa, M. (1989) *Nihonteki Keiei no Meian* [Light and Darkness of Japanese Management], Tokyo: Chikuma Shobo.

Lam, A. (1992) *Women and Japanese Management: Discrimination and Reform*, London: Routledge.

Larke, R. (1994) *Japanese Retailing*, London: Routledge.

Lebra, T. S. (1992a) 'Self in Japanese Culture', in N. Rosenberger (ed.) *Japanese Sense of Self*, Cambridge: Cambridge University Press.

—— (1992b) *Japanese Social Organization*, Honolulu: University of Hawaii Press.

Lincoln, E. (1988) *Japan: Facing Economic Maturity*, Washington, DC: The Brookings Institution.

Lo, Jeannie (1990) *Office Ladies, Factory Women: Life and Work at a Japanese Company*, New York and London: Sharpe.

McCormack, G. and Sugimoto, Y. (ed.) (1988) *The Japanese Trajectory – Modernisation and Beyond*, Cambridge: Cambridge University Press.

McLendon, J. (1983) 'The Office: Way Station or Blind Alley?' in D. Plath (ed.) *Work and Life-course in Japan*, Albany: State University of New York Press.

MacPherson, K. (ed.) (1998) *Asian Department Stores*, Richmond: Curzon.

Marshall, B. K. (1967) *Capitalism and Nationalism in Prewar Japan: The Ideology of the Business Elite, 1868–1941*, Stanford: Stanford University Press.

Martinez, D. P. (ed.) *The Worlds of Japanese Popular Culture: Gender, Shifting Boundaries and Global Cultures*. Cambridge: Cambridge University Press.

Mathews, G. (1996) *What Makes Life worth Living? How Japanese and Americans Make Sense of Their Worlds*, Berkeley: University of California Press.

Matsunaga, L. (2000) 'Spiritual Companies: Corporate Religions' in P. B. Clarke (ed.) *Japanese New Religions in Global Perspective*, Richmond: Curzon.

Mitsuyama, M. (1991) '*Pātotaimā senryokuka to kigyōnai kyōiku*' [Utilisation of part-time workers and training within firms], *Nihon Rōdō Kyōkai Zasshi* (Monthly Journal of the Japan Institute of Labour) 33(3): 28–36.

Miyake, Y. (1991) 'Doubling Expectations: Motherhood and Women's Factory Work under State Management', in Gail Lee Bernstein (ed.) *Recreating Japanese Women 1600–1945*, Berkeley: University of California Press.

Moeran, B. (1984a) 'One over the Seven: Sake Drinking in a Japanese Pottery Community', *Journal of the Anthropological Society of Oxford*, 15(2): 83–100.

—— (1984b) 'Individual, Group and *Seishin*: Japan's Internal Cultural Debate', *Man* (NS) 19: 252–66.

—— (1986) 'The beauty of violence: jidaigeki, yakuza, and 'eroduction' films in Japan', in D. Riches (ed.) *The Anthropology of Violence*, Oxford: Basil Blackwell.

—— (1989) *Language and Popular Culture in Japan*, Manchester: Manchester University Press.

—— (1996) *A Japanese Advertising Agency: an Anthropology of Media and Markets*, Richmond: Curzon.

—— (1998) 'The Birth of the Japanese Department Store' in K. MacPherson (ed.) *Asian Department Stores*, Richmond: Curzon.

Molony, B. (1991) 'Activism among Women in the Taisho Cotton Textile Industry', in G. L. Bernstein (ed.) *Recreating Japanese Women 1600–1945*, Berkeley: University of California Press.

—— (1993) 'Equality versus difference: the Japanese debate over 'motherhood protection', 1915–50', in J. Hunter (ed.) *Japanese Women Working*, London: Routledge.

Moore, H. (1988) *Feminism and Anthropology*, Cambridge: Polity Press.

Morita, A. (1987) *Made in Japan*, London: Collins.

Mouer, R. and Sugimoto, Y. (1981) *Japanese Society: Stereotypes and Realities*, Melbourne: Japanese Studies Centre.

—— (1986) *Images of Japanese Society: A Study in the Structure of Social Reality*, London: Routledge and Kegan Paul.

—— (1989) 'A Multi-dimensional View of Stratification: a framework for comparative analysis', in R. Mouer and Y. Sugimoto (eds) *Constructs for Understanding Japan*, London: Kegan Paul.

Mouer, R. and Sugimoto, Y. (eds) (1989) *Constructs for Understanding Japan*, London: Kegan Paul.

Mulhern, C. I. (1991) 'The Japanese Business Novel', introduction to S. Arai *Shoshaman: A Tale of Corporate Japan,* Berkeley: University of California Press.

Naganawa, H. (1999) 'From School to Workplace: Changes in the Labor Market for New Graduates', *Japan Institute of Labour Bulletin*. Online. Available http://www.jil.go.jp/bulletin/year/1999/vol 38 – 10/05.html (6 December 1999).

Nagy, M. (1991) 'Middle-Class Working Women During the Interwar Years', in G. L. Bernstein (ed.) *Recreating Japanese Women 1600–1945*, Berkeley: University of California Press.

Nakamura, Tadashi (1988) *Nihon no rōdō jijō*, Tokyo: Nihon Rōdō Kenkyūkai.

Nakamura, Toshio (1998) *Oishii Furiita, Pāto dokuhon* [Manual for tasty *furiita* and part-time work], Tokyo: Kou Business.

Nakamura, M. (1990) '*Pātotaimu Rodo*' [Part-time Labour] *Nihon Rōdō Kyōkai Zasshi* (Monthly Journal of the Japan Institute of Labour) 32(1): 40–1.

Nakane, C. (1967) *Kinship and Economic Organisation in Rural Japan*, London: Athlone Press.

—— (1970) *Japanese Society*, Berkeley: University of California Press.

Noguchi, P. (1990) *Delayed Departures, Overdue Arrivals: Industrial Familism and the Japanese National Railways*, Honolulu: University of Hawaii Press.

Nolte, S. H. and Hastings, S.A. (1991) 'The Meiji state's policy toward women, 1890–1910', in G. L. Bernstein (ed.) *Recreating Japanese Women, 1600–1945*, Berkeley: University of California Press.

Ogasawara, Y. (1998) *Office Ladies and Salaried Men: Power, Gender and Work in Japanese Companies*, Berkeley: University of California Press.

Ohnuki-Tierney, E. (1984) *Illness and Culture in Contemporary Japan: an Anthropological View*, Cambridge: Cambridge University Press.

Oka, T. (1994) *Prying open the Door: Foreign Workers in Japan*, Washington DC: Carnegie Endowment for International Peace.

Ong, A. (1987) *Spirits of Resistance and Capitalist Discipline: Factory Women in Malaysia*, New York: State University of New York Press.

Ouchi, W. (1981) *Theory Z*, Massachusetts: Addison-Wesley.

Pascale, R. T. and Athos, A. G. (1981) *The Art of Japanese Management*, London: Allen Lane.

Pharr, S. (1984) 'The Tea-Pourers' Rebellion', in E. S. Krauss, T. Rohlen, and P. Steinhoff (eds) *Conflict in Japan*, Honolulu: University of Hawaii Press.

Plath, D. (ed.) (1980) *Long Engagements*, Stanford: Stanford University Press.

—— (1983) *Work and Life-course in Japan*, Albany: State University of New York Press.

Rebick, M. (1998) 'The Japanese Labour Market for University Graduates: Trends in the 1990s', *Japan Forum* 10(1): 17–29.

Roberson, J. (1998) *Japanese Working Class Lives: An Ethnographic Study of Factory Workers*, London: Routledge.

Roberts, S. (1979) *Order and Dispute: an Introduction to Legal Anthropology*, Oxford: Martin Robertson.

Roberts, G. (1994) *Staying on the Line: Blue-collar Women in Contemporary Japan*, Honolulu: University of Hawaii Press.

Rohlen, T. (1970) 'Sponsorship of Cultural Continuity in Japan: a Company Training Program', *Journal of Asian and African Studies* 5(3): 184–92.

—— (1973) 'Spiritual training in a Japanese bank', *American Anthropologist* 75(5): 1542–62.

—— (1974) *For Harmony and Strength: Japanese White-collar Organization in Anthropological Perspective*, Berkeley: University of California Press.

Rosenberger N. (ed.) (1992) *Japanese Sense of Self*, Cambridge: Cambridge University Press.

Said, E. (1978) *Orientalism*, New York: Pantheon Books.

Saito, S. (1993) *Tsumatachi no Shishuki* [The Melancholy of Wives], Tokyo: Iwanami Shoten.

Sakuta, T. (1990) *Japan's Distribution System*, Cambridge MA: Harvard University Press.

Sako, M. (1997) 'Forces for homogeneity and diversity in the Japanese Industrial Relations System', in M. Sako and H. Sato (eds) *Japanese Labour and Management in Transition: Diversity, Flexibility and Participation*, London: Routledge.

Sako, M. and Sato, H. (ed.) (1997) *Japanese Labour and Management in Transition: Diversity, Flexibility and Participation*, London: Routledge.

Saso, Mary (1990) *Women in the Japanese Workplace*, London: Shipman.

Scott, James C. (1985) *Weapons of the Weak: Everyday Forms of Peasant Resistance*, New Haven: Yale University Press.

Schodt, F. L. (1983) *Manga! Manga!: The World of Japanese Comics*, New York: Kodansha International.

Seidensticker, E. (1983) *Low City, High City: Tokyo from Edo to the Earthquake: How the Shogun's Ancient Capital Became a Great Modern City 1867–1923*, New York: Alfred A. Knopf.

—— (1990) *Tokyo Rising: The City since the Great Earthquake*, New York: Alfred A. Knopf.

Shirahase, S. (1995) 'Diversity in Female Work: Female Part-time Workers in Contemporary Japan', *The American Asian Review* 13(2): 257–82.

Shirai, T. (ed.) (1983) *Contemporary Industrial Relations in Japan*, Wisconsin: University of Wisconsin Press.

Sievers, S. (1983) *Flowers in Salt: The Beginnings of Feminist Consciousness in Modern Japan*, Stanford: Stanford University Press.

Silverberg, M. (1991) 'The Modern Girl as Militant', in G. L. Bernstein (ed.) *Recreating Japanese Women 1600–1945*, Berkeley: University of California Press.

Smith, R. J. (1987) 'Gender Inequality in Contemporary Japan', *Journal of Japanese Studies* 13(1): 1–25.

Smith, T. C. (1988) 'The Right to Benevolence: Dignity and Japanese Workers, 1890–1920', in T.C. Smith (ed.) *Native Sources of Japanese Industrialisation*, Berkeley: University of California Press.

Standish, I. (1998) '*Akira*, Postmodernism and Resistance', in D. P. Martinez (ed.) *The Worlds of Japanese Popular Culture: Gender, Shifting Boundaries and Global Cultures*, Cambridge: Cambridge University Press.

Steven, R. (1983) *Classes in Contemporary Japan*, Cambridge: Cambridge University Press.

Tabata, H. (1998) 'Community and Efficiency in the Japanese Firm', *Social Science Japan Journal* 1(2): 192–215.

Takeuchi, H. (1982) 'Working Women in Business Corporations – the Management Viewpoint', *Japan Quarterly* 29:319–23.

Tanaka, Y. (1988) 'Nuclear Power and the Labour movement', in G. McCormack and Y. Sugimoto (eds) *The Japanese Trajectory – Modernisation and Beyond*, Cambridge: Cambridge University Press.

Tobin, J. (1992a) 'Japanese pre-schools and the pedagogy of selfhood', in N. Rosenberger (ed.) *Japanese Sense of Self*, Cambridge: Cambridge University Press.

Tobin, J. (ed.) (1992b) *Remade in Japan: Everyday Life and Consumer Taste in a Changing Society*, New Haven: Yale University Press.

Turner, C. (1995) *Japanese Workers in Protest: An Ethnography of Consciousness and Experience*, Berkeley: University of California Press.

Uchihashi, K. and Sataka, M. (1991) *Nihon Kabushiki gaisha Hihan* [Criticisms of Corporate Japan], Tokyo: Shakaishiso-sha.

Ueno, C. 'Seibu Department Store and Image Marketing: Japanese Consumerism in the post-war period', in K. MacPherson (ed.) *Asian Department Stores*, Richmond: Curzon.

Umetani, S. (1980) *Education and Vocational Training in Japan*, Hamburg: Institut für Asienkunde.

Uno, Kathleen S. (1991) 'Women and Changes in the Household Division of Labor', in G. L. Bernstein (ed.) *Recreating Japanese Women 1600–1945*, Berkeley: University of California Press.

Upham, Frank K. (1989) *Legal regulations of the Japanese Retail Industry: the Large Scale Retail Stores Law and Prospects for Reform*, Cambridge MA: Harvard University Press.

Uy Onglacto, Mary Lou (1988) *Japanese Quality Control Circles: Features, Effects and Problems*, Tokyo: Asian Productivity Organization.

Vogel, E. (1963) *Japan's New Middle Class: the Salaryman and his Family in a Tokyo Suburb*, Berkeley: University of California Press.

—— (1979) *Japan as Number One: Lessons for America*, Cambridge MA: Harvard University Press.

Vogel, S. (1978) 'Professional Housewife: The Career of Urban Middle-Class Japanese Women', *Japan Interpreter* 12 (1): 16–43.

Wakisaka, A. (1997) 'Women at Work' in M. Sako and H. Sato (eds) *Japanese Labour and Management in Transition: Diversity, Flexibility and Participation*, London: Routledge.

Westwood, Sallie (1984) *All Day Every Day: Factory and family in the Making of Women's Lives*, London: Pluto Press.

White, Merry (1993) *Material Child: Coming of Age in Japan and America*, New York: Free Press.

White, Michael, and Trevor, M. (1983) *Under Japanese Management: the Experience of British Workers*, London: Heinemann.

Wright, S. (1994) 'Culture in Anthropology and Organizational Studies', in S. Wright (ed.) *Anthropology of Organizations*, London: Routledge.

Yahata, S. (1997) 'Structural Change and Employment Adjustment in the Post-bubble Recession', *Japan Forum* 9(2): 138–49.

Yoshino, K. (1992) *Cultural Nationalism in Contemporary Japan: a Sociological Enquiry*, London: Routledge.

Yoshimoto, Banana (1994) *Kitchen*, New York: Simon and Schuster.

## Government, press, and trade organisation publications

Asahi Shinbun (1998) *Japan Almanac 1999*, Tokyo: Asahi Shinbun publishing company.

Asian Productivity Organization (1972) *Japan Quality Control Circles*, Tokyo: Asian Productivity Organization.

Distribution Economics (1971) *Outline of Japanese Distribution Structures*, Tokyo: Distributions Economics Institute.

Japan Chain Stores (Undated) *Outline of the Japanese Distribution Industry Association and the Present Situation of JCA*, Tokyo: Japan Chain Stores Association.

Japan Chain Store Association (1998) *Chēn Stoa hanbai tōkei nenpō* [Annual report of sales statistics for chain stores], Tokyo: Japan Chain Stores Association.

Japan External Trade Organization (1991) *Nippon 1991: Business Facts and Figures*, Tokyo: JETRO.

Japan Institute of Labour (1990) *Japanese Working Life Profile: Statistical Aspects*, Tokyo: Japan Institute of Labour.

Japan Institute of Labour (1998a) *Japanese Working Life Profile: Labour Statistics*, Tokyo: Japan Institute of Labour.

Japan Institute of Labour (1998b) *White Paper on Labour (Summary)*, Tokyo: Japan Institute of Labour.

Japan Institute for Social and Economic Affairs (1990) *Japan 1991: An International Comparison*. Tokyo: Keizai Koho Centre.
Nihon Keizai Shinbun (1985) *Kaisha nenkan*, Tokyo: Nihon Keizai Shinbunsha.
—— (1991)*Ryūtsū Keizai no Tebiki*, Tokyo: Nihon Keizai Shinbunsha.
—— (1992) *Ryūtsū Keizai no Tebiki*, Tokyo: Nihon Keizai Shinbunsha.
—— (1994) *Ryūtsū Keizai no Tebiki*, Tokyo: Nihon Keizai Shinbunsha.
—— (1999) *Ryūtsū Keizai no Tebiki*, Tokyo: Nihon Keizai Shinbunsha.
Nikkei Business (1989) *Yoi kaisha*, Tokyo: Nihon Keizai Shinbunsha.
Nikkei Weekly (1999) *Japan Economic Almanac*, Tokyo: Nihon Keizai Shinbunsha.
Statistics Bureau, Management and Coordination Agency (1991) *Statistical Handbook of Japan*, Tokyo: Japan Statistical Association.

## Newspapers

*Asahi Evening News* 16 June 1991, 16 July 1991.
*Asahi Shinbun* 15 February 2000.
*Daily Yomiuri* 11 December 1991.
*Japan Times* weekly wews roundup 12–18 February 2000. Online.
    http://www.japantimes.co.jp/wnr/2000/wnr7.html
*Mainichi Shinbun* 21 May 1991.

# Index